D0825600

COMIC
TRANSFORMATIONS
IN
SHAKESPEARE

RUTH NEVO

→COMIC TRANSFORMATIONS IN SHAKESPEARE

METHUEN & CO. LTD
LONDON AND NEW YORK

For Natan

First published in 1980 by
Methuen & Co. Ltd
11 *New Fetter Lane, London* EC4P 4EE
Published in the USA by
Methuen & Co.
in association with Methuen, Inc.
733 *Third Avenue, New York,* NY 10017
© 1980 *Ruth Nevo*
Phototypeset in V.I.P. Sabon by
Western Printing Services Ltd, Bristol
Printed in Great Britain
at the University Press, Cambridge

British Library Cataloguing in Publication Data
Nevo, Ruth
Comic transformations in Shakespeare.
1. Shakespeare, William – Comedies
I. Title
822.3'3   PR2981   80-40238

ISBN 0-416-73880-X
ISBN 0-416-73890-7 Pbk

CONTENTS

ACKNOWLEDGEMENTS

Versions of Chapters VI and XI were read while the book was in the making at conferences in Stratford in 1978, in Jerusalem in 1979 and Aberdeen in 1980; the gist of Chapter I formed part of a Shakespeare Association of America seminar held at San Francisco in 1979, and was published by the New York Literary Forum in a collection of essays on Shakespearean Comedy edited by Maurice Charney. On all these occasions alert fellow travellers set mis-emphases right and suggested new perspectives some of which were subsequently happily incorporated. To all these necessarily anonymous aiders and abetters I am most grateful, as I am, also, to those hardy annuals, my students. But most of all to my endlessly patient, meticulously critical friends and readers – Professor H. M. Daleski, without whose eagle eye I would feel completely bereft, Dr Shlomith Rimmon and Dr Elizabeth Freund, who resolutely keep me up to date, and Professor A. A. Mendilow, whose masterly comments at a very early stage of my thinking about comedy had a formative effect upon the whole carriage of the work.

Shakespearean scholarly debts are notoriously impossible to discharge in full. The most immediate and proximate are recorded in the notes, but for the rest – a great concourse – I must simply hope that my creditors find, as I do, in the pleasure and the honour of membership in such a company, a silent recompense.

The text that I have used throughout for citation is *The Riverside Shakespeare*, ed. G. Blackemore Evans (Boston: Houghton Mifflin, 1974).

I

SHAKESPEARE'S
NEW COMEDY

The chapters which follow are basically interpretative studies of
Shakespeare's ten early comedies; but they lean upon a theory of
the dynamic of comic form and they yield a hypothesis concerning
the development of Shakespeare's art from early to mature, more
detailed and specific than the ascriptions of apprenticeship or
tutelage and 'masterpiece', respectively, provide. Shakespeare's
early comedies are a gallimaufry of experiments, but each plays its
part in the gradual conquest of the medium, the increasing mastery of its complex expressive capacities. Not that any straight line
leads from *The Comedy of Errors* to *Twelfth Night*, and then
through the tragi-comedies to the final romances; there are leaps
and dashes forward, *reculers pour mieux sauter* and detours. The
story is that of a mighty river, fretting out its channels to the sea,
skirting and circumventing and deviating, dividing and rejoining,
wherever topographical obstacles, so to speak, lie in its path.

Out of his Renaissance Roman and Renaissance romance
materials Shakespeare wrought a form of comedy unmistakeably
his own. It is the function of two inconstant variables: the Donatan formula for comic plots, which serves as model for a multitude
of variations; and the battle of the sexes which constitutes the
underlying motivation of his variegated romantic-courtship
stories. The formula was derived by the fourth century gram-
marian Donatus from his study of Terence and ceaselessly re-

peated and revised by the humanist scholars of the Italian Renaissance. In one of its many formulations it was expounded in the 1550 edition of the *Andria*, a text which was very possibly used in the Stratford Grammar School of Shakespeare's day. 'Comedy', the formula runs, 'ought indeed to be five-parted, the first of which unfolds the argument . . .' (in another version: 'contains either the peril, the anguish or some trouble'); 'the second completes the same. The third has the increment of turbations and contentions . . .' (or: 'brings on the perturbations, and the impediments and despair of the desired thing'); 'the fourth seeks a medicine for the turbations' (or: 'brings a remedy for the impending evil') 'and is a preparation for the catastrophe, which the fifth demands by right for itself.'[1]

The 'telos' of this Terentian plot is the finding – discovery or recovery – of what was missing, that is, imperfect, at the start. I borrow the metaphysical term from Northrop Frye who, in a fine article, distinguishes between 'the teleological plots' of the Roman (originally Menandrine) New Comedy and the 'dialectical plots' of the Aristophanic Old Comedy, 'a more existential form in which the central theme is mockery and its distinguishing feature the agon or contest'.[2] The latter type of comedy has returned in the twentieth century, following a New Comedy hegemony of extraordinary tenacity and longevity, in the form of those extravaganzas of the absurd to which dramatists like Giraudoux, Dürrenmatt and Ionesco have accustomed us. Northrop Frye's distinction is stimulating and useful but not entirely felicitous. It overlooks the telos of dialectic itself and it overlooks the element of dialectic in the teleological New Comedy plots, where opposing temperaments, sexes, classes, generations, generate conflict. In Terence's *The Brothers*, for instance, the contest between the prim and the indulgent father of, respectively, the country cousin and the town spark, structures the entire action and the comic resolution. In Shakespeare, it will be part of my case to argue, the dialectic is particularly strong and subtle. I shall want to show later how, with the haphazardry of creative genius, its advances, its retreats, its fruitful digressions, he grows towards a form which joins the severed halves of Frye's dichotomy. But the distinction neatly emphasizes the concrete goal or aim towards

which the protagonists of New Comedy consciously direct themselves, the play coming to an end with its attainment, and it leads
me into my subject. The ends the plays of Plautus and Terence, or rather their
characters, have in view are specific and concrete indeed. Brides
(with substantial dowries), complaisant courtesans or purchased
flute girls, a parasite's pickings, the exposing of a braggart or
impostor or cheating procurer, the outwitting of a heavy father or
a light son. They aim at the wealth, pleasure, freedom, or at least
praise, or at least a prize, which life does not in general provide
equally for all. They go about to achieve these ends with the aid of
tricky manipulations, disguises, pretences, bed-tricks, simula-
tions and dissimulations, the wily slaves themselves being the
chief functionaries, if not originators, of the whole contrivance;
which, however, so far from achieving what is wished brings
about a thickening web of accidents and miscomprehensions, and
is accompanied by considerable verbal violence (especially in the
less polite Plautus) as abuse, threat and invective are lavishly and
hyperbolically distributed. The ends that are finally brought
about are consonant with the original desires of the protagonists,
but in excess of them. They get more, and better, than they
bargained for, and this on account of a series of fortunate coinci-
dences and discoveries: lost foundlings, wrecks, rings, caskets,
birthmarks, in short, all the paraphernalia of the fortunate
unforeseen, the lucky chances of which, in our precarious existences, we are in direr need than of any gift of birth or intellect.

These stratagems of the New Comedy supplied Europe with its
comic fictions for two millennia; longer, if we include subtle and
profound inversions like those of Ibsen and Chekov, witty
parodies like *The Importance of Being Earnest*, *Major Barbara*,
and *The Confidential Clerk*, fantasias like *The Playboy of the
Western World*, and the steady stream of musical comedy and
soap opera, let alone the secondary proliferating life led by
dramatic forms in the novel since the eighteenth century. They
also provided Shakespeare with his plots from *The Comedy of
Errors* to *The Tempest*.

It is worth remarking at this point that the distinction between
'plot' and 'story' (roughly equivalent to the Formalist distinction

between '*sjuzet*' and '*fabula*') was not unknown to the ancients. Horace recommended to dramatists that they employ an 'artificial order' whereby chronological sequence is disrupted for the sake of dramatic effects.[3] By the last of the final romances Shakespeare will have bettered his instruction in this respect. But if Shakespearean devices for creating a simultaneity of past and present, for irradiating present by past and for effecting multiple ironies while cunningly advancing or retarding the solutions to his characters' bewilderment finally surpass those of the ancients, it is as well to remember that the procedure is inherent in New Comedy plots as such, whether in their original form of drama or in the later development of romance narrative.

The Tempest is a palimpsest of Plautus' *The Rope*, which starts with a description of a tempest and has a prologue in which Arcturus explains how he has 'stirred up a wintry storm and raised high waves in the sea' in order to wreck the ship of the wicked procurer who decamped with the slave girl, long-lost daughter of the farmer-fisherman upon whose coast the wrecked travellers are washed up. And *The Winter's Tale* is a startlingly recognizable transformation of the fragment by Menander called *The Arbitration*, in which a charcoal burner and a goatherd dispute the ownership of trinkets found by the latter when he picked up an abandoned baby, later depositing it with the former whose wife had just given birth to a still-born child. The Arbitrator in the dispute, as it so happens, turns out to be the foundling's own grandfather, whose daughter, it seems, in the heat of a quarrel with her husband, inadvertently mislaid her baby. Whatever the obscure, primordial origins of such stories may be, whether they have their source in the myths of Dionysos or in the Athenian custom of infant-exposure, the lost or abandoned child whose lot is to be found again becomes, as Kerenyi tells us, basic to the entire genre of New Comedy.[4]

In the early *Comedy of Errors* just such a Menandrine narrative of separation and reunion encases the brisk Plautine mistakings and unmaskings of the *Menaechmi*; and this has tempted criticism to become preoccupied with the question whether the meandering romance narrative of marvellous reunions (*Apollonius of Tyre*, for instance) or the tight Roman structure of mistakes and unravellings took precedence in Shakespeare's imagination. The fact of the matter is that both were contained in Plautus, and the historical bifurcation into medieval romances on the one hand and dramas of intrigue on the other is largely a matter of theatrical convenience. The plays foreground the tangle of errors; the romances – they have the time to do so – foreground the precedent vicissitudes. Whatever permutations and combinations come to be devised it is to the basic linkage that the term New Comedy usefully applies. However, in application to Shakespeare, a further parameter comes into play.

After the initial sally of *The Comedy of Errors* the wandering narrative of long-lost children and family reunions disappears until the final romances, save for an evocation of 'sea-sorrow' vicissitudes in *Twelfth Night* with its pair of twins fished out of the sea. The modern and fashionable in Shakespeare's day comprised not only the Roman comedies which had been enthusiastically resuscitated and interpreted by the humanist eruditi of the Renaissance and popularized by that ebullient off-shoot, the *commedia dell' arte*, but also the specifically courtly branch of romance. The romance of courtship, medieval in its first impulse, had recently been trimmed and spruced up, Peele'd, Greene'd, Lylyfied and Euphuized, and had made a new and elegant début in the theatre.[5] It is therefore these courtly or courtship comedies, particularly the 'supposes' combination of mistakings and matings which dominate Shakespeare's playwriting till the turn of the century. And it is in these comedies that the specific and distinctive form of Shakespearean comedy is to be discovered.

The later post-tragic romances come under the powerful gravitational pull, so to speak, of the tragedies themselves and require separate discussion. They are indeed comedies – New Comedies – by Wittgensteinian family resemblance, for in them, too, losses are restored and sorrows end; in them, too, families are reunited and reconstructed. *The Winter's Tale* defeats shipwreck, emotional and actual, with its 'green world' renewal,[6] the healing and revitalizing powers of great creating Nature, its miraculous restoration of survivors, and a great gift for Leontes. In *The Tempest*, the green world, 'whose sweet airs give delight and hurt not', is a whole island of survivors, but its ending reopens further vistas, and its ironies decreate. Its final note in fact is dispossession: a bare island (like the island salt and bare of Milton's displaced Eden), and every third thought the grave. Nevertheless, the telos of *The Tempest* too is recovery, if only of whatever compensations or consolations can be found for the fears and wounds, oppressions and misfortunes which have been endured.

In these post-tragic time-dominated tragi-comic comedies generations are spanned and the flux of passion and vicissitude, of grief and loss enacted or recalled. And the transformations Shakespeare's sea-change works upon his models are more marvellous perhaps even than the pearls and coral of Ariel's ditty. But in the younger plays 'placing' is far more the modality of the action than 'timing'. Their protagonists are engaged in finding their place in the world, and in placing what they find in a hierarchy of values. Rightly to be placed and rightly to place – oneself and others – engrosses a good deal of their attention and involves them in the erotic sparrings and duellings, the positionings and counter-positionings of the sexual battle in its refined and elaborated courtly form.[7]

The telos of Shakespeare's early comic plots then is recovery: the finding of what was missing or lacking at the start. And here the first great novelty is at once apparent – Shakespeare's protagonists do not know what they want, except in the most superficial sense. They discover as they go along, and so transform the rather arid Donatan scheme into a heuristic device of immense potency and flexibility. When his protagonists, like the Romans in their happy ends, get more than they bargained for, it is not simply the bonus (admittedly considerable) of a son's light of love turning out to be respectable, or an Athenian citizen, or even the long-lost daughter of the father's best friend, but an illumination of their entire lives. Leo Salingar expresses this extremely well, if impressionistically, when he speaks of a

> fundamental innovation which in its general effect distinguishes Shakespeare's plays from all previous comedies, that he gives his people the quality of an inner life. Their inner life, with their capacity for introspection, changes the whole bearing of

the incidents that make up a traditional comic plot. It is as if Shakespeare separates the events that composed the plot from the centres of consciousness in his leading characters, so that the plot-machinery operates on a different plane, the plane where the characters are being 'transformed' . . . carried out of their normal selves . . . observe themselves passing into a new phase of experience.[8]

It is not only the language of the inner life, however (important though it is), which 'changes the whole bearing of the incidents that make up a traditional comic plot.' The effect is the consequence of a radical and consistent employment of what Bertrand Evans has taught us to recognize as a particularly subtle and pervasive form of dramatic irony: the exploitation of a gap in awareness between the characters (or some of them) and the audience.[9] This is a major heuristic technique in all of Shakespeare's plays, but in the comedies particular profit is derived from the close co-ordination between the audience's knowledge and the character's ignorance and from an overt display of the device as such. The audience is given intelligence of matters which are concealed from the characters (or some of the characters) in such a way or by such means that progressive disclosures for the former are synchronous with progressive deceptions, confusions, mystifications, for the latter. Puck's application of the magic juice, for example, puts the audience in the know and the lovers into bafflement at one and the same stroke, as does the eaves-dropping scenes in *Much Ado*. But to this central comic device I shall presently return.

The audience's possession of superior knowledge ensures that comedies of this kind never surprise. Or rather, the 'surprises' they supply are of the kind characteristic of good spectator sports: perfectly expected in principle but always admirably unforeseen in practice. They are the fruit of the finesse, versatility, verve, and skill whereby goals are achieved, situations saved, gambles pulled off in despite of the difficulties set up by the conventions of the game itself. Once again the point has been tellingly made by Northrop Frye:

All art is conventionalised but where the convention is most obvious and obtrusive the sense of play, of accepting the rules of a game, is at its strongest. . . . The comedies as a single group . . . seem more like a number of simultaneous chess games, played by a master who wins them all by devices familiar to him, and gradually, with patient study, to us, but which remain mysteries of an unfathomable skill.[10]

Shakespeare's implementation of the Terentian scheme (in the first ten comedies) runs as follows.

Whatever the predicament sets forth as missing at the start, be it a twin, or an obedient wife, or matched couples to make up a foursome, or the secret of a 'living art', or requited love, or love and a fortune, or a good match for a daughter and a punishment for a jealous husband, or a match for a wayward cousin, or a place in the sun for a dispossessed young man, or mastery in love, it will be found. The plot's formal coherence depends on this, and so does the audience's perception of the play's coherence. Since, as has been noted, the protagonists are themselves seekers, and only partly, or not at all cognizant of what they seek, the formal development is a continual, unfolding process of disclosure, during which, however, the protagonist and audience are proceeding at different rates, that of the protagonist being positively retarded by tumults and confusions on the way, that of the audience proceeding apace by inferences and hypotheses.

Therefore, when the plot is finally resolved by some appropriate recognition which enables objectives to be attained, the *anagnorisis* is retrospective as well as immediate for the protagonists and holistic or integrative for the audience. The recognition invites in effect a second order or interpretative, re-evaluative reading of events for both. The solving event, of which the audience too has not had full advance notice, produces hindsight on two levels. Scales fall from the protagonists' eyes in terms of whatever mistaken identity or reunion is now disclosed, and from the audience's in terms of the entire 'journey into the interior'[11] the protagonists' adventures can now be seen to have been. The manifest purposes, desires, goals and motivations of the protagonists reveal their inner, previously concealed, or veiled, or latent implications. What the protagonists see will not altogether of course coincide with what the audience sees. The audience has more material to unify, to knit into coherence, than any single character. But the approach of the protagonists' knowledge to the level of the audience's at the end of the play is what gives the recognitions of the dénouement their telling effect. And it is one of the marks of the progressive Shakespearean mastery of dramatic speech that protagonists become more self-perceptive, more aware of themselves both as having been fooled or foolish, and also as having gained in wisdom or insight.

In the Roman New Comedy the author or implementer of the comic device – the deception or pretence or bluff or imposture – which precipitates the comic process of involution and evolution, and creates the gap between audience's knowledge and protagonist's, is usually the trickster slave. In Shakespeare trickery has gone up in the world. And though he has tricky servants, like Puck, they are not markedly successful and have to have their chestnuts pulled out of the fire for them by their royal employers in the end. The freeing of the comic device from its strictly utilitarian Roman deceptions, however, has great advantages for variety and flexibility. In *The Comedy of Errors* the comic device is nature's own – the freakish identicalness of twins – but thereafter we have psychological one-upmanship, a girl as page, crossed letters, the delusive juice of a flower, three deceptive caskets, a wifely trick to catch a cuckold, a series of eavesdroppings, girls in disguise.

The comic device meshes in marvellously intricate, varied and eye-opening ways with the comic disposition of human beings to be deluded, deceived, mistaken, unreasonable, perverse, irrational and subject to every kind of folly. This produces what the neoclassical theorists of the Renaissance, following Donatus, called the *incrementum processusque turbarum*, the increase and progression of perturbations, or 'the forward progress of the turmoils',[12] that is to say, confusion worse confounded or the knot of errors. The reversals, shocks, absurdities, displacements and disorientations of this stage strike the protagonists as having turned their world upside down, or into dream, and result eventually in a double exhaustion. The comic device is exhausted; that is to say, it has fulfilled (or over-filled), its function. It is not usable any more, or it is about to be exposed. But also, and at the same time, the privations or perversities which bred the entanglements ultimately to be dissolved or resolved, have undergone a process of hyperbolic excess which has reached the point of exhaustion.

This process is itself remedial, and is the internal equivalent of the providential remedy which dissolves the knot of errors and issues in the recognitions of the dénouement, and the comic resolution or recovery. The providential remedies are in the first instance the immediate local solutions to the impasses, the enigmas and the errors induced by the involutions of the plot, what Donatus called 'the infolding of the argument'. That they come about at all is the happy chance, the good luck, the fortuitous and fortunate circumstances which is comedy's presiding genius, as the fatal error and its inevitabilities are tragedy's. Thus the presence of the disguised abbess, a convenient occasion for demonstrative obedience, true love in disguise, the healing flower, the legal loophole, cover for the elopement of the young lovers, the captured villain, the fortunate encounter and a change of heart, the arrival of a lost twin – such stuff as spells out the bitter anguish of 'too late' in the tragedies – here provide solutions to the problems, dilemmas, embarrassments, mishaps, mistakings, deceptions and imbroglios, and potential disasters, of the *processus turbarum*. This is their technical function. But as they close the gap opened by the play's beginning, they provide the audience with means for a full and final retrospective intelligence of the nature, in all its inwardness, of the desirable, the pleasurable, the good, the absence of which motivated the story. They enable us to transcend, if we will, the comedy-game aspect of the play, and to move, in the words of Paul Ricoeur, 'from what it says to that of which it speaks'.[13] The power of Shakespeare's comic creations lies in the simultaneous formal complexity and naturalistic verisimilitude with which he deploys these canonical elements of comic form. The remedies solve and resolve, illuminate the whole human condition for the audience while they enact the particular repair, or cure the particular folly or set of follies, or species of folly, or privation or perversity presented in a particular play. The insights that these remedies generate or precipitate are thus endowed with a double validity.

We do not, it must be insisted, devive these insights from our 'identification' with a favourite character as is often carelessly or loosely supposed. We participate rather in a dynamic process, acting out imaginatively, and restructuring, impulses as often as not dialectically opposed. Identification with a protagonist would short-circuit a fully intelligent participation and it is for this essential purpose – the creation of a detachment, of aesthetic distance – that the fools are provided. But they are provided also for fun. It is to the knotty problem of the nature and function of Shakespeare's fools that I now turn.

These fools, that great company of the commonalty – menials, professional jesters, solid citizens – who carry on their quotidian, absurd and good-natured existences in the most subtle disrelation with the official plot, grow in stature as Shakespeare proceeds. They are the catalysers of the comic disposition to be deluded, deceived, mistaken, affected, conceited, pretentious, inept, maladroit or perverse, and, in short, foolish. Foolery, as Feste says, 'doth walk about the orb like the sun'. It is the fools that, to pursue the metaphor, focus its rays. Because they are not tricksters – Shakespeare's orientation is aristocratic and his plotters are dukes and princes and witty heroines – they are not tied to the exigencies of plot and are therefore free to improvize plays and parody their betters. They do this directly, if they are witty fools whose folly is a stalking horse; or indirectly if they are foolish would-be wits, simply by being in their own blithe unawareness what their betters are in their ridiculous essence.

The question of how foolish a Shakespearean fool really is, is always a good question. Who, for instance, is mocking whom when the complacent Jaques mockingly exults at having met a fool in the forest? It is a fool, at all events, whose foolish philosophy bears an uncanny resemblance to Jaques' own nihilistic obsessions. The dramatic duplicity here is like Bottom's dream, so called, it will be remembered, because it hath no bottom. Face and mask, illusion and imposture are the dubieties out of which a profoundly ironic intelligence generates its ironies, the world of the theatre and the theatre of the world reflecting each other in manifold ways. By dissonance and by consonance, by diminishing or by augmenting, by simulation or by dissimulation, by infirmities and by recoveries, the fools entertain us ceaselessly, and we entertain them; that is to say, we entertain a diversity of perspectives and proportions. They may not themselves always be witty – some may indeed fairly be rated under-achievers – but they are certainly the cause that wit is in others. And the constant mediation between opposing temptations: between head and heart, rational and irrational, between the defences of the ordering intellect and the defences of immersion in dissolving emotion, has much to do with the exquisite equipoise of Shakespearean remedies. Through them fantasies of the unconscious and fantasies of the ideal are both enacted and reduced to viable proportion.

One is often struck by the multi-facetedness of even the simplest of Shakespeare's clowns, by their complementarity with other characters and by their refusal to be disposed of by a dichotomous wits/butts or knaves/gulls classification, or in terms of besetting and extravagant 'humours'. The only way I can discover to account for this peculiarity of Shakespeare's fools is by recourse to an ancient Greek insight concerning three comic manners, or dispositions, or modes of conduct or characters (*ethoi*), namely, the Bomolochos, the Eiron and the Alazon: Buffoon, Ironical Man and Impostor. These are the three possible producers of the ludicrous and pleasureable according to the fourth-century *Tractatus Coislinianus*,[14] the fragment which tantalizes us with its glimpse into the missing Aristotelian treatise on Comedy. Tripartite divisions of the soul are common and frequently overlap conceptually, Freud's having often been shown to have more than a superficial resemblance to Plato's. The *Tractatus* for its part, lends itself to the notion of a mock or burlesque theatre of the psyche, with Plato's charioteer as Eiron/Ego, his spirited part as Alazon/Superego and his appetitive part the buffoonish Bomolochos/Id. What the appellations mean we have a fair idea from other Greek texts, in particular the *Nichomachean Ethics*. Alazon or Boaster is 'a charlatan or impostor who pretends to have distinguished qualities which he either does not possess at all or possesses less fully than he would have us believe' (book IV, chapter VII). Bomolochos is a facetious wag, exhibits an excess of wit, must be funny come what may and can't resist a joke in or out of season (book IV, chapter VIII). Eiron is notoriously hard to pin down. In the *Nichomachean Ethics* he is the self-deprecator, the understater (like Socrates) who disclaims the possession of distinguished qualities (chapter VII). But Socrates himself, according to Alcibiades in the *Symposium*, adds an important proviso: he is Silenus, the large-bellied, coarse, ridiculous image within which is hidden divine wisdom. The formulations of the *Nichomachean Ethics* (and even more of Theophrastus' *Characters* in the next generation) are ethically-orientated descriptions, prescriptions, of ways of behaving in society. Alazon and Eiron, for instance, are, respectively, the excess and defect of the virtue of plain truth-speaking. Bomolochos represents the excess of affability, against the dour and humourless Agroikos who is its defect (chapter VIII).[15] But consider the threesome functionally, as does the *Tractatus*, as laughter-producers, and it becomes at once evident that they are all necessary and complementary elements in the perception of absurdity. Alazon is a fool for pretending to wisdom or virtue he does not have, but there must be an Eiron present to make this apparent. Bomolochos is a fool because he is always fooling or playing the fool, but again, always for someone's benefit and enjoyment, and at someone's cost, if only his own. Eiron masks true wisdom by pretending to be a fool in order to expose the mock wisdom of wisdom's ape. All 'humours', excesses, defects, fixations and compulsions are, of course, foolish from either a rational or an ethical point of view. But what distinguishes the archetypal threesome is that they are inter-related functions, depending on and varying with each other; and they can reflect and modify and duplicate each other in infinite combinations of deception and pretence, imitation and parody, masking and unmasking, resembling nothing so much as the antics performed, modern mythology tells us, by their equivalents – Ego, Id and Superego – in the comedies of our own discomfitures.

Shakespeare's fools exhibit just this complementarity of the quasi-Aristotelian triad, thus proving it as natural as folly itself (since Shakespeare had no written source) and justifying the Greek insight. And just as the three primary colours under the laws of optics behave – the complement of red being green, for instance, which is a mixture of blue and yellow; or the complement of blue being orange, a mixture of red and yellow – so, after the initial essays in the Terentian servant couple – one dumb and one clever – Shakespeare's fools tend to pair off in exactly analogous ways: Touchstone and Jaques, for instance, Feste and Malvolio, Aguecheek and Sir Toby, Armado and Costard. The complement and opponent of a braggart like Armado is Costard – a mixture of mocker and fool. The mocking Puck has for his complement the foolish and bossy Bottom, impostor-lover of a Fairy Queen; Feste the wit complements the foolish Alazon Malvolio. If the complement of an ironic impostor like Sir Toby is a fool simple, Aguecheek admirably fills the bill. Don John, cunning impostor, is out-witted (ironically) by no other than the virtuous, but assified Dogberry. In the darker tonality of *Troilus and Cressida*, Thersites, scurrilous mocker, stands over against Pandarus, complacent and over-reaching fool. The ironic Hamlet faces the pompous fool Polonius, and when he becomes his own buffoon it is to outwit the sardonic impostor, his uncle. One could multiply instances. But for fear of a digression on fools of Shandyean proportions, perhaps by some contamination from the subject matter, I turn instead to Falstaff and to the question raised by that fat knight, who is composite Buffoon, Alazon and Eiron. What does his Folly enact? What do his comic energies nourish and foster? Having more flesh than another man he has therefore more frailty, but what are the pleasures we derive from his easy morals and immense belly?

According to Bakhtin, in *Rabelais and his World*, Falstaff would be the supreme example of what he calls the 'grotesque realism' of Renaissance comic art, the sole function of which is to degrade or debase the dogmatic, the authoritarian, the official or ideal, the pompous or pretentious, the 'finished and polished'. 'Folly', says Bakhtin, 'is a form of gay, festive wisdom, free from all laws and restrictions, as well as from preoccupations and seriousness.'[16] This comic degradation, this 'uncrowning' as Bakhtin calls it in his brilliant analysis of the language and imagery of the comic, brings down to earth, to the lower stratum of the body – belly, bowels, phallus – turns into flesh, materializes. The essence of comedy, he claims, is contained in the 'Rabelaisian complex': laughter, food, procreation, abuse. It is rooted in folk

carnival with its Billingsgate abuse, its gay licence, its indecent
irreverence, its violence and scatology, its presentation of the
body not as a harmoniously proportionate form, but all belly, as a
prodigy of cavities, excrescences and protuberances; but also as
itself grave and seed bed, matrix of both disintegration and
renewal: Falstaff's Hallowe'en Spring.

Against Bakhtin's radical medievalism (reminiscent of Victor
Hugo's preface to *Cromwell*) it is instructive to place the neoclassical rationalism of Castelvetro, who, in 1576[17] adduced four
sources for the risible in an analysis which is startlingly anticipat-
ory of modern post-Freudian views like Koestler's, for instance, in
The Act of Creation.[18] As a first source for laughter, not essentially comic, such as that of a mother welcoming her children,
Castelvetro placed affection. Next came deception, mainly the
mishaps and miscalculations of others, but he does include self-
deception such as boasting or pretension, which rebounds
boomerang fashion. Third, a physical or moral defect or deficiency, wittily exposed; and lastly, obscenity, cunningly covert.

Falstaff is certainly a very Prince of Libido and of mockery. Both these caps fit, though one fits Falstaff as object of
derision, the other as subject. But what neither Castelvetro nor
Bakhtin explains is precisely the duality, the doubleness, of comic
pleasure when laughter, or the risible, is deliberately, brilliantly,
histrionically engineered, rather than simply embodied or expressed. Falstaff is a multi-impersonator, and in this he draws
upon a source of pleasure, not exclusively and disjunctively the
property of comedy, but anterior to all other comic pleasure: the
art of mimicry. He impersonates 'Monsieur Remorse', pious pat-
riot, valiant soldier, plays at being misunderstood, long-suffering.
There is nothing he will not impersonate in fact, and this is the
secret of his wit. For the pleasure of imitation, as Aristotle knew,
is the primary pleasure of knowledge as power. Consciously to
imitate is to understand, to grasp the distinguishing principle, to
strip away all that is excrescent or accidental, to have recognized. While Falstaff thus performs he has two audiences: the
stage audience, duped or unduped; the theatre audience,
unduped. Falstaff rejoices in the gulling of the dupes. The theatre
audience rejoices both in the gulling of the dupes and in the

counter-gulling of Falstaff, thus emotionally having its libidinous, disinhibitory cake and eating it with a good moral conscience. The theatre audience rejoices in the actor's histrionic skill, in the fictive Falstaff's skill, in Hal's greater skill (or vice versa), in Shakespeare's skill in providing the text which generates these skills, and in its own skills of perception. Since it is never oblivious for a moment of the open and palpable fabrication, it is never the victim of Plato's most heinous of deceptions: the presentation of appearances as if they were reality. Whether we rejoice with trickster-victim or with trickster-victor, our love is really love for the artist, masked and transferred to his creations. We love the inventor of these marvellous inventions.

Such clowning gives us double indemnity: we escape with the hare and hunt with the hounds; we mock and affirm; we delight in witty intelligence and in unwise impulse, in high spirits and low designs; in the laxities of infantile fantasy, and in the astringencies of ironic reality. For the two hours' traffic of the stage we are not trapped in the disjunctions of our mortality; and this in itself is therapeutic. A benign doubling and redoubling is a mark of comedy; its emblem, Falstaff, doubling, redoubling and multiplying his buckram men for the delectation of his double audience. There are twins and quasi-twins, double-faced rogues and jokers, double plots doubly complicating each other, *doubles entendres* and dual sexual roles for disguised heroines. But where doubling in life, we are told, is often a sign of a failure in integration, in comedy, mankind's dramatized dream of a second chance, doubling is the essential vehicle for its dialectic of wisdom and folly.

Falstaff is a complete and composite comic figure – hence his popularity – but, alas, history and its chronicles are mirrors, not of things made over in the image of desire, but of disjunctive mortality and its exclusive alternatives. Therefore, Falstaff must be cast out of Hal's kingdom. The pleasures of catharsis give place to the catharsis of pleasure. Polity cannot survive this demon of jest, subversive and anarchic. If Shakespeare has no illusions about the house of Lancaster he has none about the power of unrestraint to heal a kingdom 'sick with civil blows' either. Falstaff must go. And his creator must find new channels in which the comic energies can nourishingly run, the pleasure principle and the reality principle fruitfully interlock.

I see the Falstaff plays as constituting a great watershed in the progress of Shakespeare's comedy. Of the first five comedies, the two early farces, *The Comedy of Errors* and *The Shrew*, the interesting but abortive *Two Gentlemen of Verona* and the subtly counterpointed *Love's Labour's Lost* culminate in the brilliant achievement of *A Midsummer Night's Dream*. Twinships, rivalries, ambivalences, tamings and matings, the sameness and difference that hides under the notion of identity, all coalesce in the harmonies of *A Midsummer Night's Dream*. I see also, however, *Love's Labour's Lost* and *The Merchant of Venice* in juxtaposition. *Love's Labour's Lost*, though possibly drafted as early as 1594, was revised for performance (and for the Good Quarto of 1598) in 1597, the year after the conjectured date of composition of *The Merchant*. In both, the necessary senex of New Comedy is replaced, very significantly, by 'the will of a dead father', for Portia and the Princess at least (who are really remarkably alike), though in *The Merchant*, of course, there is another irate father and a very intractable one indeed. Both plays exhibit in their different ways disrupted or ruptured comic forms, and an uncertain or inconclusive role for the main woman protagonist; but in connection with the latter play I also take up the problem of the scapegoat figure which I believe is alien to Shakespeare's *comic* genius. That 'scapegoating' as it has come to be called in some of the newer criticism[19] is essentially tragic – drawing all a play's elements ineluctably towards the tragic pole like a magnet drawn across iron filings – is an insight Shakespeare might indeed have acquired from the Greeks but in fact appears to have discovered for himself. And in this respect it is of exceptional interest that *The Merchant* is followed by the Falstaff plays – the two histories and then (or concurrently, according to recent conjecture) *The Merry Wives*. Discussion of *The Merry Wives* entails further reflection upon scapegoats and Greek origins, and upon the interesting reversal of the usual New Comedy roles for men and women in the plottings at Windsor. There I shall argue the case for the part played by Falstaff in the emergence of a grand new comic protagonist: no longer Bacchanalian trickster and rogue, but infinitely resourceful anti-'romantic' romantic heroine, possessed of an ironic wit and exhibiting the 'higher folly' of an individual, differentiated inner life.[20] The three masterpieces which follow: *Much Ado, As You Like It* and *Twelfth Night*, are Shakespeare's Praise of Folly and exhibit an Erastian transvaluation of values in its most exemplary form – as a battle of the sexes in which neither contender is defeated: each possesses a heroine who is the final product of a long dialectic, during the shifts and turns of which traditional antithetical sexual roles have been challenged, subverted, polarized, reversed, exchanged, to be finally transcended in a new synthesis and a new harmony. The three plays represent the summit of Shakespeare's achievement in the invention of a New Comedy which is one of the human triumphs.

But I think of it as a moment's achievement, hard-won, and no sooner achieved than abandoned or dismantled, and then in the post-tragic period, re-deployed in new explorations. Like all great artists, perhaps, Shakespeare was in constant struggle with his medium, making of it an instrument of incessant enquiry, of the incessant furthering of perception; seeing always through the achieved, the not yet achieved, the still to do. Michelangelo, whose captives struggle to emerge from within the obdurate rock, provides us with an icon both of the artist *agonistes* and of his art. I believe that Shakespearean comedy can be understood, not as a collection of particular plays, each *sui generis*, nor as unified by some extrapolated thematic, but as a whole immense heuristic enterprise, an unceasing experiment of the imagination upon dread and upon desire.

I hope to show that the three perspectives, theoretical, developmental and interpretative, complement each other, providing tests and checks and a system of internal balances for speculations which, in response to so rich and multifarious a field, might otherwise be in danger of surfeiting in their own excess. Because so laminated a study requires as firm a base as possible, I have tied my discussion of the plays as closely as seemed feasible to the concrete and the specific – the events, the *personae* and the language of the texts themselves.

NOTES

1 See T. W. Baldwin, *Shakespeare's Five-Act Structure* (Urbana: Illinois University Press, 1947), pp. 232–3, 249, and passim. Also Martin Herrick, *Comic Theory in the Sixteenth Century* (Urbana: University of Illinois Press, 1964).

2 Northrop Frye, 'Old and New Comedy', *Shakespeare Survey*, vol. 22 (1969), p.1.

3 *Ars Poetica*, lines 146–52; and recommended by Sir Philip Sidney, *Apologie for Poetry*, ed. G. G. Smith, *Elizabethan Critical Essays* (Oxford: Oxford University Press, 1904) vol. 1, p. 198.

4 C. Kerenyi, *Dionysos: Archetypal Image of Indestructible Life* (New Jersey: Princeton University Press, 1976), pp. 343–67.

5 The accounts of the Shakespearean background I have found most helpful and informative are M. C. Bradbrook, *The Growth and Structure of Elizabethan Comedy* (London: Chatto & Windus, 1955; reprinted Peregrine, 1963) and Leo Salingar, *Shakespeare and the Traditions of Comedy* (Cambridge: Cambridge University Press, 1974).

6 In the valuable sense set out by Northrop Frye in *The Anatomy of Criticism* (New Jersey: Princeton University Press, 1957), third essay, 'Theory of Myths', passim.

7 In 'The Argument of Comedy' (*EIE*, ed. D. A. Robertson, New York: Columbia University Press, 1949, p. 61) there is a more cogent and coherent theory of comedy than the later development in *The Anatomy*, where Frye's proliferating categories tend to lead a dance of their own.

8 Salingar, *Shakespeare and the Traditions of Comedy* p. 222.

9 Bertrand Evans, *Shakespeare's Comedies* (Oxford: Oxford University Press, 1960).

10 Northrop Frye, *A Natural Perspective* (New York: Columbia University Press, 1965), pp. viii and 4–5.

11 I am indebted to Dame Helen Gardner for this striking phrase.

12 Evanthius, *De Fabula*. During the sixteenth century this essay was ascribed to Donatus and published together with the latter's *De Comoedia* under the title *De Comoedia et Tragoedia*.

13 Paul Ricoeur, 'Metaphor and the Main Problem of Hermeneutics', *NLH*, vol. 6, no. 1 (Autumn 1974), p. 106.

14 Translated and discussed by Lane Cooper in his attempt to reconstruct an Aristotelian theory of comedy in *An Aristotelian Theory of Comedy* (New York: Harcourt Brace, 1922).

15 Frye (*The Anatomy of Criticism*, p. 172) borrows Agroikos from the Ethics in order to make up, with the triad of the *Tractatus*, 'two opposed pairs' of comic character types. Despite the appeal of symmetry this move obscures the issues and seriously confuses Frye's account of comic character. Of course the surly Agroikos can provide the basis for humours characters and frequently did in comedies of the Latin tradition – Surly, Morose, Malvolio, are cases in point. So were Eiron, Buffoon and Alazon susceptible of development and realization in any number of ethically-based ways. Comic transformations are legion, as many as there are varieties of temperament, sensibility, morality. They may be as rarefied and refined as Lyly's pert pages or as randy and rambunctious as Panurge. We learn a great deal about their powers of proliferation from the improvizations of the Arlechinni, the Scarramucci and Pulcinelli of the *commedia dell' arte*. Giacomo Oreglia, *The Commedia dell' Arte* (London: Methuen, 1968) lists no fewer than thirty recognized sub-Harlequins (himself a strange pot-pourri of demon-lover, foolish zanni, bawdy buffoon and merry dreamer) and names half-a-dozen famous individualized impersonations. Like organic substance itself they subdivide and proliferate, break apart and reintegrate in kaleidoscopic re-configurations of traits. More orderly and respectable theatres fixate these volatile creations into rationally determined or ethically consistent 'characters' and from time to time these solidify into a cast of familiar categorizations: the charlatans, knaves and gulls of Jacobean city comedy, or the fops, rakes and coxcombs of the Restoration. But the comic complementarity obtains only between the three primary laughter-producing functions. In other words an Agroikos, in order to be funny, will have to have a touch of Eiron, Buffoon or Alazon in his

dour disposition, or a neighbour to point out that he has!

16 Mikhail Bakhtin, *Rabelais and his World*, trans. H. Iswolsky (Cambridge, Massachusetts: M.I.T. Press, 1968), pp. 19–23, 260 and passim.

17 Quoted in Herrick, *Comic Theory*, p. 53, and in Allan H. Gilbert, *Literary Criticism: Plato to Dryden* (New York: American Book Co., 1940), p. 314.

18 A. Koestler, *The Act of Creation* (London: Macmillan, 1964). The theory is conveniently summarized by Koestler himself in the *New Encyclopedia Brittanica*, under 'Humour and Wit'.

19 The latest issue of *Diacritics: A Review of Contemporary Criticism*, vol. 8, no. 1 (Spring, 1978), is devoted entirely to the topic, and the influence upon it of the work of René Girard.

20 Alexander Leggatt's fine book *Shakespeare's Comedy of Love* (London: Methuen, 1974) in its emphasis on the dialogue the plays conduct between conventional and colloquial dramatic idioms illuminates this point.

II

'MY GLASS
AND NOT
MY BROTHER'

If it were not so funny, Shakespeare's first comedy would read like a schizophrenic nightmare: identities are lost, split, engulfed, hallucinated, imploded.[1] Apparently solid citizens (solid at least to themselves) suffer 'ontological uncertainty' in acute forms, wandering about unrecognized by all they encounter. During this chapter of accidents servants are subjected to assault and battery upon their persons and masters are subjected to the severest undermining of their sense of their own identity. A respectable citizen is shut out of his own house by his own wife and servants, abused by his merchant associates, arrested on charges of false-hood, taken for insane, given over for cure into the hands of a mountebank pedant and, in general, experiences the collapse of all the familiar social and cognitive foundations of his life and his sense of reality. At the same time a displaced, disorientated voy-ager is so alarmed by the inexplicable behaviour of all Ephesians, including the object of his new affections, that he becomes con-vinced he has taken leave of his senses, or is the victim of witch-craft. The disintegrating effects of this frenzy of errors are such as to cause one brother to be incarcerated as a raving lunatic and the other to take flight in panic.

These zany events are often dismissed as 'farce', a youthful malady Shakespeare was to grow out of. The New Shakespeare editor says, 'as yet, farce and romance were not one "form" but

two separate stools; and between them in *The Comedy of Errors*
he fell to the ground'.[2] Quiller-Couch's half-truth misleads.
As I have argued in the previous chapter, farce and romance appear, in
varying proportions but indivisibly interlocked, in Shakespeare's
New Comedy models; and while it would be simply foolish to
deny the increasing refinement of artistry with which he manu-
factured 'one form' out of his heterogeneous materials, nevertheless in *The Comedy of Errors*, I suggest, not only did he *not* fall
between two stools, he laid the foundations for all his subsequent
essays in the comic mode. It is precisely the farcical phase of *The
Comedy of Errors* which, so far from requiring apology, confers
upon it a genuine primacy.

I wish to argue that in this first of the comedies Shakespeare's
fundamental, generating comic strategy is manifest, and that this
is what we must seek if we are to understand the comicalness of
Shakespearean comedy. The initiating privation is that created by
the losses of the various limbs of a family body. A husband has
lost a wife, a wife a husband, parents their children, children their
parents, and brothers each other. At the immediate opening of the
play we hear of poor Egeon's further loss of his one remaining
son, and the threat of death by a harsh and retributive law. All
that is required to save Egeon is a thousand marks but the extremity of his situation is the lack of anyone to pay it. Egeon's first
speech, therefore is expressive of his total adversity, isolation and
bereavement. He is a being so dispossessed that he welcomes
his fate:

> Yet this my comfort, when your words are done,
> My woes end likewise with the evening sun.
>
> (I. i. 26–7)

The Comedy of Errors begins Shakespeare's long exploration
of this danger zone with the issue which constitutes the basic
condition of personal integrity, of personal identity: sameness
and difference, pinpointed, in the doubleness of twins, in its most
overt and pantomimic form. The loading of the dice in this
direction is made clear by a moment's glance at the *Menaechmi*,
where the complete family plays no part, the likeness of the twins
to each other is the occasion of merely technical errors, and the

motivations of both sturdily pragmatic. Menaechmus I is engaged in keeping wife, mistress and parasite in that stage of tenuous equilibrium which makes life possible and Menaechmus II is speedily persuaded of the advantages of a courtesan's free hospitality however inexplicable. The climactically hilarious scene in which one twin simulates the madness everyone believes him to suffer from, in order to escape the attentions of a wife and a father-in-law, and the other *acts* madly out of the sheer fury and frustration induced by the unaccountable events, is totally devoid of reverberations which could suggest the dimension of inner experience. Compare the speech 'He that commends me to mine own content' of the melancholy, voyaging Antipholus of Syracuse:

> He that commends me to mine own content,
> Commends me to the thing I cannot get:
> I to the world am like a drop of water,
> That in the ocean seeks another drop,
> Who, falling there to find his fellow forth
> (Unseen, inquisitive), confounds himself.
> So I, to find a mother and a brother,
> In quest of them (unhappy), ah, lose myself
>
> (I. ii. 33–40)

This is followed by the first *pas-de-deux* of mistaken identities – of being 'unseen': he is called to a mysterious dinner by his servant who has unaccountably taken it into his head to chatter about mistresses and sisters instead of telling him where his money is bestowed.

When this same Dromio returns home to report to his mistress he does so with perhaps less than complete accuracy but with great pantomimic verve; and it so happens that his tale presents her with just what the feelings of a neglected wife need to inflame them:

> When I desir'd him to come home to dinner,
> He ask'd me for a [thousand] marks in gold:
> ''Tis dinner-time,' quoth I: 'My gold!' quoth he.
> 'Will you come?' quoth I: 'My gold!' quoth he;

'Where is the thousand marks I gave thee, villain?'
'The pig,' quoth I, 'is burn'd': 'My gold!' quoth he.
'My mistress, sir,' quoth I: 'Hang up thy mistress!
I know not thy mistress, out on thy mistress!'

(II. i. 60–8)

Adriana is a stout warrior against double standards ('Why should their liberty than ours be more?' and has tart replies to her sister's conservative pieties concerning women's place and the virtues of obedience, patience and meekness. But Dromio's tale confirms her worst suspicions, throws her into a paroxysm of self-pity and exacerbates the conjugal battle of the sexes between Adriana and her husband:

His company must do his minions grace,
Whilst I at home do starve for a merry look:
Hath homely age th' alluring beauty took
From my poor cheek? Then he hath wasted it.

What ruins are in me that can be found,
By him not ruin'd?

(II. i. 87–90; 96–7)

When we hear her appeal to her once devoted, now (apparently) wayward husband it must come as something of a surprise that she uses the very language of the Antipholus she is in fact addressing in the belief that he is her husband:

How comes it now, my husband, O how comes it,
That thou art then estranged from thyself?
Thyself I call it, being strange to me,
That, undividable incorporate,
Am better than thy dear self's better part.
Ah, do not tear away thyself from me;
For know, my love, as easy mayst thou fall
A drop of water in the breaking gulf,
And take unmingled hence that drop again,
Without addition or diminishing,
As take from me thyself and not me too.

(II. ii. 119–29)

Much has been made of the interesting recurrence, and interesting indeed it is. What I believe we are able to construct both from the recurrence as such and from the import of the ocean-waterdrop relation, is the restless, schizoid condition of Ephesians and Syracusans alike. Antipholus' baffled quest for himself – for the mother and the brother through whom he will realize himself – is the inverted mirror image of Adriana's almost rapacious 'incorporation' of her husband into herself, a frantic, possessive dependence. What is lacking in both is self-possession. Neither is his own man, with a composed and secure sense of his own independent separate identity and, in consequence, of the boundaries between himself and others. She is estranged from her husband; he is a stranger in a strange land. Neither sees him or herself as clearly and distinctly autonomous. Neither possesses the detachment of the drop, and both, in consequence, fear oceanic engulfment.

The beautiful farcical point of the play's whole evolution is that precisely oceanic engulfment, the great dread, overcomes them and their fellow protagonists, in the hyperbolic and comic-monstrous forms of fantasy. In the alien Antipholus, the tendency to be confused about who one is and where one is reaches a point where 'alienation' might well be a medical diagnosis. The disorientation and bewilderment of the Syracusan pair is referred to in terms which, while appropriate to the legendary Ephesus, transform the depth of their bafflement into a pathological paranoia: cozenage, sorcery, witchcraft, demonic possession; they are surrounded, so they believe, by cheats, mountebanks, 'goblins', 'owls', 'sprites', 'fiends', Satan himself, or 'the devil's dam' in the shape of the comforting courtesan. The resident twin becomes 'estranged from himself' in a sense no less radical.

The more they lose themselves in a spiralling whirligig of misapprehensions, the more their latent selves emerge, or are acted out. This is the fundamental Shakespearean discovery. The *processus turbarum* educes, brings out, exacerbates and enlarges the comic disposition, the maladies, frailties, fears and obsessions of the protagonists, and in so doing, brings remedy about. Both the comic fury of Ephesian Antipholus and the comic consternation of his twin illustrate the process. And when Adriana expresses her outrage in abuse of her errant husband:

> He is deformed, crooked, old, and sere,
> Ill-fac'd, worse-bodied, shapeless everywhere;
> Vicious, ungentle, foolish, blunt, unkind,
> Stigmatical in making, worse in mind.
>
> (IV. ii. 19–22)

and Luciana very sensibly enquires:

> Who would be jealous then of such a one?
> No evil lost is wail'd when it is gone.
>
> (IV. ii. 23–4)

Adriana's reply is significant:

> Ah, but I think him better than I say;
> And yet would herein other eyes were worse.
> Far from her nest the lapwing cries away;
> My heart prays for him, though my tongue do curse.
>
> (IV. ii. 25–8)

By the same token Adriana's simultaneous welcoming of one twin and rejection of the other can be seen as an externalization of the real ambivalence of her feelings. The knot of errors, the *processus turbarum*, turns the world of the protagonists upside down, and discovers them to us in all their comical, previously hidden ambivalences, violences and consternations. It also minimally, and as yet, inchoately, reveals them to themselves.

By the end of the play Antipholus will have found not only his mother, brother and father, but himself – a will and an orientation – through the familiar alchemy of romantic love; and Adriana, in the second plot, will have been neatly duped into a recognition of her own weaknesses and a capacity to realize her own genuine lovingness, through the cunning cross-examination of the Abbess. But for these bonuses of insight there is a price, the price of ridicule. Antipholus' courtship of Luciana is ridiculous because the lady in question is under the impression that he is her brother-in-law, who has taken leave of his morals as well as of his senses. It is one thing for a Petrarchan lover to find himself, his own self's better part, his eye's clear eye, his dear heart's dearer heart, his food, his fortune, his sweet hope's aim, his sole earth's heaven, and his heaven's claim in his mistress's visage, and quite another when the lady believes herself his sister-in-law and dashes off indignantly to fetch his wife to berate him.

Similarly, the Abbess's disguise (otherwise merely perfunctory) is made the means of the Abbess's tricky and therapeutic exposure of Adriana to herself. Trapped by the Abbess into a self-confession, Adriana recognizes as in a mirror her own face in the figure of the nagging wife. 'She did betray me to my own reproof', she says, acknowledging the remedial, truth-producing power of benign deceit. We never hear whether her husband's solid bourgeois complacency and fiery temper have been in any way chastened by his experiences, but the lively account of Dr Pinch's drubbing provides, as we shall see, a ludicrous, safety-valve catharsis.

The play's comic device is not strictly a 'device'. It is not invented by anyone. The identicalness of two sets of twins – two different identities under one appearance – is a tricky stratagem at best on the part of nature, not art, and a device only in the sense that the comic dramatist exploits it for his comic purposes. It is, as Harry Levin puts it, 'a practical joke conceived and executed by providence'.[3] But the question of sibling doubles lies at the heart of much persistent human questioning of identities and essences and appearances; questioning which found expression in folklore and literature before the philosophers and anthropologists and psychologists made of it their special province. In *The Comedy of Errors* the matching of violently severed family bonds with the Dromios' burlesque imitation of their masters' consternations and perplexities: 'Do you know me sir?' demands Syracusan Dromio of (this time!) Syracusan Antipholus. 'Am I Dromio? Am I your man? Am I myself?' make problems of identity at the level of mere identification comment ironically upon, or wryly illuminate problems of identity at the level of personal ontology. The Dromios, as they march back and forth with their messages, and their missions, their rope ends and their masters' purses, fated to miscarry and constantly belaboured by their irate masters, function to defuse by laughter the dire personal threat of traumatic non-entity, or total chaotic non-being.

The *processus turbarum*, with its accelerating and cumulative whirl of errors, produces, in the fullness of time, its own remedies. It also produces most of the sheer risibility of Shakespeare's comedies. It will be statutory for the funniest, most farcical, most palpably ridiculous scenes in Shakespearean comedies to occur when the tumult of errors is at its 'hiest and hottest', in Act III, and in IV, while the latter 'begins to bring about the remedy'.

One of the funniest moments, for instance, occurs outside the Antipholus house when Ephesian Dromio yells for 'Maude, Bridget, Marian, Cicely, Gillian, Ginn' and receives a mock echo from his mirror-image within: 'Mome, malt-horse, capon, coxcomb, idiot, patch', (III. i. 31–2) and one radical source of comic pleasure – mimicry – is neatly yoked to the whole question of who's who in a name-calling pantomime of excess.

Freud's calculus of the comic economy explains why we find funny both over and under expenditure of physical (in relation to mental) energy.[4] The argument is well known and it will suffice to recall no more exacting instances than the routines of a country bumpkin armed with a sledgehammer lunging ponderously about after a fly, or a professor totally absorbed in the mental construction of a sophisticated electronic device for the undoing of the same vexing insect. What farce does is to multiply such situations and propel them, in a rhythm of increasing intensity, towards some point of explosion or collapse. I find in a recent study two excellently expressive terms for the double dynamic of farcical pleasure: riot and deadlock; riot for the hyperbolic whirl of comically excessive, usually disinhibitory actions, and deadlock for the no-exit cul-de-sac into which protagonists are man-oeuvred and from which they must be extricated.[5] Farce, thus understood, may be instrumental in strategies of festive celebration, of satiric invective or of cathartic fantasy.

Farce is also, as its etymology tells us, stuffing;[6] and the structure of comic pleasure demands that a farce be stuffed indeed, to satiety, by its own exuberance. It is the achievement of Shakespeare's farce to exploit that exuberance for ends far beyond the immediate requirements of risibility, of celebration, or of satire. Ralph Berry has wittily summarized the relation between characters and situations in The Comedy of Errors as 'a study of the reactions of people to the farce in which they find themselves'.[7]

But I would prefer to say, 'to the farce *through* which they find themselves', stressing therapy as final cause. Shakespeare's farcical *processus turbarum* is a working-out of psychic material – the obsessions, compulsions, fantasies which, unresolved, unremedied, would represent catastrophe.

Put in non-psychological terms, this is to say no more than that the *processus turbarum* exhibits and enacts the besetting errors of the *dramatis personae*, and that the play's real and formal remedy is the convergence of the entire family at the Abbey where Antipholus' and Egeon's recovery and all the reunions can take place. One pair of twins has taken refuge there, and is produced to confront the other pair upon their arrival, following the violent overthrow of Dr Pinch, and Adriana's hotfoot pursuit of her 'poor distracted husband'. Errors are unpeeled like onions as each plaintiff in turn appeals to the Duke, and he in turn to the Abbess. Then the fortuitous presence of the Abbess transforms loss into restoration, grief into joy, ignorance into knowledge, alienation into homecoming, and imminent death into metaphorical rebirth.

> Thirty-three years have I but gone in travail
> Of you, my sons, and till this present hour
> My heavy burthen [ne'er] delivered.
> The Duke, my husband, and my children both,
> And you the calendars of their nativity,
> Go to a gossip's feast, and go with me –
> After so long grief, such nativity!   (v. i. 401–7)

She, the mother, is the matrix in which the whole family's individual identities are recovered; all are seen to be who they are, while the frontier between harm and remedy, the danger zone which is the territory of comedy, has been luridly marked by the doomed Egeon on his way to the nearby scaffold.

But, as I have indicated, Shakespeare proceeds consistently towards a conception of these follies and of their exhibition, as themselves remedial. His characters act out all manner of absurdities and these are, it turns out, the very stuff of human imperfection; the underside of the drama of psychic life. And the tumult they cause is at once expressive and therapeutic. By becoming absurd, the protagonists objectify their folly. Fooled, they become, to whatever degree, aware of themselves as selves and as fooled, and so have a basis for the regaining of control. And in this connection the episode of Dr Pinch is extremely interesting. Dr Pinch attempts to cure his client by the exorcism, in approved medieval mountebank manner, of the devils by whom he is, clearly, possessed. But since he is not in fact possessed by any devils at all, he turns the tables upon Dr Pinch and beats him prodigiously. The messenger's account of the breaking loose and the revenge of master and man, in v. i. 168–77, is uproariously comic, but what is of particular interest is the counterpoint treatment of remedy in this early comedy. Dr Pinch's cure for Antipholus' ills is a travesty of the true remedy which the play is enacting.

The complex and delicate transformation of perception, which lies at the heart of Shakespeare's comic method, is mediated by the Shakespearean fools, and is, indeed inconceivable without them. They are the common against which we measure the uncommon; they are the sense against which we measure nonsense; they are the natural against which we measure the unnatural; and they are the foolish against which we measure the wise.

Richard Levin, in his valuable study of multiple plots in Renaissance drama[8] provides useful categories for a theory of clowns. Clowns, he says, 'imitate' their betters, in actual practice or by formal analogy, giving a low comic version of what the serious, main protagonists are up to. But, as in any analogy, either difference or similarity can be stressed, or both, alternately. And it is in the play of complementaries, of difference and likeness, that the variety, interest and multiplicity of effect of Shakespeare's clowns lie. If, says Levin, it is the difference that is stressed, the ineptitude, rambunctiousness and amorality of, for instance. Pistol, Nym and Bardolph in *Henry V*, so that the skill, nobility and morality of the King's parallel activities are enhanced, then the clowns are acting as foils. If, on the other hand, it is the striking resemblance between the doings of the manifestly lower characters and the behaviour of the gentry that is stressed, then the higher characters will be disparaged, debased, assimilated and drawn down to the level of the foolish or ridiculous, and the clowns will have functioned as parodies. He quotes the Robin and Dick and Horse Courser episodes in *Dr Faustus* and notes that there will be differences in critical decision on whether their function is that of foil or parody according (mainly) to the reigning critical *zeitgeist*.

Two other possibilities are indicated by Levin. A clown's or clown plot's effect may function simultaneously in contrary directions with reference to two different higher characters. Pistol's cowardly bluster elevates Hal's soldiership by contrast, and ridicules the Dauphin's by similarity. And a clown or clown-plot may function simultaneously in contrary directions with respect to the same higher character or group of characters. In this, the most complex case, the parody is only apparent; it is, in Empson's terms, 'pseudo-parody', which disarms anti-sentimental responses by taking them into account in anticipation.[9] Mercutio's bawdy in Act II of *Romeo and Juliet* would be an example, the result of which is to confirm the validity of Romeo's romantic passion, to enhance and not to debase it. Levin spells out the interesting resultant paradox: it is the foil clowns (Touchstone, for instance) not the parodic ones who are themselves literary, or literally, parodists – conscious and deliberate mockers. The further effect is that of a lightning conductor – 'which works directly as a foil to set off an elevated main action, while it is working indirectly to attract and draw away those potential reactions hostile to that elevation'. And this effect is what he calls magic, like a ritual mock curse to ward off the evil eye, or to reduce its powers by playing something of its part ahead of time.

> For the clown's roles as child-idiot-lout, as Saturnalian ruler, and as ritual mocker all seem to operate in this manner by sanctioning the release through the subplot of our anarchic impulses and feelings, under controls which prevent them from threatening the adult, civilized norms of the main plot.
>
> (p. 146)

The Dromios, unlike their masters, whose fate they share, keep their wits about them and are never without some impudent repartee or wry observation, thus making their master's plight even more ridiculous than their own. They are, therefore, like their Terentian prototypes, Eiron-Buffoons. In terms of the

Shakespearean law of complementarity this makes the fooled Antipholuses a species of impostor. And so they are, indeed – the visiting Antipholus welcomed to bed and board none of his, and the resident Antipholus *treated* as an impostor by his frustrated creditors. The Dromios are the characteristic Shakespearean fools though the subtlety, obliquity and variety of the mimetic mockery deployed by later members of the class will grow immeasurably. In Syracusan Dromio's account of the 'wondrous fat marriage' apparently in store for him, upon which he expatiates with an Aristophanic verve, there is a good early example of Levin's 'lightning conductor' principle:

> Marry, sir, she's the kitchen wench and all grease, and I know not what use to put her to but to make a lamp of her and run from her by her own light. I warrant, her rags and the tallow in them will burn a Poland winter: if she lives till doomsday, she'll burn a week longer than the whole world.
>
> (III. ii. 95–100)

The analogy is to Adriana's claims upon Syracusan Antipholus as her supposed husband, and the similarity is certainly deflating. It has, moreover, an immediate absurd effect in that the dialogue precipitates Antipholus' beating of a retreat from a place apparently inhabited solely by comic-monstrous witches. But Dromio's diatribe, a ribald vilification of the fat wench's charms, is at the furthest possible remove downwards from the ambience of the relationship which has been developing between the peregrine Antipholus and his ostensible sister-in-law:

> It is thyself, mine own self's better part:
> Mine eye's clear eye, my dear heart's dearer heart
>
> (III. ii. 61–2)

and therefore functions as foil to the latter.

Luciana's 'gentle sovereign grace', her 'enchanting presence and discourse' (III. ii. 160–1) is left not only intact but enhanced, while the abusive, wittily anti-erotic catalogue drains off a good measure of the sexual aggression triggered by the volatile situation which has been developing in Ephesus. Traversi says with caution:

The introduction, through the twin Dromios, of a comic underplot, including a burlesque upon marriage itself in the pursuit of the Syracusan by the kitchen maid of Ephesus, presents yet another standpoint from which the central theme can be considered.[10]

The point at issue, however, is not the 'theme' of marriage but the dignity or absurdity of the protagonists, a matter which it is the function of Shakespearean comedy to place in exquisite and precarious poise.

Nothing is more revealing of his comic art, or of the directions it will take than the final moments of the play. The last words are, significantly, Dromio's. Says the Ephesian twin, complacently marching off with his brother: 'Methinks you are my glass and not my brother:/I see by you I am a sweet-fac'd youth' (v. i. 418–19). The whole little episode is a deliciously comic forerunner of a Lacanian *stade du miroir*.[11] But it is also a parody of self-discovery. And it punctures the whole grand remedial idea of regenerated, enlightened, separate, complete and viable personalities with the impermeable lunatic logic of its narcissism. Punctures, and yet reaffirms, since the contentment of Dromio with his inability to acquire a separate self at all is, our laughter tells us, the most reassuring antidote to insanity Ephesus could possibly supply.

Shakespeare's next investigation into the acquiring of separate selves – *The Two Gentlemen* – both complicates and deepens the issues. But in the meantime there are rivalries afoot in Padua, the settling of which will forge a vital link in the dramatist's portrayal of the battle of the sexes.

NOTES

1 The terms are R. D. Laing's in his celebrated study of the structure and imagery of the schizophrenic personality, *The Divided Self* (London: Tavistock Publications, 1960; reprinted New York: Pantheon, 1965).

2 The New Shakespeare edn (Cambridge: Cambridge University Press, 1922), p. xxii. A brilliant recent psychoanalytic

study of *The Comedy of Errors* (Barbara Freedman, 'Errors in Comedy: A Psychoanalytic Theory of Farce', Shakespearean Comedy issue of *New York Literary Forum*, ed. Maurice Charney, New York: Jeannine Plottel, 1980 [expected]), which came to my attention too late to be fully taken into account, agrees in the defence of farce. It is 'a strategic denial and displacement of meaning' through absurdity and the disjunction of cause and effect precisely in order for repressed libidinal material to find an acceptable outlet. 'Farce enacts', says Freedman, 'a primitive superego punishment for its characters' transgressions in the form of a maniacal plot which both arranges libidinal gratification and punishes for it'. The initial transgression in the case of *The Comedy of Errors* is Egeon's abandonment of his wife, and the twins represent the consequent splitting up of his psychic personality into the restless wanderer and the delinquent stay-at-home. The play is obsessed with confronting, punishing and forgiving debts — Egeon's which is actual and monetary but meaningless, and the twins' which are basically marital, mistaken and meaningful. Barbara Freedman's richly suggestive study extends, and confirms, my own at many points; but in her emphasis upon the 'one original, meaningful plot which can be retrieved' from the dispersions and denials of the farcical working through, that is, the plot of Egeon's rehabilitation or reintegration, she pays perhaps too little attention to the diversified, individualized dramatic material of the play.

3 H. Levin, introduction to the Signet edn of *The Comedy of Errors* (New York: New American Library, 1965), p. xxvi.

4 'Jokes and their Relation to the Unconscious', *The Standard Edition of the Complete Psychological Works of Sigmund Freud*, trans. James Strachey (London: Hogarth Press 1953–1966, vol. VIII, p. 236.

5 Zvi Jagendorf, 'Happy End'. Unpublished Doctoral Dissertation, Hebrew University of Jerusalem (1977), pp. 16–20.

6 See Robert C. Stephenson, 'Farce as Method', *Tulane Drama Review*, vol. 5, no. 2 (1961), pp. 85–93; and Eric Bentley, 'Farce' in *The Life of Drama* (New Jersey: Atheneum, 1964), pp. 219–56.

7 Ralph Berry, *Shakespeare's Comedies* (New Jersey: Princeton University Press, 1972), p. 25.

8 Richard Levin, *The Multiple Plot in English Renaissance Drama* (Chicago: University of Chicago Press, 1971), pp. 109–47.

9 William Empson, *Seven Types of Ambiguity* (reprinted 1930; Penguin, 1961) p. 52.

10 Derek Traversi, *Shakespeare: The Early Comedies* (London: Longman Green, 1960), p. 12.

11 In the now famous article which heralded Parisian neo-Freudianism, '*Le Stade du Miroir*' (1949), Lacan writes of the child's experience of himself when placed in front of a mirror, compared with that of a monkey which does not recognize itself, as indicative of the fundamental 'ontological structure of the human world'. 'It suffices to comprehend the *stade du miroir* as an identification in the full sense of this term in analysis – that is, the transformation produced in the subject when he assumes an image. . . . The joyful assumption of his specular image of a being still unable to control his motor functions and still dependent on his mother to nurse him . . . therefore seems to me to reveal in an exemplary situation the symbolic matrix in which the *je* precipitates itself in a primordial form, before it becomes objectified in the dialectic of the identification with the other, and before language restores to it in the universal, its function as subject.' Trans. Anthony Wilden, *The Language of the Self* (Baltimore: Johns Hopkins University Press, 1968), p. 135.

III

'KATE OF
KATE HALL'

A more gentlemanly age than our own was embarrassed by *The Shrew*. G. B. Shaw announced it 'altogether disgusting to the modern sensibility'.[1] Sir Arthur Quiller-Couch of the New Shakespeare, judged it

> primitive, somewhat brutal stuff and tiresome, if not positively offensive to any modern civilised man or modern woman, not an antiquary. . . . We do not and cannot, whether for better or worse, easily think of woman and her wedlock vow to obey quite in terms of a spaniel, a wife and a walnut tree – the more you whip 'em the better they be.[2]

It will be noticed, however, that Q's access of gallantry causes him to overlook the fact that apart from the cuffings and beatings of saucy or clumsy *zanni* which is canonical in Italianate comedy, no one whips anyone in *The Taming of the Shrew*, violence being confined to Katherina who beats her sister Bianca, and slaps Petruchio's face. Anne Barton has done much to restore a sense of proportion by quoting some of the punishments for termagant wives which really were practised in Shakespeare's day. Petruchio comes across, she says,

> far less as an aggressive male out to bully a refractory wife into total submission, than he does as a man who genuinely prizes

Katherina, and, by exploiting an age-old and basic antagonism between the sexes, manoeuvres her into an understanding of his nature and also her own.[3]

Ralph Berry reads the play rather as a Berneian exercise in the Games People Play, whereby Kate learns the rules of Petruchio's marriage game, which she plays hyperbolically and with ironic amusement. 'This is a husband-wife team that has settled to its own satisfaction, the rules of its games, and now preaches them unctuously to friends.'[4] In our own day, the wheel, as is the way with wheels, has come full circle and the redoubtable feminist, Ms Germaine Greer, has found the relationship of Kate and Petruchio preferable to the subservient docility of that sexist projection, the goody-goody Bianca.[5]

With all this fighting of the good fight behind us, we may approach the play with the unencumbered enjoyment it invites. As Michael West has excellently argued 'criticism has generally misconstrued the issue of the play as women's rights, whereas what the audience delightedly responds to are sexual rites'.[6] Nothing is more stimulating to the imagination than the tension of sexual conflict and sexual anticipation. Verbal smashing and stripping, verbal teasing and provoking and seducing are as exciting to the witnessing audience as to the characters enacting these moves. It is easy to see why The Shrew has always been a stage success, and so far from this being a point to be apologized for it should be seen as exhibiting Shakespeare's early command of farce as the radical of comic action, a mastery temporarily lost as he struggled to absorb more rarefied material in The Two Gentlemen and only later recovered. The mode, however, of the sexual battle in The Shrew is devious and indirect and reflects a remarkably subtle psychology. Petruchio neither beats his Kate nor rapes her − two 'primitive and brutal' methods of taming termagant wives, but neither is his unusual courtship of his refractory bride simply an exhibition of cock-of-the-walk male dominance to which in the end Katherina is forced to submit. Michael West's emphasis upon wooing dances and the folklore of sexual conquest is salutory, but Petruchio's conquest of Kate is far from merely a 'kind of mating dance with appropriate struggling and biceps

flexing'. Nor is she simply 'a healthy female animal who wants a
male strong enough to protect her, deflower her, and sire vigorous
offspring' (p. 69).

Only a very clever, very discerning man could bring off a
psychodrama so instructive, liberating and therapeutic as Petruchio's, on a honeymoon as sexless (as well as dinnerless) as
could well be imagined. Not by sex is sex conquered, nor for that
matter by the witholding of sex, though the play's tension spans
these poles. Christopher Sly, one recalls, is also constrained to
forgo his creature comforts, a stoic *malgré lui*, and thereby a foil
and foreshadower of the self-possessed Petruchio.

In the Induction, the page Bartholomew plays his part as Lady
Sly to such effect that Sly pauses only to determine whether to call
the lovely lady 'Al'ce madam, or Joan madam?' (Ind. II. 110) or
plain 'madam wife' before demanding 'Madam, undress you, and
come now to bed' (Ind. II. 117). Bartholomew must think fast, of
course, and does: '[I] should yet absent me from your bed', he
says, lest '[you] incur your former malady', and hopes that 'this
reason stands for my excuse' (Ind. II. 124). Sly clearly has his own
problems: 'Ay, it stands so that I may hardly tarry so long. But I
would be loath to fall into my dreams again. I will therefore tarry
in despite of the flesh and the blood' (Ind. II. 125–8). But Christopher Sly's 'former malady' is, of course, an imposed delusion: it
is not as anamnesic lord that he is himself but as drunken tinker.
Katherina's, we will finally learn to perceive, was self-imposed,
and requires the therapies of comedy – 'which bars a thousand
harms and lengthens life' – not the tumbling tricks of a 'Christ-
mas gambold' for its cure. This lower level functions as foil to the
higher yardstick and guarantor of the latter's reality.

The play's formal *telos* is to supply that which is manifestly
lacking: a husband for the wild, intractable and shrewish daughter
of Baptista. But how shall Katherina herself not perceive that
this husband is sought in order to enable her younger sister
to be happily married to one of *her* numerous suitors? The situation of inflamed and inflammatory sibling rivalry which the
good signor Baptista has allowed to develop between these
daughters of his is suggested with deft economy. Her very first
words:

> I pray you, sir, is it your will
> To make a stale of me amongst these mates?
>
> (I. i. 57–8)

speak hurt indignity, an exacerbated pride. Her response when
Baptista fondles and cossets the martyred Bianca:

> A pretty peat! it is best
> Put finger in the eye, and she knew why.
>
> (I. i. 78–9)

indicates her opinion that if Bianca is long suffering she is also
extracting the maximum benefit and enjoyment from that state.
Nothing that Baptista says or does but will be snatched up and
interpreted disadvantageously by this irascible sensitivity:

> Why, and I trust I may go too, may I not? What, shall I be
> appointed hours, as though (belike) I knew not what to take
> and what to leave? Ha!
>
> (I. i. 102–4)

These first glimpses already invite us to infer some reason for the
bad-tempered, headstrong, domestic tyranny Kate exercises, but
when we find her beating her cowering sister, screaming at her for
confidences about which of her suitors she most fancies, and
turning on her father with

> What, will you not suffer me? Nay, now I see
> She is your treasure, she must have a husband;
> I must dance barefoot on her wedding-day,
> And for your love to her lead apes in hell.
> Talk not to me, I will go sit and weep,
> Till I can find occasion of revenge.   (II. i. 31–6)

we surely do not require inordinate discernment to understand
what ails Katherina Minola. It is a marvellous touch that the pious
Bianca, defending herself from the wildcat elder sister (with no
suitor), says:

> Or what you will command me will I do
> So well I know my duty to my elders.
>
> (II. i. 6–7)

Bianca, it may be supposed, is not the only younger sister who has got her face scratched for a remark like that.

All of Padua, we are given to understand, is taken up with the problem of finding someone to take his devilish daughter off Baptista's hands, leaving the field free for the suitors of the heavenly Bianca. And this is precisely a trap in which Kate is caught. She has become nothing but an obstacle or a means to her sister's advancement. Even the husband they seek for her is in reality for the sister's sake, not hers. When she says: 'I will never marry' it is surely because she believes no 'real' husband of her own, who loves her for herself, whom she can trust, is possible. How indeed could it be otherwise since patently and manifestly no one does love her? Because (or therefore) she is not lovable. And the more unlovable she is the more she proves her point. Katherina of Acts I and II is a masterly and familiar portrait. No one about her can do right in her eyes, so great is her envy and suspicion. No one can penetrate her defences, so great her need for assurance. So determined is she to make herself invulnerable that she makes herself insufferable, and finds in insufferability her one defence. This is a 'knot of errors' of formidable proportions and will require no less than Petruchio's shock tactics for its undoing.[7]

The undoing begins with the arrival of Petruchio, to wive it wealthily in Padua. No doubts are entertained in Padua about the benefits of marriage where money is, but it will be noted that no one is banking on a rich marriage to save him from the bankruptcy courts. All the suitors are wealthy; Lucentio, potentially at least. The contrast that Shakespeare sets up between Petruchio and Lucentio is an interesting ironic inversion of that obtaining in the Terentian tradition. In Terence the second (liaison) plot entailed tricky stratagems for acquiring money in order to buy (and keep) the slave girl. The main (marriage) plot on the other hand hinged upon the fortunate discovery of a true identity, which meant both legitimizing the affair and acquiring the dowry. Here, in the case of Bianca and Lucentio the mercenary mechanics of match-making are masked by Petrarchan ardours on Lucentio's part (or Hortensio's, until the appearance of the widow):

> Tranio, I burn, I pine, I perish, Tranio,
>
> . . . let me be a slave, t'achieve that maid
> Whose sudden sight hath thrall'd my wounded eye.

(I. i. 155; 219–20)

and by angelic docility on Bianca's part; while Petruchio's affairs are deromanticized by the unabashed, unmasked worldlines of his motivation:

> I come to wive it wealthily in Padua;
> If wealthily, then happily in Padua.

(I. ii. 75–6)

and the formidable temper of Kate.

To Petruchio's incontinent and precipitate request to draw up the 'covenant' between them, Baptista demurs:

> Ay, when the special thing is well obtain'd,
> That is, her love; for that is all in all.

(II. i. 128–9)

and the reply is unequivocal:

> Why, that is nothing; for I tell you, father,
> I am as peremptory as she proud-minded;
> And where two raging fires meet together,
> They do consume the thing that feeds their fury.
> Though little fire grows great with little wind,
> Yet extreme gusts will blow out fire and all;
> So I to her, and so she yields to me,
> For I am rough, and woo not like a babe.

(II. i. 130–7)

And again: 'For I will board her, though she chide as loud/As thunder when the clouds in autumn crack' (I. ii. 95–6). Final recognitions will reverse these evaluations: the nakedly mercenary relationship will prove itself productive of affection and of spirit as well as sheer animal spirits; the romantic will prove hollow, its Petrarchanism a mere mask.[8]

In *The Shrew*, Shakespeare's characteristic handling of multiple levels is already to be discerned. The main protagonists are the agents of the higher recognitions, the middle groups function as screens on which are projected distorted mirror images of the main couples – images in a concave mirror; while the lower orders ridicule the middle by the parody of imitation, and act as foils for the higher by providing a measure of qualitative difference.

Though *The Shrew* fails to integrate Christopher Sly satisfactorily and indeed abandons him altogether after Act I, such a function for him, as I have already indicated, is adumbrated. Shakespeare, it seems, felt more comfortable with the playlet-within-the-play of *Love's Labour's Lost* and *A Midsummer Night's Dream* for his clowns, or with the parenthetic internal comment of a cunning and a foolish servant combination like Grumio/Tranio or Launce/Speed than with the clown-frame, to which he does not return. But the flurry of disguisings and contrivings, 'supposes' and role-playings in Baptista's middle-class household, resolved finally by nothing more complex than natural selection and substantial bank balances, do set off admirably the subtler, more complex and interiorized transformations of the Petruchio-Katherina relationship.

Petruchio's first speech in reply to Katherina's haughty insistence on her full name, is richly expressive:

> You lie, in faith, for you are call'd plain Kate,
> And bonny Kate, and sometimes Kate the curst;
> But Kate, the prettiest Kate in Christendom,
> Kate of Kate-Hall, my super-dainty Kate,
> For dainties are all Kates, and therefore, Kate,
> Take this of me, Kate of my consolation –
> Hearing thy mildness prais'd in every town,
> Thy virtues spoke of, and thy beauty sounded,
> Yet not so deeply as to thee belongs,
> Myself am mov'd to woo thee for my wife.
>
> (II. i. 185–94)

Ironic, mocking, amused and appreciative, it invites us to infer a certain relief, to say the least. Though he has stoutly affirmed his priorities:

> Be she as foul as was Florentius' love,
> As old as Sibyl, and as curst and shrowd
> As Socrates' Xantippe, or a worse . . .
>
> I come to wive it wealthily in Padua;
> If wealthily, then happily in Padua.
>
> (I. ii. 69–71; 75–6)

the spirited, bonny dark lass Baptista's terrible daughter turns out to be cannot but cause him a lift of the heart. She, for her part, does not of course respond immediately to his good-humoured teasing, but we may surely assume a certain vibration to be caused by this note of a tenderness which her obsessive fear of not finding has consistently put out of court. But she has built up sturdy bastions and will certainly not imitate her conciliatory sister. Combat is her chosen defence, and that these two are worthy opponents the set of wit which follows shows. Then comes the cut and thrust of the clash between her proud-mindedness and his peremptoriness. She misses no ploy, is outrageously provocative and brazenly impolite, verbally and even physically violent. He trips her up with a bawdy pun, she dares him to return a slapped face, and it is by no means certain to anyone that he will not. His strategy of mock denial:

> 'Twas told me you were rough and coy and sullen,
> And now I find report a very liar;
> For thou art pleasant, gamesome, passing courteous . . .
>
> (II. i. 243–5)

contains an infuriating sting in its tail:

> But slow in speech, yet sweet as spring-time flowers.
>
> (II. i. 246)

so that she is criticized for being what she most prides herself on not being, and consoled by being told she is what she most despises. Again:

> Why does the world report that Kate doth limp?
> O sland'rous world! Kate like the hazel-twig
> Is straight and slender, and as brown in hue

As hazel nuts, and sweeter than the kernels.
O, let me see thee walk. Thou dost not halt.

(II. i. 252–6)

And poor Kate must be beholden to him for patronizing defence
against the alleged detractions of a despised world, and finds
herself judiciously examined for faults much as if she were a
thoroughbred mare at a fair. It is no wonder that in reply to his

> Father, 'tis thus: yourself and all the world,
> That talk'd of her, have talk'd amiss of her.
> If she be curst, it is for policy,
> For she's not frorward, but modest as the dove;
> She is not hot, but temperate as the morn;
> For patience she will prove a second Grissel,
> And Roman Lucrece for her chastity;
> And to conclude, we have 'greed so well together
> That upon Sunday is the wedding-day.

(II. i. 290–8)

she can only splutter 'I'll see thee hanged on Sunday first'; a
response which is immediately interpreted by Petruchio, for the
benefit of the spectators, as a secret bargain between lovers:

> 'Tis bargain'd 'twixt us twain, being alone,
> That she shall still be curst in company.
> I tell you 'tis incredible to believe
> How much she loves me. O, the kindest Kate,
> She hung about my neck, and kiss on kiss
> She vied so fast, protesting oath on oath,
> That in a twink she won me to her love.
> O, you are novices! 'tis a world to see
> How tame, when men and women are alone,
> A meacock wretch can make the curstest
> shrew.   (II. i. 304–13)

Round one thus ends indeed with 'we will be married a'Sunday'.

Sunday, however, brings not the marriage that has been prepared for in the Minola household, but a mummer's carnival.
Petruchio arrives inordinately late, and in motley. Of the uproar

he produces in the church we hear from Gremio, in a lively description containing the shape of things to come:

> Tut, she's a lamb, a dove, a fool to him!
> I'll tell you, Sir Lucentio: when the priest
> Should ask if Katherine should be his wife,
> 'Ay, by gogs-wouns,' quoth he, and swore so loud
> That all amaz'd the priest let fall the book,
> And as he stoop'd again to take it up,
> This mad-brain'd bridegroom took him such a cuff
> That down fell priest and book, and book and priest.
> 'Now take them up,' quoth he, 'if any list.'
> *Tranio*   What said the wench when he rose again?
> *Gremio*   Trembled and shook; for why, he stamp'd and swore
> As if the vicar meant to cozen him.
> But after many ceremonies done,
> He calls for wine. 'A health!' quoth he, as if
> He had been aboard, carousing to his mates
> After a storm, quaff'd off the muscadel,
> And threw the sops all in the sexton's face . . .
>
> This done, he took the bride about the neck,
> And kiss'd her lips with such a clamorous smack
> That at the parting all the church did echo.
>
> (III. iii. 157–73; 177–9)

All of this is prologue to the first open clash of wills between these fiery newly-weds. He will instantly away, she 'will not be gone till I please myself':

> The door is open, sir, there lies your way:
> You may be jogging whiles your boots are green.
>
> (III. ii. 210–11)

> Father, be quiet, he shall stay my leisure.

> Gentlemen, forward to the bridal dinner.
> I see a woman may be made a fool,
> If she had not a spirit to resist.
>
> (III. ii. 217; 219–21)

This is Petruchio's cue:

They shall go forward, Kate, at thy command.
Obey the bride, you that attend on her.

But for my bonny Kate, she must with me.
Nay, look not big, nor stamp, nor stare, nor fret,
I will be master of what is mine own.
She is my goods, my chattels, she is my house,
My household stuff, my field, my barn,
My horse, my ox, my ass, my any thing;
And here she stands, touch her whoever dare,
I'll bring mine action on the proudest he
That stops my way in Padua. Grumio,
Draw forth thy weapon, we are beset with thieves;
Rescue thy mistress if thou be a man.
Fear not, sweet wench, they shall not touch thee, Kate!
I'll buckler thee against a million.

(III. ii. 222–3; 227–39)

And he snatches her off, sublimely indifferent to anything she
says, insisting upon his property rights, benignly protective, mind
you, of his bonny Kate, turning all her protests to his own pur
poses and depriving her of any shred of self-justification by his
indignant defence of her.

Stage-manager and chief actor, master of homeopathy – 'He
kills her in his own humour' as Peter says – Petruchio's play-
acting, his comic therapy, provides the comic device. One of a
long line of Shakespearean actor-protagonists he holds the mirror
up to nature, and shows scorn her own image. The tantrums that
she has specialized in throwing he throws in super-abundance,
forcing her to see herself in the mirror he thus holds up.

Grumio's tale of the saga of the journey:

. . . hadst thou not cross'd me, thou shouldst have heard how her
horse fell, and she under her horse; thou shouldst have heard in
how miry a place, how she was bemoil'd, how he left her with the
horse upon her, how he beat me because her horse stumbled,
how she waded through the dirt to pluck him off me; how
he swore, how she pray'd that never pray'd before; how I cried,
how the horses ran way, how her bridle was burst; how I lost

my crupper, with many things of worthy memory, which now shall die in oblivion, and thou return unexperienc'd to thy grave.   (IV. i. 72–84)

prepares for the continuing hubbub in the Petruchean dining-hall. That Petruchio's strategy has the additional advantage of an austerity regime as far as food and sleep and 'fine array' is concerned is all to the good. Petruchio is canny and will leave no stone unturned. Also, he has tamed hawks. But it is not physical hardship which will break Kate's spirit, nor does he wish it, any more than a spirited man would wish his horse or his hound spiritless. And Petruchio, we recall, wagers twenty times as much upon his wife as he would upon his hawk or his hound. Significantly, Kate's recurrent response to his carrying on is to fly to the defence of the cuffed and chivvied servants. Crossing her will, totally and consistently, under the guide of nothing but consideration for her desires, confuses and disorients her, as she complains to Grumio:

> What, did he marry me to famish me?
> Beggars that come unto my father's door
> Upon entreaty have a present alms,
> If not, elsewhere they meet with charity;
> But I, who never knew how to entreat,
> Nor never needed that I should entreat,
> Am starv'd for meat, giddy for lack of sleep,
> With oaths kept waking, and with brawling fed;
> And that which spites me more than all these wants,
> He does it under the name of perfect love;
>   (IV. iii. 3–12)

Katherine gets the point, but fails to get from Grumio even one of the mouth-watering items from a hearty English menu with which he tantalizes her. When she, listening hungrily to Petruchio's 'sermon of continency', and knowing not 'which way to stand, to look, to speak,' is 'as one new-risen from a dream', she might well rub her eyes and say, with Christopher Sly, . . . 'do I dream? Or have I dream'd till now?' (Ind. ii. 69).

What subtle Dr Petruchio has done is to drive a wedge into the steel plating of Kate's protective armour, so that he speaks at oncc to the self she has been and the self she would like to be; the self she has made of herself and the self she has hidden. The exchange of roles, with herself now at the receiving end of someone else's furies, takes her, as we say, out of herself; but she also perceives the method of his madnesses. Petruchio's remedy is an appeal to Kate's intelligence. These are not arbitrary brutalities, but the clearest of messages. And they are directed to her with undivided singleness of purpose.

In Act IV the remedy comes to fruition and Kate enunciates it:

> Then God be blest, it [is] the blessed sun,
> But sun it is not, when you say it is not;
> And the moon changes even as your mind.
> What you will have it nam'd, even that it is,
> And so it shall be so, for Katherine.   (IV. v. 18–22)

And then it is enacted, with considerable verve, as she addresses Vincentio, on cue from Petruchio, as 'young budding virgin, fair, and fresh, and sweet' and then promptly again, on cue, undoes all. Kate has yielded to a will stronger than her own and to an intelligence which has outmanoeuvred her, but the paradoxical, energizing and enlivening effect of the scene is that the laughter is directed not against her as butt or victim, but, through her prim performance, towards the disconcerted Vincentio. The *senex* is made fun of, in effect, by a pair of tricksters in some subtle alliance with each other not clear to him, but clear to the audience. Partly this response is structured by New Comedy paradigms. As Grumio puts it in Act I: 'Here's no knavery! See, to beguile the old folks, how the young folks lay their heads together!' (I. ii. 138–9). But mainly I believe it is due to our sense of liberation from deadlock. Petruchio has enlisted Kate's will and wit on his side, not broken them, and it is the function of the final festive test to confirm and exhibit this. It is also to be noted that the arrival in Padua of Vincentio 'exhausts' Lucentio's wooing devices, just as Petruchio's taming device exhausts its function; and it is a dexterous turn of composition which balances the mock non-recognition of Vincentio on the way to Padua, and his encounter with his Mantuan proxy, with the unmasking and recognition of the true Katherina, and the true Bianca, at the banquet.

That Kate is in love by Act V, is, I believe, what the play invites us to perceive. And indeed she may well be. The man she has married has humour and high spirits, intuition, patience, self-command and masterly intelligence; and there is more than merely a homily for Elizabethan wives in her famous speech:

> A woman mov'd is like a fountain troubled,
> Muddy, ill-seeming, thick, bereft of beauty,
> And while it is so, none so dry or thirsty
> Will deign to slip, or touch one drop of it.
> Thy husband is thy lord, thy life, thy keeper,
> Thy head, thy sovereign; one that cares for thee,
> And for thy maintenance; commits his body
> To painful labor, both by sea and land;
> To watch the night in storms, the day in cold,
> While thou li'st warm at home, secure and safe;
> And craves no other tribute at thy hands
> But love, fair looks, and true obedience –
> Too little payment for so great a debt.
>
> (v. ii. 142–54)

She wins her husband's wager but the speech bespeaks a generosity of spirit beyond the call of two hundred crowns. We have just heard Bianca snap at Lucentio mourning his lost bet: 'The more fool you for laying on my duty', and it seems that the metamorphosis of folly into wisdom which the comic action performs makes an Erastian reversal. More fool the Paduans indeed, in their exploitative hypocrisies and meannesses, than this madcap pair.

The very un-Petrarchan Petruchio has been the initiator of remedies in *The Taming of the Shrew* as well as the temperamental suitor; Katherina largely a responder and a foil. These positions will be reversed in *As You Like It* but not without a number of intermediate moves. *The Two Gentlemen of Verona* which follows *The Shrew* allows very little scope for the presentation of independent action on the part of Julia (despite her notable independence) and no occasion for courtship at all. Nevertheless, the growth of perceptions which make later developments possible proceeds through this next play, and is positively advanced by its explorations in the ambivalent and mimetic rivalry of the gentlemen.

NOTES

1 *Shaw on Shakespeare*, ed. Edwin Wilson (1961; reprinted Penguin, 1969), p. 198.
2 Introduction, The New Shakespeare edn (Cambridge: Cambridge University Press, 1928), p. xv.
3 The Riverside Shakespeare, ed. G. Blakemore Evans (Boston: Houghton Mifflin, 1974), p. 106.
4 Ralph Berry, *Shakespeare's Comedies* (New Jersey: Princeton University Press, 1972), p. 7.
5 Germaine Greer, *The Female Eunuch* (New York: McGraw Hill, 1971), pp. 220–1. 'The submission of a woman like Kate is genuine and exciting because she has something to lay down, her virgin pride and individuality: Bianca is the soul of duplicity . . .' (p. 221).
6 Michael West, 'The Folk Background of Petruchio's Wooing Dance: Male Supremacy in *The Taming of the Shrew*', *Shakespeare Studies*, vol. VII (1974), p. 71.
7 This vicious circle of the psyche is strikingly similar in form, to those delineated by R. D. Laing in his 'anthology of human bondage' as he calls *Knots* (New York: Random House, 1970). For instance:

> She has started to drink
>   as a way to cope
>   that makes her less able to cope
>
> the more she drinks
>   the more frightened she is of becoming a drunkard
>
> the more drunk
>   the less frightened of being drunk
>
> the more frightened of being drunk when not drunk
>   the more not frightened drunk
>   the more frightened not drunk . . .   (p. 29)

8 The contrast between hollow mercenariness, or the lower folly of ordinary existence and what Erasmus called the 'higher folly of the inner life' is further developed in *Much Ado*, and in *As You Like It*. See P. O. Kristeller, *The Classics and Renaissance Thought* (Cambridge, Massachusetts: Harvard University Press, 1955), pp. 62–3 and W. J. Kaiser, *Praisers of Folly* (Cambridge, Massachusetts: Harvard University Press, 1963).

IV

THE TWO GENTLEMEN
OF VERONA

In *The Two Gentlemen*, the doubling structure of *The Comedy of Errors* is repeated with some elaboration, but the scene of operations, so to speak, is thoroughly interiorized. The issue of mistaken identities is now predominantly within, a question of psychic identity rather than optic identification, a question of the self that the self chooses, or is driven, to be. Much has been written on the 'friendship literature', the cult of friendship and its conflict with the cult of love, from which *The Two Gentlemen* is said to derive.[1] But it may be profitable to consider these themes from the point of view of a deeper structure. For the purpose of examining the choice of selves and self-images, twins are conveniently replaced by friends, and by that aspect of the friendship of young men which is a matter of likeness and liking, of imitation and rivalry.[2]

In *The Comedy of Errors* there were two identical twin servants; here, there are two antithetical servants, one artless and one witty, chiastically arranged to match their masters, one witty, one foolish. Speed, the pert servant, a witty beggar who is later to reappear in Feste, in point of character would have been better matched with Proteus, and indeed at the beginning, in one of the play's notorious inconsistencies, he does carry letters from Proteus to Julia. Possibly Shakespeare changed his mind at some stage of his ruminations[3] when he saw the advantages of cross-matching his servants. In *The Comedy of Errors* there were two ladies (sisters), one married and betrayed, one unwed and available. Here the two ladies are spiritual sisters, both in fact unwed, but one is betrothed and betrayed. Both young men are transformed and metamorphozed – truly, not apparently – but Valentine is the equivalent of the travelling Antipholus who discovers love; Proteus of the (apparently) shape-shifting resident twin, who despises the love he possesses. The freeing of the relationships from the strictly determining family roles and the raising of affairs of the heart to the level of courtly ardour and artifice gives the play an added interest and resonance, while it advances the critique of Petrarchanism; but the trouble with *The Two Gentlemen* is that the farcical, exorcist principle has got lost in the elaboration of the sentimental reversals.

The usual complaint against farce is that it is too 'situational'; but in *The Two Gentlemen* there is not enough comedy of situation to render the reversals theatrically ludicrous however susceptible of interpretation as mockery or satire they may be.[4] Partly this is because there is no central comic device – no trick or stratagem to breed deceptions, and evoke or exacerbate follies. Julia's disguise comes too late for this and is the effect rather than the cause of Proteus' treacheries. As a consequence, there is no central comic protagonist-trickster – a Petruchio or an Oberon – to engineer and exhibit absurdities. And the result is that the deracination of folly is not mediated by means of mockery, but is merely announced. *The Two Gentlemen* is rich in comic potentiality, as its implied contrasts between *amour propre* and love proper, and its reversals, suggest; but for this particular collection of ills and follies Shakespeare has not yet found the right form of remedial exposure, though, as I hope to show in the following pages, he is within a stone's throw of his own best discovery.

*

Briefly, the story which *The Two Gentlemen* recounts concerns the replacing of one triangular relationship in a group of four by another, and the eventual emergence of two couples. Valentine is odd man out at the start. Symmetry reigns briefly when he falls in love with Sylvia, and each Jack has his Jill, as Puck would have said. Then, when Proteus abandons his Julia to pursue Valentine's Sylvia, Julia, now odd man out, sets off in disguise in pursuit of her love. Sylvia defiantly follows her now banished lover as well, and in the wood relations, already criss-crossed, are dizzily disrupted: Proteus is about to violate romantic propriety and Sylvia's honour by raping her; Valentine, rescuing her, repudiates his false friend. The latter repents, and Valentine's response to the challenge of that friend's repentance is the magnanimous renunciation of Sylvia. This pleases no one, neither the renouncer nor the renounced nor the recipient of the renunciation, since repentant Proteus will presumably no longer be content with a virtual rape victim in place of an adored mistress, nor the onlooker – the disguised and rejected Julia.

In Act V of *The Two Gentlemen* there is an intensified accumulation of the kind of switchback reversal which has structured the plot all along in the interchange of partners and rivals; the possibilities of further reversal are fairly exhausted or deadlocked by Proteus' bid for violence and Valentine's total renunciation. The only possible further move is for Proteus to refuse to accept the renunciation, thus outdoing his friend in magnanimity. And then? Either Valentine gets the girl, and Proteus is left forlorn, himself now odd man out, or both continue to vie with each other in magnanimity with poor Sylvia as pawn between them. Julia's unmasking following her swoon (which has been read as deliberate),[5] her appearance in her own presence to be recognized and to bring about resolution and reconciliation, is clearly what the plot demands for its remedy, and the initial deficiency for its correction. It is the logically satisfying closure for the initial asymmetrical situation. Proteus is disabused of 'delusions' as was Antipholus of Ephesus, and the ecstatic pair are free to continue to find themselves in each other. Yet there is little comic profit in this remedy because the accumulation of errors and ills, the 'increase and progression of perturbations' has not been shown to generate its own panaceas by virtue of its own absurdity and so, in effect, to exorcize itself as it progresses cumulatively and giddily towards exhaustion. Towards the accomplishment of this secret of his craft Shakespeare's early comedies make uncertain and erratic progress. And *The Two Gentlemen*, though richer and more diversified in surface features than *The Comedy of Errors*, manages its comic structure less surely.

The *Two Gentlemen* is particularly interesting in that it contains in inert state much of what is afterwards to be so memorably galvanized. Scarcely anything happens in the play that does not reappear later, transformed, reworked, re-imagined. It is an inventory of Shakespearean transformations. To exhaust the list would require another chapter. Some belong to the stock-in-trade of the Italian *novelle* from which Shakespeare drew his stories, or the New Comedy from which they derived, or the conventions of the *commedia dell' arte*, or Lyly: the witty servants, for instance, or Speed's mockery of the lover's demeanour, Valentine's rope-ladder, Julia's page disguise, Valentine's banishment and Sylvia's flight to the forest from her angry father, Proteus' recognition of an incriminating ring. Even the bandits. But the most significant Shakespearean transformations are those generated from the friend–rival relationship between the two gentlemen, and from the as yet partial transfer of the comic initiative to the ladies. The way in which Julia's errand to Sylvia with Proteus' message becomes Viola's to Olivia in Act II, scene v of *Twelfth Night* is paradigmatic for the development of Shakespearean comedy.

The *Two Gentlemen* is properly named, as are the two gentlemen themselves. For this is still a play in which the masculine view and the masculine initiative dominates. The differentiation between these two – friends and rivals – is, it turns out, a standard antithetical contrast between foolish virtue and cunning knavery transposed into the key of romantic love. Valentine is the credulous simpleton (witness the letter scene) and Proteus guilefully deceitful (witness his exploitation of Valentine's banishment). But this is itself a reversal of what appeared to be their original posture, when Valentine preached worldly wisdom to Proteus' 'homely wits'. Speed openly mocks the slower wits of Valentine, while Launce, the dunce, who serves the too-quick-witted Proteus, graphically depicts for us situations which point parodically to the moral deficiencies of his master by way of remonstrances and complaints over the faithless Crab:

my mother weeping, my father wailing, my sister crying, our

maid howling, our cat wringing her hands, and all our house in
a great perplexity, yet did not this cruel-hearted cur shed one
tear. He is a stone, a very pibble stone, and has no more pity in
him than a dog.   (II. iii. 6–11)

In the matter of love one is votary and one is heretic – the
interest will be in the comic reversal of a notable lover into, as
Launce would have it, 'a notable lubber' (II. v. 42–6), and of an
anti-lover into an emblem of love. The play is going to examine
the effects of love, the folly of love. So it says. But this is not
exactly what it does. It examines the remedial and beneficent
power of the ladies' love, and the uncertain, image-dependent,
wavering, volatile nature of the gentlemen's. And as a result of
this shift of the centre of gravity, so to speak, it examines the way
two gentlemen become themselves when possessed of quite mistaken initial notions of what becomes them. This is a fascinating
theme and a truly Shakespearean outcome, but it is as if this early
comedy does not quite know what it is about, and therefore does
not quite realize its own inherent possibilities.

Folly in *The Two Gentlemen* is identified by fancy-free Valentine. It is to be in love, he says, interpreting the signs:

> where scorn is bought with groans;
> Coy looks with heart-sore sighs; one fading moment's
>   mirth
> With twenty watchful, weary, tedious nights:
> If happ'ly won, perhaps a hapless gain;
> If lost, why then a grievous labor won;
> However – but a folly bought with wit,
> Or else a wit by folly vanquished.   (I. i. 29–35)

So, by your circumstance, you call me a fool, says Proteus, getting,
not surprisingly, the point. And against the folly of love Valentine
proposes the wisdom of foreign travel. Seeing the wonders of the
world broadens the mind – shapes the mind, he says. Proteus will
wear out his youth dully sluggardized at home, for 'Home-keeping
youth have ever homely wits' (I. i. 2). Thus is romantic love, the
finest flower of Renaissance courtship, nominated sluggardry by
Valentine. Proteus, replying to Valentine, is curiously ambiguous:

> Yet writers say: as in the sweetest bud
> The eating canker dwells, so eating love
> Inhabits in the finest wits of all.   (I. i. 42–4)

Proteus grants Valentine's point at the very moment when he defends his condition by appeal to the good company he keeps. The very finest wits are affected – so he defends himself. But by what? By an eating canker!

Proteus, left alone on the stage, entirely reflects his friend's view. 'He after honour hunts, I after love.' Proteus is a chameleon, a colour- and shape-shifter, as his name tells us. His desires are reflections of what he believes others desire. Therefore self-improvement, Valentine's aim, at once appears to him infinitely desirable. Thus, too, it is Valentine's denigration of love which is at once reflected in Proteus' change of mood:

> I [leave] myself, my friends, and all, for love.
> Thou, Julia, thou has metamorphis'd me,
> Made me neglect my studies, lose my time,
> War with good counsel, set the world at nought;
> Made wit with musing weak, heart sick with
>   thought.   (I. i. 65–9)

He is a perfect example of what René Girard has called 'triangular desire'[6] – the desire of an object because it is desired by another – and interestingly enough, he is fully conscious of this when he finds himself in love with Valentine's chosen mistress:

> Even as one heat another heat expels,
> Or as one nail by strength drives out another,
> So the remembrance of my former love
> Is by a newer object quite forgotten.
> [Is it] mine [eye], or Valentinus' praise,
> Her true perfection, or my false transgression,
> That make me reasonless, to reason thus?
>   (II. iv. 192–8)

When Speed says to Valentine of the 'deformed' Sylvia: 'If you love her, you cannot see her . . . Because Love is blind. O that you had mine eyes, or your own eyes had the lights they were wont to have when you chid at Sir Proteus for going ungarter'd!' (II. i 68–73) and tells him, moreover, what he should see: 'Your own present folly, and her passing deformity, . . .' (II. i. 75–6) he is himself possessed of defective vision because, as it transpires, Valentine's love for Sylvia is entirely justified. She is as good and devoted and loyal as she is beautiful. The joke is ultimately on Speed. But Speed nevertheless points to an important principle in all of Shakespeare's romantic comedies: love looks not with the eyes, but with the mind, as Helena is later to complain. The object of desire is mediated by Psyche no less than by Cupid, and the mind is a rag-bag of obliquities, mimicries, posturings and self-delusions.

The Girardian analysis makes good sense of the names. Proteus, amorphous, identity-less like his namesake, turns himself into Valentine, first by falling in love with the same girl, then by becoming Valentine's proxy suitor when Valentine is banished, and finally by violently attempting to take Valentine's physical place. Valentine, whose essence is love, seeking self-improvement, finds Sylvia.

Proteus' desire for what the envied other desires is set off against Valentine's total self-absorption in his own newly-discovered raptures:

> why, man, she is mine own,
> And I as rich in having such a jewel
> As twenty seas, if all their sand were pearl,
> The water nectar, and the rocks pure gold.
> Forgive me, that I do not dream on thee,
> Because thou seest me dote upon my love.
>
> (II. iv. 168–73)

The two gentlemen are each other's doubles, or mirror images, as Speed points out, obligingly explaining to Valentine how he knows the latter is in love:

Marry, by these special marks: first, you have learn'd, like Sir Proteus, to wreathe your arms, like a malecontent; to relish a love-song, like a robin-redbreast; to walk alone, like one that had the pestilence; to sigh, like a schoolboy that had lost his

ABC; to weep, like a young wench that had buried her gran-
dam; to fast, like one that takes diet; to watch, like one that
fears robbing; to speak puling, like a beggar at Hallowmas.
You were wont, when you laugh'd, to crow like a cock; when
you walk'd, to walk like one of the lions; when you fasted, it
was presently after dinner; when you look'd sadly, it was for
want of money; and now you are metamorphis'd with a mistress, that when I look on you, I can hardly think you my
master.   (II. i. 18–32)

For Valentine only Sylvia, his *alter ego*, can illuminate and
enliven the world. He has lost himself in her:

> Except I be by Silvia in the night,
> There is no music in the nightingale;
> Unless I look on Silvia in the day,
> There is no day for me to look upon.
>   (III. i. 178–81)

And when he gives her up to Proteus the reversal of roles is
complete.

For Proteus, the world is well worth losing for self-
gratification:

> I cannot leave to love, and yet I do;
> But there I leave to love where I should love.
> Julia I lose, and Valentine I lose:
> If I keep them, I needs must lose myself;
> If I lose them, thus find I by their loss –
> For Valentine, myself; for Julia, Silvia.
> I to myself am dearer than a friend,
> For love is still most precious in itself,
> And Silvia (witness heaven, that made her fair)
> Shows Julia but a swarthy Ethiope.
> I will forget that Julia is alive,
> Rememb'ring that my love to her is dead;
> And Valentine I'll hold an enemy,
> Aiming at Silvia as a sweeter friend.
> I cannot now prove constant to myself,
> Without some treachery us'd to Valentine.
>   (II. vi. 17–32)

But the self Proteus thus gains becomes a perverse masochism of monstrous proportions, filling his world:

> Already have I been false to Valentine,
> And now I must be as unjust to Thurio:
> Under the color of commending him,
> I have access my own love to prefer –
> But Silvia is too fair, too true, too holy,
> To be corrupted with my worthless gifts.
> When I protest true loyalty to her,
> She twits me with my falsehood to my friend;
> When to her beauty I commend my vows,
> She bids me think how I have been forsworn
> In breaking faith with Julia whom I lov'd;
> And notwithstanding all her sudden quips,
> The least whereof would quell a lover's hope,
> Yet, spaniel-like, the more she spurns my love,
> The more it grows, and fawneth on her still.
>
> (IV. ii. 1–15)

Valentine's loss of the worldly world on the other hand gains him 'this shadowy desert, unfrequented woods' which he 'better brook[s]' than 'flourishing peopled towns' (V. iv. 2–3). Both are thus contrarily isolated: Valentine in the forest deprived of the 'thou that dost inhabit in [his] breast' (though he does at least gain the brotherhood of the bandits), and Proteus within his obsession.

It is the cause of this sorry state and one possible remedy which is parodied by Launce's clown pantomime of canine faithlessness and dogged devotion:

> When a man's servant shall play the cur with him, look you, it goes hard: one that I brought up of a puppy; one that I sav'd from drowning, when three or four of his blind brothers and sisters went to it. I have taught him, even as one would say precisely, 'Thus I would teach a dog'. I was sent to deliver him as a present to Mistress Silvia from my master; and I came no sooner into the dining-chamber but he steps me to her trencher and steals her capon's leg. O, 'tis a foul thing when a cur cannot keep himself in all companies! I would have (as one should say)

one that takes upon him to be a dog indeed, to be, as it were, a dog at all things. If I had not had more wit than he, to take a fault upon me that he did, I think verily he had been hang'd for't; sure as I live he had suffer'd for't. You shall judge: he thrusts me himself into the company of three or four gentleman-like dogs, under the Duke's table. He had not been there (bless the mark!) a pissing-while, but all the chamber smelt him. 'Out with the dog', says one. 'What cur is that?' says another. 'Whip him out', says the third. 'Hang him up', says the Duke. I, having been acquainted with the smell before, knew it was Crab, and goes me to the fellow that whips the dogs: 'Friend', quoth I, 'you mean to whip the dog?' 'Ay, marry, do I', quoth he. 'You do him the more wrong', quoth I, 'twas I did the thing you wot of'. He makes me no more ado, but whips me out of the chamber. How many masters would do this for his servant? Nay, I'll be sworn, I have sat in the stocks for puddings he hath stol'n, otherwise he had been executed; I have stood on the pillory for geese he hath kill'd, otherwise he had suffer'd for't. Thou think'st not of this now. Nay, I remember the trick you serv'd me, when I took my leave of Madam Silvia. Did not I bid thee still mark me, and do as I do? When didst thou see me heave up my leg and make water against a gentlewoman's farthingale? Didst thou ever see me do such a trick?

(IV. iv. 1–39)

Structurally, this comic remonstrance is crucially placed: the faithlessness of Proteus has been laid bare; that of both Thurio and Sir Eglamour (Love's Philistines, as Harold Brooks has called them)[7] to the doctrine and discipline of courtly love is still to come; the faithful devotion of Valentine (and both Silvia and Julia) are in the process of trial and testing. It is an excellent example of what Levin has described as simultaneously foil and parody.[8] If an ungrateful cur is parodic proxy for Proteus, the rustic buffoon his owner is foil for Julia, his unconquerable good nature acting not to undercut but to underwrite Julia's 'folly'. It is the play's richest comic counterpoint, and its foolishness casts an exquisitely ludicrous light upon the courtly company.

Moreover, Act IV, as Shakespeare knew, 'exhibits the desperate state of the matter' and 'seeks a medicine for the turmoils'.[9] Act IV of *Two Gentlemen* excellently exemplifies certain Shakespearean ways of reflecting, and reflecting upon, that which his play presents as remedial in the situation which it depicts. Act IV, scene i introduces the outlaws, opening a window upon a world antithetical to the cultivated, spurious, accommodating and deceptive court. Nearer, as Charlton pointed out,[10] to the Pirates of Penzance than to any seriously-entertained image of natural simplicities, nevertheless their Spenserian and Italian pastoral antecedents are evident and their intended connotations plain enough. This presence is the informing spirit of Act IV. The specifically Shakespearean therapy of the forest is no more than germinal in this early play, but it is to be noticed that events in the forest do bring the absolutism of excluded middles in which the gentlemen are deadlocked to a crisis and an exhaustion. Proteus' threat of rape is a maximization of egoism, Valentine's renunciation – of Silvia, who is his essence – an ultimate in absolute altruism. The logic of either/or has by then run the play into a logical *cul-de-sac*, from which only the devoted presence of Julia can save it.

Once Valentine has been accepted into the outlaws' company (on the rather odd grounds of his linguistic accomplishments) we move to Silvia's window, where the devious Proteus serenades his friend's beloved, ostensibly for Thurio's sake. This double betrayal is rejected by Silvia with the contempt it deserves and witnessed by the abandoned Julia herself, in disguise.

The unknowing encounter between Julia and Silvia is the high point of the Act. And in it is realized the beneficent, saving irrationality which in blithe defiance of the law of excluded middles plunges toward solutions. Julia's speech sets out her dilemmas:

> Because he loves her, he despiseth me;
> Because I love him, I must pity him.
> This ring I gave him when he parted from me,
> To bind him to remember my good will;
> And now am I (unhappy messenger)

> To plead for that which I would not obtain,
> To carry that which I would have refus'd,
> To praise his faith which I would have disprais'd.
> I am my master's true confirmed love;
> But cannot be true servant to my master,
> Unless I prove false traitor to myself.
>
> (IV. iv. 95–105)

The antitheses echo Proteus:

> I cannot now prove constant to myself,
> Without some treachery used to Valentine.
>
> (II. vi. 31–2)

and Valentine's despairing

> To die is to be banished from myself,
> And Silvia is myself: banish'd from her
> Is self from self, a deadly banishment!
>
> (III. i. 171–3)

But it ends with the illogic of compromise:

> Yet will I woo for him, but yet so coldly
> As heaven it knows, I would not have him speed.
>
> (IV. iv. 106–7)

This is consonant with Julia's vividly-rendered vacillations over the letter from Proteus in Act I, scene ii. And there, too, the character is built up by the need to play a part. She is pretending to Lucetta that she has no interest in the letter. Carried away by the playing of the part she goes so far as to tear it up, only to fall frantically to trying to put it together again the moment her mocking maid is out of the room. Not consistency but inconsistency is the secret of dramatic character, and that of Julia deserves a more accomplished play.

In Act IV, scene iv, Julia, telling Silvia of Proteus' abandoned lady and inspired by the playing of her page's part, improvizes the story of the pageant ostensibly to justify her assessment of the lady's height – 'about my stature', but actually, we are invited to infer, to cloak her own scarcely controllable tears:

About my stature; for at Pentecost,
When all our pageants of delight were play'd,
Our youth got me to play the woman's part,
And I was trimm'd in Madam Julia's gown,
Which served me as fit, by all men's judgments,
As if the garment had been made for me;
Therefore I know she is about my height.
And at that time I made her weep agood,
For I did play a lamentable part.
Madam, 'twas Ariadne passioning
For Theseus' perjury and unjust flight;
Which I so lively acted with my tears
That my poor mistress, moved therewithal,
Wept bitterly; and would I might be dead
If I in thought felt not her very sorrow.

(IV. iv. 158–72)

This, for the first time, is the density and vivacity of characterization by impersonation to which later comedies will accustom us. It is, paradoxically, out of the rendering of dissimulation that the impression of a genuine personality emerges. The gap between the ostensible (the story of the pageant) and the inferred (what we know of the speaker and her possible motives) is such as to provoke and exercise the imagination of the audience, and it is this exercise of the imagination which creates the mimetic illusion. The effect, of course, is foregrounded by the disguise, but the page disguise is not indispensable, as the first scene shows.

The girl-boy disguise device of the *novelle* may well have represented itself to the dramatist as an invaluable bonus in the development of a sophisticated character portrayal, but it also precipitates the imagining of a complex and double point of view. So, in Julia's soliloquy upon the portrait of Silvia – that 'virtuous gentlewoman, mild and beautiful' – she promises herself an auburn wig to take the place of her own 'perfect yellow' (if that is what is required) and concludes with lines of resonant and reflective maturity almost sufficient to persuade us that she might make a reality even of Proteus' cardboard love if she should ever regain it:

> Come, shadow, come, and take this shadow up,
> For 'tis thy rival. O thou senseless form,
> Thou shalt be worshipp'd, kiss'd, lov'd, and ador'd;
> And were there sense in his idolatry,
> My substance should be statue in thy stead.
>
> (IV. iv. 197–201)

Shadow and substance, image and idol: these recurrences point to a preoccupation which later comedies will explore and immensely deepen. *The Two Gentlemen* moves on the threshold only of these later concerns; but in its song to Silvia gives lyric expression to what the discovery of Julia dramatizes. In this context 'Who is Silvia, what is she/That all our swains commend her?' is a key question; and 'Love doth to her eyes repair/To help him of his blindness' a key remedy which later comedies will wonderfully explore.

Though *The Two Gentlemen* does not live up to its comic potentialities, its resolution is an interesting foreshadowing. The scandal of Act V (Quiller-Couch says, with Victorian primness, 'there are by this time *no* gentlemen in Verona'[11] has distracted attention from the real significance of the play's resolution. The intended rape, however, is no more than the moment of incipient danger and harm which is statutory in Shakespearean comedy to demarcate its frontiers and mark its remedy. It might even be argued, since human deficiencies generate tragedy as readily as comedy, that the remedies of comedy require no less than a deliberate, perilous skirting of harm and danger. The real trouble is the absence, in their speech, of nuance, of an expressive self-awareness.

However, when Julia defends her disguise on the grounds that modesty finds women's shape-changing a 'lesser blot' than men's mind-changing, Proteus exclaims:

> 'Than men their minds?' 'tis true. O heaven, were man
> But constant, he were perfect; that one error
> Fills him with faults; makes him run through all th' sins:
> Inconstancy falls off ere it begins.
> What is in Silvia's face, but I may spy
> More fresh in Julia's with a constant eye?   (v. iv. 110–15)

The speech has been faulted for lack of eloquence but there is a certain disingenuous, uncouth vehemence in its exclamatory confirmation of the primacy of 'mind' over 'eye' that does carry conviction. Proteus blames his 'inconstancy', but audience hindsight, collating all it has seen, comprehends at a higher level of generality the nature of the folly or comic disposition of Verona's young men. To neither gentlemen at the start of the play was love anything but a fashion, or an imitation. They use the language of metamorphosis, but their adolescent attachment to each other is largely unchanged. As Nietzsche said, everything absolute belongs in the realm of pathology; and their compulsive vacillations between disjunctive alternatives: either be him or kill him, either all or nothing, is certainly that.

When Julia faints, however, at the climax of Act V and then produces her ring and is recognized, she is the living proof that exclusive-alternative catastrophe can be eluded, given a certain feminine capacity for waiting upon the event, nourishing and fostering it, till it ripen in its own good time. In Julia craft and constancy, spontaneity and morality, are no longer irremediably sundered as they have been for the two gentlemen, nor self and other doomed to a polarity of identity or non-entity. Julia *is*, it appears, the excluded middle it was their folly not to perceive, and an admirable remedy for the gentlemen's ills. But she lacks, as yet, the Shakespearean trickster-heroine's freedom and élan.

Shakespeare's next essay in the comic mode is by way of being two steps forward and one back. The tendency to disjunctive alternatives, among other intellectual disabilities, is exhibited at large among Navarre's young men, who also vie with each other in extremist zeal and do not always clearly distinguish between the recipients of their respective affections. A new departure is the critic in the company who provides occasion for counter-turns and counterpoint which double discomfiture, and, of course, the marvellous elaboration of the comics. The ladies in the case are witty wenches, self-assertive and wise enough to tease the scales from their suitors' eyes; yet no comic resolution ensues. And this, the stubborn fact of a non-comic, even anti-comic conclusion to *Love Labour's Lost* surely requires explication.

NOTES

1 See, for example, Muriel Bradbrook, *Shakespeare and Elizabethan Poetry* (London: Chatto & Windus, 1951), p. 151, passim.

2 Compare Thomas E. Scheye's stimulating paper, 'Two Gentlemen of Milan', *Shakespeare Studies*, vol. VII (1969).

3 On the inconsistencies and their explication, see Clifford Leech, editor of the New Arden edn (London: Methuen, 1969), introduction, pp. xiii–xxxv.

4 Hereward Price, 'Shakespeare as a Critic', vol. XX (1941), pp. 390–9, took the reversals as intended to 'prove Valentine a fool' and the trend towards a satiric reading has gained ground in recent criticism. See, for example, Leech in the New Arden edn, and Alexander Leggatt, *Shakespeare's Comedy of Love* (London: Methuen, 1974), pp. 21–40.

5 New Arden edn, introduction, p. lxvii.

6 René Girard, *Deceit, Desire and the Novel: Self and Other in Literary Structure*, translated by Yvonne Freccero (Baltimore: Johns Hopkins University Press, 1965); cf. Scheye, 'Two Gentlemen of Milan'.

7 Harold F. Brooks, 'Two Clowns in a Comedy (to say nothing of a Dog): Speed, Launce (and Crab) in The Two Gentlemen of Verona', *Essays and Studies* (1963).

8 Richard Levin, *The Multiple Plot in English Renaissance Drama* (Chicago: University of Chicago Press, 1971), ch. IV. On the parodic element in Launce's speech, see also Brooks, 'Two Clowns', p. 99, and Leech, introduction, p. lxvi.

9 Willichius, in the Commentary to Terence's *Andria*, 1550 edition: quoted in T. W. Baldwin, *Shakespeare's Five-Act Structure* (Urbana: University of Illinois Press, 1947), p. 715. See also Marvin Herrick, *Comic Theory in the Sixteenth Century* (Urbana: University of Illinois Press, 1964), pp. 119ff.

10 H. B. Charlton, *Shakespearian Comedy* (London: Methuen, 1938), p. 40.

11 A. Quiller-Couch, to The New Shakespeare edn (Cambridge: University Press, 1921) introduction, p. xiv.

V

NAVARRE'S
WORLD OF WORDS

'The distinctive human problem', says Ernest Becker in *The Denial of Death*, 'has been the need to spiritualize human life, to lift it onto a special immortal plane, beyond the cycles of life and death that characterize all other organisms.'' His words would have been heartily endorsed by Shakespeare's King of Navarre. But Navarre and his bookmen are not content with declarative statements of general import. 'Our late edict shall strongly stand in force', says the King. 'Navarre shall be the wonder of the world;/Our court shall be a little academe,/Still and contemplative in living art' (I. i. 11–14). 'Still and contemplative', but with a wary eye upon that most flattering of the great humanist motivations:

> Let fame, that all hunt after in their lives,
> Live regist'red upon our brazen tombs,
> And then grace us in the disgrace of death;
> When spite of cormorant devouring Time,
> Th' endeavor of this present breath may buy
> That honor which shall bate his scythe's keen edge,
> And make us heirs of all eternity. (I. i. 1–7)

In these first words both the King's project 'to live laborious days' and his characteristic habit of mind are succinctly conveyed. Present rewards will be renounced so that future gains – immortal increments – be ensured. But the particular appeal the project has for the King is rendered in a euphuistic figure called by Renaissance rhetoricians Polyptoton: 'When ye turn and tranlace a word into many sundry shapes, as the Tailor doth his garment, and after that sort display with him in your dittie'.[2] Peacham's explanatory image of sartorial display throws no inconsiderable light, as we shall see, upon *Love's Labour's Lost*. Such a figure is 'And then grace us in the disgrace of death', or 'Your oath is pass'd to pass away from these' (I. i. 49). It is a favourite of the King's and, to anticipate, one of the play's most effective moments occurs when the King's favourite figure conspicuously lets him down. Mercade has delivered his news, the bereaved Princess is bidding Navarre farewell. The King's speech is a mélange of embarrassment and awkwardness: 'The extreme parts of time extremely forms/All causes to the purpose of his speed, . . .' (v. ii. 740–1), to which the Princess replies simply (and significantly) 'I understand you not, my griefs are double' (v. ii. 752), and it takes the dexterous Berowne to attempt reclamation:

> Honest plain words best pierce the ear of grief,
> And by these badges understand the King.
>
> (v. ii. 753–4)

But this later on.

At the outset Longaville and Dumain, enthusiastic warriors against their own affections and the huge army of the world's desires, yearn to banquet the mind, not the body, to die to love, wealth, pomp. In this they are unlike the practical Costard, who hopes, if he has to fast, to do it on a full stomach. He is foil to the King and his entourage who dream of a spiritualized world of words. The fame they seek is itself a linguistic phenomenon – words engraved to all eternity upon the graves which hold mere mortal remains. The King and his bookmen we perceive, are compulsive not only about the performatives – edicts and oaths and vows – but also about the whole immense array of rhetorical schemes and tropes with which – in which – they delight to disport themselves. For the King even a signature (by way of a zeugma) has illocutionary force:

and now subscribe your names,
That his own hand may strike his honor down
That violates the smallest branch herein.

(I. i. 19–21)

But he does not sufficiently reckon with the presence of a fifth
column within his own ranks. The courtiers' heroic enterprise is
challenged by the sceptical odd man out in the fraternity. To live
and study three years with the King, yes, says Berowne. But there
are those ancillary observances which he hopes are not enrolled –
'not to see ladies, study, fast, not sleep'. 'I swore in jest', he
protests, welshing; and equivocates shamelessly. He will swear to
study things 'hid and barred from common sense' – a description
of study's arcane and godlike recompense that he has extracted
from the King – but only if somewhat differently defined: where
to dine well, meet a fine mistress, how to break oaths and get away
with it (I. i. ff.). He rises to a vehement eloquence in defence of his
pragmatism:

Study me how to please the eye indeed
By fixing it upon a fairer eye,
Who dazzling so, that eye shall be his heed,
And give him light that it was blinded by.
Study is like the heaven's glorious sun,
That will not be deep search'd with saucy looks;
Small have continual plodders ever won,
Save base authority from others' books.
These earthly godfathers of heaven's lights,
That give a name to every fixed star,
Have no more profit of their shining nights
Than those that walk and wot not what they are.

(I. i. 80–91)

So forceful indeed is this pragmatical view that the King resorts to
his favourite figure with some unwilling envy: 'How well he's
read, to reason against reading', and is echoed faithfully and
parisonically by his acolytes: 'Proceeded well, to stop all good
proceeding'; and 'He weeds the corn and still lets grow the weed-
ing'. Berowne parries ironically with suitably similar form and

unsuitably dissimilar matter: 'The spring is near when green geese are a-breeding', and Dumaine falls into the trap. 'How follows that?' he asks. Berowne rubs in the green geese part with 'Fit in his place and time', and Dumaine's clumsily defensive, 'In reason nothing' gives Berowne the opportunity for a scoffing riposte: 'Something then in rhyme'. The King, intent upon his beloved scheme, joins in with acerbity: 'Berowne is like an envious sneaping frost/That bites the first-born infants of the spring', and Berowne nimbly picks up the cue and turns it to his own advantage with a pointed reference to the unseasonability of the King's desire to study.

Sets of wit, a stylized power game, have been standard fare in courtly comedy since Lyly, with a word or figure tossed back and forth between players who gain points with each shift of meaning or extension of meaning. Nor was an interest in the powers, effects and devices of rhetoric confined to Navarre in the sixteenth century. The point is rather that in *Love's Labour's Lost* Shakespeare has created laboratory conditions, so to speak, for comic enquiry concerning the way of a man with a word.

As everyone will remember, the academicians, intent upon their monastic vows, overlook in their enthusiasm certain ambassadorial functions which the management of the Kingdom of Navarre continues inconveniently to demand. Therefore all that the play requires for their discomfiture is the arrival of a bevy of charming ladies on embassy from France. The solemn oaths are put to the instant test, they crumble at a touch, the bookmen come out in a rash of sonnets, and a number of low attempts are made on the part of each in turn to break his oath without his companions knowing of his treachery.

What is lacking at the outset of this comedy – what the King seeks – is plainly stated:

> Navarre shall be the wonder of the world;
> Our court shall be a little academe,
> Still and contemplative in living art.   (I. i. 12–14)

It is the secret of this 'living art' which is wanting. And the oxymoron (life/art) makes it clear that the prescription is not to be easily found, even if we could suppose its seekers to be endowed

with a greater degree of common sense and more sense of proportion than the courtiers of Navarre. More specifically, however, the comic disposition in Navarre might well be described as
the tendency to take oneself too seriously or not seriously enough,
or both, at unseasonable times and places; and the cardinal error
which the comedy explores, exposes, exacerbates and proposes to
remedy is the conviction that the world is made of words.

That the loss of her tongue (Longaville's ingenious penalty
clause) will be the fate that awaits a lady daring to come within a
mile of the court is a comic exposure of the company's besetting
obsession. That the lady could lose nothing more important is
a chief tenet in their communal creed; but that she would be
'frighted hence' by only hearing of that dread penalty is not only
evidence of a truly remarkable faith in verbal power, but a
'dangerous law against gentility' as Berowne (of course) is quick
to point out. The King describes Armado, who will amuse them,
as a man that hath a mint of phrases in his brain:

> One who the music of his own vain tongue
> Doth ravish like enchanting harmony;   (I. i. 166–7)

But by the time we hear this, we find that the description cuts
neatly both ways, applying with equal validity to the designator
and the nominee.

Ironic Berowne, accomplished rhetorician, sceptical libertine,
pragmatical sophist and (but the matter is, as we shall see, in
doubt) lover, is the chief vessel of the play's enquiry. He agrees to
take the oath, it will be recalled, precisely at the moment when the
Princess has arrived, and 'not to see ladies' is already a broken
article. 'Necessity will make us all forsworn' he announces cheer-
fully, knowing even before Jaquenetta and Costard produce
incontrovertible evidence, that

> every man with his affects is born,
> Not by might mast'red, but by special grace.
>
> (I. i. 151–2)

But, though he speaks for 'barbarism', he is too convivial to
renounce the collective pursuit of 'angel knowledge', and is
moreover complacently assured that

If I break faith, this word shall speak for me:
I am forsworn 'on mere necessity'.   (I. i. 153–4)

To this debonair young man life is a language game he is confident
he can win. It is therefore cunningly consonant with the play's
theme that crossed *letters* constitute the comic device which punctures conceit and reveals truths, exposing at once the deception
practised by both Berowne and his comic double, Armado.

The originality of *Love's Labour's Lost* lies in the transformation of the slippery power of language into the dialectical comic
theme itself. Word-play and wit-work, jest and earnest, reciprocally test, define and illuminate each other during the comic progress of the play, itself an extravagant display of verbal exuberance; and it is the learned fools, Armado and Holofernes, who
direct our perception to this. They owe their origin no doubt to
the unprecedented language explosion of the Elizabethan period.
But their functionality in the play is surely an inspiration on
Shakespeare's part. Middle class, and transparent in their motivations, they are preposterous, hyperbolic imitations of the courtiers, grotesque mirror images of the heroic furor of arms and
arts. The hierarchy of comic resemblance, in earlier plays limited
to master and servant, acquires through them a further layer, and
a new middle-level possibility is opened up. The result is a masterpiece of indirect analogy. The social scene of the play is also
extended in range in this way, but chiefly their effect is that of
parody.

They, too, the preposterous pair, do things with words,[3] rather
more prosaic and mundane things, perhaps, but of a revealingly
similar kind. They jockey for positions, fantasize, outbid, outwit,
compete. The degree to which Armado's peacock display of finery
in the shape of flowers of rhetoric is a form of conspicuous
consumption – the only kind he can afford, it transpires – is
glaringly evident, but Holofernes' ecstasy of schoolmastering is
also something of a paying proposition if the adulation of Sir
Nathaniel is any indication: 'And thank you too; for society, saith
the text, is the happiness of life' (IV. ii. 161–2). Thus Nathaniel
unctuously accepts Holofernes' invitation to a free dinner, supplied by a pupil's father in return for an exhibition of literary criti-

cal skills: Holofernes will prove Berowne's verses to be very 'un-learned, neither savoring of poetry, wit, nor invention' (IV. ii. 160). They dined well, if post-prandial conviviality is any indication. The beauty of Shakespeare's invention is that these uncon-scious parodists, playing their language games transparently for prizes and praises, and to be 'singuled from the barbarous' (v. i. 81–2), use every known and conceivable vice of language recog-nized in the rhetoric books of the day. The aberrations of lan-guage of these fops thus parallels the aberration of mind of the courtiers. In them the verbal dandyism of Navarre is, metaphori-cally, substantiated. For them words are 'most dainty epithets' to be mouthed and tasted and eaten, too, as if words and their powers were the basic stuff of life. If it is a case of the courtiers feasting their minds, these underlings are busy minding the feast, and the inverted caricature is mirrored in the comic catachreses of the play's language itself. 'They have been at a great feast of languages, and stol'n the scraps', observes the diminutive Moth, receiving for his pains Costard's retort to the effect that his master might well have eaten him for a word. But he agrees, nevertheless: 'they have liv'd long on the alms-basket of words' (IV. i. 36); while the toady Nathaniel outdoes him in a denigratory apology for poor Dull: 'Sir, he hath never fed of the daintics that are bred in a book;/He hath not eat paper, as it were; he hath not drunk ink; his intellect is not replenished' (IV. ii. 24–6). Berowne joins the chorus when he says of Boyet, 'This fellow pecks up wit as pigeons pease' (v. ii. 315) and cheeky, lively Moth provides an offbeat counter-point in his advice to Armado on the conduct of his amorous affairs: 'sigh a note and sing a note, sometime through the throat, [as] if you swallow'd love with singing love, sometime through [the] nose, as if you snuff'd up love by smelling love; . . .' (III. i. 13–17).

Bomphiologia (it is our loss to have allowed this particular inkhorn term to lapse into antiquity) is Armado's characteristic vice. It was, according to Peacham, an inflation of both words and matter

when trifling matters be set out with semblaunt and blazing wordes, used of none but of such as be eyther smell-feasts, and

Parasites, which mayntayne their good cheere with counter-feyted prayses, or of great bosters and craking souldyours, as of Thraso in Terence, and such lyke persons in Comodyes.[4]

But he is also not innocent of *Soraismus*, the mingle-mangle, or mixture of tongues: 'but we will put it (as they say) to *fortuna della [guerra]*' (v. ii. 530). These were recognized vices, and make their users butts for the mocking amusement of the courtiers. But there are other recognized vices – Solecisms, Tapinoses, and general breakings of Priscian's head which the pedant is quick to notice in lesser mortals like Costard and Dull, thus producing a double quota of comic pleasure for the audience.

The comicality of the learned clowns' 'maggot ostentation' is further augmented by the marvellous complacency with which they display their bombast, their pomposity, their self-conceit and their affected foppery. Their capacity for self-congratulation is practically unlimited. 'This is a gift that I have', says Holofernes modestly, 'simple; simple, a foolish extravagant spirit, full of forms, figures, shapes, objects, ideas, apprehensions, motions, revolutions. . . . But the gift is good in those [in] whom it is acute, and I am thankful for it' (IV. ii. 65–72). Self-congratulation also takes the form of a capacity to bask in reflected light, however delusive. One of the engaging things about them is the prodigality of their praise for their partners' witty sallies. Except for the one occasion when Armado becomes inexplicably incensed about an eel, he has nothing but praise for the felicities of his tender juvenal, though that ingenious and well-educated infant is very far from invariably on his master's side. Nathaniel is perpetually thanking God for the profundities of Holofernes' learning, his singular choice epithets, his sharp and sententious reasons, his fund of elegancies, and in general the profit accruing to any common-wealth fortunate enough to count him among its pedagogues. Moth and Armado, Nathaniel and Holofernes constitute indeed a pair of mutual admiration societies, highly competitive and volu-bly critical of each other, mind you, though Armado does succeed in extracting a compliment from Holofernes for his 'posteriors of the day': 'The posterior of the day, most generous sir, is liable, congruent, and measurable for the afternoon. The word is well cull'd, chose, sweet and apt, I do assure you, sir, I do assure' (v. i. 91–4). They exist in a narcissitic glow produced, one feels, by no more than the sheer profusion of self-enhancing, self-gratifying euphoric speech acts. And in this way the vices of rhetoric parody the vice of Rhetoric. In its mimesis of linguistic absurdities, obsessions, compulsions and self-fulfilling delusions, the play is itself a superb linguistic *jeu d'esprit*.

At the base of the pyramid are the fools proper. And they, too, function in complex ways both as parodies and foils. The outer limits of Navarre's language territory are defined by Dull, who is for the most part completely out of his depth. Like the later Verges, he 'reprehends' the Duke's own person (i. i. 183), clings doggedly to his old grey doe (iv. ii. 12ff.) as the one familiar landmark in the mists of Holofernes' Latinity, and is apologized for by Nathaniel as one who has never fed of the dainties that are bred in a book. Costard, on the other hand, though an unlettered and small-knowing soul in Armado's opinion (i. i. 250) is, in his own modest and plebeian fashion also something of a wit. Costard is a stage in the ramification of Shakespeare's impenetrable wise fool from, first, the undifferentiated Dromio twins, and then the clever/foolish split pair, Speed and Launce. In this new compound of Buffoon and Eiron — an achievement in ironic duplicity — it is as often as not impossible to distinguish between ingenuous naive foolishness and deadpan ironic fooling. Shrewd and unlearned, these are figures through whom mockery pointedly turns around upon the learned (and in this case the mock-learned as well), who show up as impostors against these *ingénu* ironists. Costard exposes humbug or affectation at both the social levels superior to him in the play. In a play of heroes he is a cock-eyed anti-hero, a faint foreshadowing of Puntila's hired man.[5] The linguistic appurtenances of learning as well as the ascetic platonism of the courtiers, come apart under his invincible literal-mindedness. He was taken with Jaquenetta he announces under questioning, 'in manner and form following: he was seen with her in the manor-house, sitting with her upon the form, and taken following her into the park' (i. i. 205). He is the play's paradoxical life-line between words and things, testing the value of 'renumerations' and 'guerdons' in solid sterling, and confident, through a barrage of verbal equivocations, that the maid, without benefit of inverted commas, will serve his turn. He is a life-line to reality, but for the audience, not the court. For the court of Navarre, too, is a mutual admiration society, securely fenced about, hermetically sealed from the least breath of reality by the bewitching power of language to delude with its figments of power.

The Princess (first cousin to Portia), has been pedagogue to princes from the start, putting them firmly and properly in their place. '"Fair" I give you back again, and "welcome" I have not yet', she replies to the King's greeting. 'The roof of this court is too high to be yours, and welcome to the wide fields too base to be mine' (II. i. 91–4). ''Tis deadly sin to keep that oath, my Lord,/And sin to break it' (II. i. 105–6). She is morally disapproving of hard riders (IV. i. 1–4) and clearly a member of the anti-blood-sport league (IV. i. 24–35). She primly checks Boyet's flattery:

> Good Lord Boyet, my beauty, though but mean,
> Needs not the painted flourish of your praise:
>
> (II. i. 13–14)

and keeps her girls in order too, adjuring them to keep their powder dry and reserve their 'sets of wit', at which they excell no less than the men, for the real battle to come. Boyet, the ladies' man, who is nearly as foppish as the Nemean lion himself, though less preposterous – Monsieur the Nice, as Berowne calls him, 'that kiss'd his hand away in courtesy' (it is a marvellous pantomimic portrait, v. ii. 315–34) provides her throughout with someone to rap over the verbal knuckles. 'Speak to be understood', she scolds, in reply to a very spruce flourish of his about blowing roses (v. ii. 294). He speaks perhaps with some personal ruefulness when he says 'The tongues of mocking wenches are as keen/As is the razor's edge invisible' (v. ii. 256–7), but for the most part the ladies' didactic efforts are directed satirically against the 'breed of wits so wondered at' of Navarre. On this topic even the decorous Princess becomes jocular.

As well she might, for the comic reversal undoes not only the courtiers' oaths, but their cherished self-images as well – at all events, Berowne's. Hence his fury at his fall. The vexation of his

confession in Act III, scene i, reveals the degree to which his own
self-complacent self-image – the detached, amused Ovidian libertine – has been impaired, and his own vanity affected:

> O, and I, forsooth, in love! I, that have been love's whip,
> A very beadle to a humorous sigh,
> A critic, nay, a night-watch constable,
> A domineering pedant o'er the boy . . .   (III. i. 174–7)

He is undone on three counts: himself in love, forsworn, and,
which is worst of all, in love with the 'worst of all': a whitely
wanton with a velvet brow and two pitch balls stuck in her face
for eyes. The wounding of social vanity adds a spice to the
humiliation of his plight, though his rhetorical virtuosity will rise
undaunted to the challenge later on. But worse is to come.
Berowne is toppled from his perch – we hear him complain of this
again in Act IV, scene iii: 'The King he is hunting the deer: I am
coursing myself. They have pitch'd a toil: I am toiling in a pitch –
pitch that defiles . . . I will not love; if I do, hang me; i'faith I will
not. O but her eye . . .' But so far only for the audiences' delectation. He has not yet been made a fixed figure for the time of scorn
to point his slow and moving finger at. This overthrow occurs
during the eavesdropping scene and he brings it upon himself.
Unable to resist the temptation to recoup his own losses at his
companions' expense, he caps the King's hypocrisy with his own:

> I that am honest, I that hold it sin
> To break the vow I am engaged in.
> I am betrayed by keeping company
> With men like [you], men of inconstancy.
> When shall you see me write a thing in rhyme,
> Or groan for Joan, or spend a minute's time
> In pruning me? When shall you hear that I
> Will praise a hand, a foot, a face, an eye
> A gait, a state, a brow, a breast, a waist,
> A leg, a limb—   (IV. iii. 175–84)

and is undone before all eyes at the height of his tirade of mock
righteous indignation by the arrival of the incriminating letter.
   There is still more, however, to the undoing of Berowne. Even

when all four woodcocks are caught in this dish and Berowne has
invoked his naturalist doctrine of young blood in their defence:

> Sweet lords, sweet lovers, O, let us embrace!
> As true we are as flesh and blood can be.
> The sea will ebb and flow, heaven show his face;
> Young blood doth not obey an old decree.
> We cannot cross the cause why we were born;
> Therefore of all hands must we be forsworn.
>
> (IV. iii. 210–15)

'What', says the King, who is a little slow on the uptake, 'did these
rent lines show some love of thine?'

> Did they, quoth you? Who sees the heavenly Rosaline,
> That (like a rude and savage man of Inde),
> At the first op'ning of the gorgeous east,
> Bows not his vassal head, and strooken blind,
> Kisses the base ground with obedient breast?
> What peremptory eagle-sighted eye
> Dares look upon the heaven of her brow,
> That is not blinded by her majesty?   (IV. iii. 217–24)

And this, the *audience* at least will remember, was the contemptuous dismisser just so many moments before, of Longaville's
'liver-vein, which makes flesh a deity,/A green goose a goddess;
pure, pure [idolatry]' (IV. iii. 72–3).

Now Berowne must play a match of wit in defence of his dark
beauty against the calumnies of gentlemen who prefer blondes,
and don't mind punishing him for his attempt to deceive them.
'Fie, painted rhetoric', says Berowne grandiloquently dismissing
the Queen of Arts as he marches from paradox to hyperbole, to
anaphora, to antimetabole, these moves dissolving into under-
graduate ribaldry, and the King's appeal to Berowne to extricate
them from the trap of their broken vows. Most critics have taken
the view that the oration of Berowne's which follows is perfectly
serious. It is, says Traversi, an 'apotheosis of love and one of the
most impressive utterances of the play':[6] Berowne has seen the
light. We have heard him inveigh against mere booklearning,
'leaden contemplation', before, but now the erstwhile philanderer

is outdoing the platonist and in the vein of Diotima herself, deriving from womens' eyes the doctrine of the true Promethean fire:

> They are the books, the arts, the academes,
> That show, contain, and nourish all the world.
>
> (IV. iii. 349–50)

He is a changed man, it is felt, and the verve and vivacity of the verse surely proves it. 'In a world of words', says C. L. Barber, 'the wine is wit',[7] and he very aptly compares Berowne's witty panegyric on love to Falstaff's on sack:

> But love, first learned in a lady's eyes,
> Lives not alone immured in the brain,
> But with the motion of all elements,
> Courses as swift as thought in every power,
> And gives to every power a double power,
> Above their functions and their offices.
> It adds a precious seeing to the eye:
> A lover's eyes will gaze an eagle blind.
> A lover's ear will hear the lowest sound,
> When the suspicious head of theft is stopp'd.
> Love's feeling is more soft and sensible
> Than are the tender horns of cockled snails.
> Love's tongue proves dainty Bacchus gross in taste.
> For valor, is not Love a Hercules,
> Still climbing trees in the Hesperides?
>
> (IV. iii. 324–38)

This is excellent, and the exhilaration experienced by the courtiers at this festive and joyous release from their bond is graphically described later by Boyet:

> One rubb'd his elbow thus, and fleer'd, and swore
> A better speech was never spoke before.
> Another, with his finger and his thumb,
> Cried, 'Via! we will do't, come what will come'.
> The third he caper'd, and cried, 'All goes well'.
> The fourth turn'd on the toe, and down he fell.
> With that they all did tumble on the ground,
> With such a zealous laughter . . . (V. ii. 109–16)

But doubts do creep in. First of all, one remembers the nature of the assignment: to prove 'Our loving lawful and our faith not torn'; to produce 'quillets . . . to cheat the devil'. That Berowne can perform such feats with *sprezzatura* is his charm, but does that make the tongue-in-cheek mock seriousness less so? Is there not for the alert the hint of an erotic *double entendre* in 'tender horns' and in 'love's tongue'? The flicker of a parody of the mighty Marlovian line in those Hesperidean trees? And if, when Love speaks, the voice of all the gods make heaven drowsy with the harmony, what are we to make of the earlier (but not all that much earlier) doctrine of the German clock?

> A woman, that is like a German [clock],
> Still a-repairing, ever out of frame,
> And never going aright, being a watch,
> But being watch'd that it may still go right!

> Ay, and, by heaven, one that will do the deed
> Though Argus were her eunuch and her guard.
>   (III. i. 190–3; 198–9)

It is religious to be thus forsworn, is Berowne's climax:

> For charity itself fulfills the law,
> And who can sever love from charity?
>   (IV. iii. 361–2)

They asked for a salve for perjury. They are certainly getting it.

> [Let] us once lose our oaths to find ourselves,
> Or else we lose ourselves to keep our oaths.
>   (IV. iii. 358–9)

It is without a doubt a forensic *tour de force*. The oath has been undone, perjury justified, faces saved, at least to their owners' satisfaction. But is it 'serious'? The King's salute, 'Saint Cupid, then' suggests that he at least is not taken in by the mock piety of the peroration. And Berowne's final words would seem to indicate a residue (at least) of his old cynic's pragmatism:

> [Allons! allons!] Sow'd cockle reap'd no corn,
> And justice always whirls in equal measure:

Light wenches may prove plagues to men forsworn;
If so, our copper buys no better treasure.

(IV. iii. 382–3)

It is a puzzle. 'Berowne', observes Muriel Bradbrook, 'plays a double game with language throughout . . . he runs with the hare and hunts with the hounds'.[8] 'Berowne calls a game a game', Barber replies. 'He plays the game and he calls it too . . . in the classic manner of Erasmus in his *Praise of Folly*; it becomes folly not to be a fool'.[9]

Traversi's view (quoted above) of the seriousness of Berowne suggests itself, I submit, as persuasively as it does, and is able to modify the sceptical view as much as it does, not because of what actually occurs in the play but because of what we expect to occur. We expect marriages. Betrothals, at least. We expect the closure of comedy to resolve our doubts (if any) and to assure us that whatever *jeux d'esprits* Berowne's virtuosity dictates, whatever high-spirited young wit's posturing remains in evidence, his heart is in the right place, and his lady knows it. Since we do not get this assurance, we are plunged into doubt and all his utterances become ambiguous.

> Although in his heart of hearts he [Berowne] knows that love gives to every power a double power . . . yet when we part from him we doubt much that this voice will echo in his soul throughout his year of penance. His fertile wit will devise many a mean to stifle it should his task to move wild laughter in the throat of death prove too irksome. His present love's labour will be lost, and Jack will never have his Jill.[10]

It is not a remark the writer would have made of Benedick, who shares with Berowne what we might call his Confirmed Bachelor Syndrome, but who inhabits a comedy which forecloses options and closes mouths with a kiss.

The pull towards the regulation comedy game ending is very strong, not only because we bring generic expectations with us to our reading, but because the play does nothing to disturb those expectations until the very end.

The 'little academe' has been turned upside down into a school for lovers, and now all seems set fair for a fiesta of collective betrothals. And nothing in the sentiments of either of the two parties would seem to preclude this. There is evidence in plenty, and in rhyme, of the state of the courtiers' affections, while the ladies do not appear to have been exactly indifferent to the charms of the bookmen from the very beginning. All these gallants are held, in the opinion of the French young ladies at all events, to be great wits. Maria knows that Longaville is esteemed a man of sovereign parts (II. i. 44); Katharine thinks that Dumain 'hath wit to make an ill shape good', supposing he were by any chance in need of such amelioration (II. i. 59). And Rosaline never spent an hour's talk with a merrier man than Berowne, whose discourse positively ravishes young and old alike (II. i. 68–76). The chorus of praise is such as to cause the Princess to exclaim 'God bless my ladies: are they all in love?', and the conditions they set at the end of the play can be regarded as no more than the delay of a betrothal willingly anticipated.

Thematically, the ending of *Love's Labour's Lost* can be accommodated, or found to be intelligible, justifiable and appropriate. The young men have perjured themselves, have been vain and frivolous, must learn responsibility, humility. There must be tests and assurances for 'world-without-end bargains' – a neat reversal of the King's importunate dedication to the eternity of fame. The play ends as it began with vows, but they are now – particularly the undertaking to 'move wild laughter in the throat of death' – another neat reversal: of the King's initial dream of a 'living art'.

The ladies' realism has shown fantasy its limits, and mortal finitude has tapped immortal longings ironically upon the shoulder. These themes have been intimated throughout, are meshed into the semantic web of the text, and capped by the seasonal songs. Whenever descriptions of nature are added epilogue fashion, they will generate, by way of metaphor or metonymy, a sense of thematic continuity. For example: the 'songs offer us a vision of true pastoral to contrast with the false pastoralism Berowne and his friends had espoused earlier'.[11] Great creating Nature (Jaquenetta two months gone), time and the seasons ridicule the pretensions and presumptions to transcendence of carnal and finite creatures. Greasy Joan keeling the pot (with real apples or milk in it) counterpoints the dainties that are bred in books.

The play is indeed obedient to its complex dialectic of nature and art, reality and illusion, jest and earnest, time and eternity. But Armado's scenario for an imperially amorous career reminds us that action as well as dialectic is required. From that learned artsman's epistle to Jaquenetta we learn that

> The magnanimous and most illustrate King Cophetua set eye upon the pernicious and indubitate beggar Zenelophon; and he it was that might rightly say, *Veni, vidi, vici*; which to annothanize in the vulgar – O base and obscure vulgar! – *videlicet*. He came, [saw], and overcame: he came, one; [say], two; [overcome], three. Who came? the king. Why did he come? to see. Why did he see? to overcome. To whom came he? to the beggar. What saw he? the beggar. Who overcame he? the beggar. The conclusion is victory; on whose side? the [king's]. The captive is enrich'd; on whose side? the beggar's. The catastrophe is a nuptial; . . .   (IV. i. 64–77)

But the catastrophe of *Love's Labour's Lost* is not a nuptial. There is delay. And it is no mere postponement for a mourning period. There are conditions, and very testing conditions at that. Nothing surely would have been simpler than to have the Princess's father arrive on some pretext connected with the Aquitaine treaty, and to have found some suitable formula which would have allowed the very attractive and eligible suitor for his daughter's hand to be forgiven 'the dear guiltiness' of his perjury. Replication would then look after the affairs of the other three couples and appropriate betrothal celebrations would close the play. The seasonal songs which are the play's epilogue would then, I suggest, truly and resonantly celebrate an interlocking of contraries, an achieved simplicity, domesticity, equilibrium and natural harmony (despite the touch of ironic realism for married men). As it is, only special pleading for a generalized lyrical – rather than a particularized dramatic – embodiment of comic resolution affords then this status. Why, we must be tempted to reflect, does the play end in this way? It is a breach of (theatrical) promise which seriously disrupts, or challenges, our retrospective reconstructions of the play's coherence. Despite thematic continuities, the play is fractured. If it is as G. B. Harrison claims, a case of 'Cupid's Revenge'[13] we have been watching, in which the young men, having turned their backs upon the 'wimpled, whining, purblind, wayward boy' (III. i. 179) are promptly brought to heel, and taken down a peg or two in the pride of their imagined imperviousness, then the extra penance is surely superfluous. And what have hospitals and almshouses and hermitages to do with the traditional and legitimate concerns of the little blind Eros? This comedy 'denies itself and refuses to behave' as Philip Edwards puts it: 'The mating quest ends not with triumphant wedding music, but with a disconsolate group of lovers dismissed to a wintry twelve-month in hermitage or hospital'.[14] If it is, however, the Abasement of the Proud King, or Heroic Raptures Transprosed, then love's labour was not, surely, lost, because love, in this model, is purely instrumental, a didactic means for the acquisition of sobriety and humility.[15] If again love is, and deservedly, lost, so that the play becomes a derisive satire against the frivolous courtiers, what of the princess' young ladies, if not the cool princess herself, who admits to 'double grief' at the news of her father's death and the parting from Navarre? And if, on the other hand, it is *their* love's labour that is 'lost', it is surely strange that it should be by their own doing, and right doing at that.

The most impressive attempt to reconcile the ending of *Love's Labour's Lost* with a consistent theory of comedy is that of C. L. Barber in his admirable *Shakespeare's Festive Comedy*. No play of Shakespeare's is more packed with references to games, sports, pastimes, revels, masques – the whole slight plot hinges upon the entertainment, with suitable festivities, of the visiting ladies, and the commissioning of a 'delightful ostentation, or show, or pageant, or antic or firework, or . . . suchlike eruptions and breakings out of mirth' to make amends to the ladies for previous breaches of hospitality and for the abortive masque of Muscovites. Since, nevertheless, Carnival is abruptly transformed into Lent at the end, the play would seem to provide a test case for the festive theory, of which, were the ending otherwise, it would be natural to suppose it no less than a paradigm.

That the play should end without the usual marriages, is exactly right, in view of what it is that is released by its festivities – the folly of amorous masquerade . . . of acting love and talking love without being in love. . . . The game of witty wooing seemed to be love: now comes clarification . . . Berowne's last line ('That's too long for a play') recognises explicitly that to have brought these people from these festivities to the full fledged event of marriage would have required a whole new development.[16]

But this will surely not do. For if non-marriage is 'exactly right' here, how can marriages be exactly right elsewhere? Why does this particular folly require more of 'a whole new development' than the various other follies and delusions that are exhibited in other comedies? It might be sobering to reflect how much time Demetrius and Helena could be conceived to need for the 'full-fledged event of marriage', not to mention Proteus and Julia or, for the matter of that Olivia and Sebastian. The argument is untenable, as reversing it at once makes clear. Had *Love's Labour's Lost* ended with marriages not one accepted statement of the play's thematic import would have required alteration. The marriages would simply have set the seal of certainty upon the reformation and illumination, in terms of nature, reality and seriousness, of Navarre's young men. What the absence of marriages does is to leave the comedy radically unfinished. I believe, for reasons that I shall presently come to, that it is better to recognize this than to attempt to cover up for it.

It is in the nature of open forms to approach a state of infinite non-finality or non-resolution. There is, precisely, no closure, and therefore counter and incompatible possibilities traverse the events of the play retrospectively like magnets across a board of iron filings. Take for example, the little problem of Armado's expiatory three years behind the plough for Jaquenetta's sweet love. Jaquenetta is two months pregnant so she is hardly in a position to expect knightly courtship of this length. Is there some strange foreshadowing here of Quixote, whose love for Dulcinea was a total figment of his imagination? This in itself is a fascinating thought, since Armado precedes his fictive countryman by at least a decade; but what light does it reflect upon the ladies' devoted suitors and *their* expiatory vows? Since the issue of the latter is inconclusive, we cannot preclude the possibility of irony, which generates further irony, the process going so far (in these degenerate and cynical times) as to cause a recent critic's suggestion that we should understand Costard to be taking the opportunity of fathering his bastard upon the gullible Don. Armado's extravagant nonsense would have functioned simply as foil for the courtier's achieved wisdom had betrothals closed the play. As it is, the ending makes it not only impossible to fathom Armado's cloudy depths, but also to decide the major issues of the play: whether the young men are to be understood as being genuinely in love with the ladies, or in love only with themselves; whether their rash of sonneteering is to be regarded as the symptom of their malady, or as the beginning of their cure.

'We are wise girls to mock our lovers so', says the Princess, as they prepare to tease the masked Russians; 'They do it but in mockery merriment'. (v. ii. 58, 139) and clearly require chastening. The fooling of the Muscovites is perhaps just what is required for homeopathic therapy – 'sport by sport o'erthrown' – the perfect remedy, indeed, for wordy intoxications.

Moreover, the pageant of the Nine Worthies, the King's amendment for his previous breach of hospitality, though it does not 'fadge' quite as was intended, could be seen, by dramatic indirections to the audience, admirably to serve such remedial purposes. For the performances of the Nine Worthies, who are engaged to perform, are in fervent earnest, while their play audience jests unmercifully at their expense. Only the ladies are compassionate: 'Alas, poor Machabeus, how hath he been baited!' (v. ii. 631). What the lord's baiting reveals behind the travesty of a pageant and the breakdown of language is the native reality of the performer. It is the real Costard we hear modestly confessing to 'a little fault in "Great"', and rushing at once to the castigation and defence of 'the world's commander', and it is the real Nathaniel we are invited to recognize in his defence of the crest-fallen Alexander:

There an't shall please you, a foolish mild man, an honest man, look you, and soon dash'd. He is a marvellous good neighbor,

faith, and a very good bowler; but for Alisander – alas, you see
how 'tis – a little o'erparted. (v. ii. 580–4)

The real Armado, who can afford nothing but woollens beneath
his fancy attire, makes a forlorn but dogged attempt to pass it
off: 'I go woolward for penance' (v. ii. 711). While the real
Holofernes, savaged by the picador courtiers, acquires dignity in
protest: 'This is not generous, not gentle, not humble' (v. ii. 629).

A jest's prosperity lies in the ear
Of him that hears it, never in the tongue
Of him that makes it. (v. ii. 861–3)

A jest, as well as an oath we are invited to perceive, and so surely
are the courtiers invited to perceive, should be taken very seriously indeed.

If this is so, then Berowne's repudiation of maggot ostentation,
his renunciation of 'taffata phrases, silken terms precise' in favour
of 'russet yeas and honest kersey noes' (v. ii. 413) would appear to
be a genuine recognition, and his love for the wench 'sound, sans
crack or flaw' (v. ii. 415). Ah, but there is the fatal giveaway –
'sans', and Rosaline catches him in the act. Does this suggest that
he is putting off affected finery but only for another garb? That he
has struck one linguistic posture after another on the question of
love and is still caught in his web of self-regarding rhetoric? Or is
it no more than 'a trick of the old rage', as he disarmingly admits,
and proof, the more endearing for its fallibility, that the ladies'
game has really been a triumphant lesson in the importance of
being earnest? But then again if that is the case the words of
Mercury are indeed harsh after the songs of Apollo.

The truth of the matter is that a betrothal delayed is an anti-
strophe, resolving nothing. 'Our wooing doth not end like an old
play:' says rueful Berowne, frustrated in his hope that russet yeas
will save the day. 'Jack hath not Gill. These ladies' courtesy/Might
well have made our sport a comedy' (v. ii. 874–6). 'Come, sir',
says the King, seeking consolation no doubt, for his own enforced
retirement from the world; 'it wants a twelvemonth an' a day, And
then 'twill end'. But Berowne: 'That's too long for a play'. Self-
reflexion of this kind, a deliberate drawing of attention from

within the represented world of the play to some alleged inade-
quacy in the artifice of its representation can only act either as a
forestalling of possible criticism, or as an invitation to consider all
that has passed in an ironic light. So glum Berowne's remark is yet
another source of possible ironic retrospection. His words are
immediately followed by Armado's leave-taking, as he sets off for
the plough, and then by the seasonal songs. We have, therefore,
instead of the anticipated Komos, a positive cluster of irony-
producing occurrences; and it will have been noticed that the
ironies are themselves conflicting, and even incompatible. They
do not point in the same direction.

I believe that these effects are inadvertent, and I venture to
suggest that Professor Barber's sense of 'exact rightness' comes to
him from his knowledge of *all* of Shakespeare's comedies. He
knows what is to come. He knows that implicit or latent elements
in *Love's Labour's Lost* will be brought out and realized in all
their dramatic plentitude in later plays, and he therefore assimi-
lates *Love's Labour's Lost* to this larger knowledge. And I wish to
conclude this discussion of *Love's Labour's Lost* with a specula-
tion of my own concerning the relation of the play to the comedies
which follow it.

The comic deficiency which the play explores is displaced from
the complexities of relations between lovers, and localized in the
follies of the mind: specifically, the belief that with words one can
do anything one wishes to do; that with words reality can be
mastered, will performed. The title misleads us if we think of the
later plays, for the play is only half, or secondarily, about love at
all; but if we remember the earliness of *Love's Labour's Lost* then
the title reveals. The 'labourers' are the men. Shakespeare's concern with love at this stage is still rooted in the absurdities and
follies of male courtly lovers, with the logic or illogic of men in the
role of lovers. The play follows *The Two Gentlemen* in this
respect though it does allow the ladies far more scope. Shakespeare's early comedies are altogether doubtful about the efficacy
of romantic love to redeem or to resolve, tending to class Petrarchan ardours with the errors rather than with the remedies; and
are markedly satirical about its effects. Love is a seizure, a sudden

malady, the symptoms of which are mockingly etched by Moth (and Speed in *The Two Gentlemen*), and gleefully gloated over by the 'lovemonger' Boyet. Love is furiously repudiated by Berowne (until the grand recantation), enacted in burlesque by Armado, and coolly criticized by the ladies. In this early comedy, as in *The Shrew* and *The Two Gentlemen* (and even initially in *A Midsummer Night's Dream*) courtly love is still a posture, and even an imposture. The play is richly and exquisitely amusing, even today when so much of the wit is dated, brilliant in its comic dialectic, accomplished in its engineering of a comic rhythm of hyperbolic accumulation. It is not yet ready, or willing (hence the evasion of closure) to take the testing of the non-seriousness of contracts and the non-seriousness of games as far as the full dramatization of the serious game of love and the serious contract of marriage. This move is imminent in the comic material but for its full development to take place individualized couples rather than symmetrical foursomes are required. And required, above all, is a comic heroine who will do more than occasion comic reversals and administer wholesome reproofs. As an independent source and originator of comic pleasure herself, she will not be simply an object of masculine attention, but an active, self-assertive improvisor of the confrontations, evasions, manoeuvres, self-discoveries, through which lovers finally, and remedially, recognize each other and transcend the power game. But this Shakespeare comedy of courtship is yet to be composed.

To what extent *Love's Labour's Lost* is transitional in the way thus suggested can perhaps be indicated by considering the notorious textual crux known as the 'Katharine-Rosaline tangle'. In the scene of introduction between the lords and ladies (II. i.) there are two teasing exchanges between Berowne and a Lady called Katharine in Q and Rosaline in F, and the same lady (or another? it is impossible to tell) named alternately Rosaline and Katharine by Boyet in reply to inquiries of Dumain and Berowne. Dover Wilson argues that the two exchanges were deleted by Shakespeare during revision. Boyet's identifications then having to be adjusted in order simply to link each lord with his own favoured lady; and that these cancellations and corrections were so confusingly or unclearly indicated that the compositor could not make them out. Dover Wilson believes that there was an original plan: to have the lords and the ladies in masks, and be teasingly deceived about their identities, and that at some point Shakespeare decided to transfer his comedy of mistaken identities to later on in the play, where it becomes the foiling of the Muscovites.[17] There, however, mistaken identities function rather differently. The men are coyly hiding behind their masks, the ladies calling their bluff. The latters' intrigue has been in the first place punitive, and not, as later stratagems in *Much Ado* or *As You Like It* for the purpose of matchmaking. As Rosaline says:

> That same Berowne I'll torture ere I go.
> O that I knew he were but in by th' week!
> How I would make him fawn, and beg, and seek,
> And wait the season, and observe the times,
> And spend his prodigal wits in bootless rhymes,
> And shape his service wholly to my device,
> And make him proud to make me proud that jests!
> So pair-taunt-like would I o'ersway his state
> That same Berowne I'll torture ere I go.
>
> (v. ii. 60–8)

Mutual sparring of exactly the same kind occurs in the encounters, masked and unmasked, between Beatrice and Benedick. Whether *Much Ado* is the lost *Love's Labour's Won* as is sometimes supposed, it certainly supplies in full measure the merry war of courtship which is half deleted, and belatedly returned to, in Act V of *Love's Labour's Lost*, which, though it does propose a (penitential) 'remedy for the great ills' does *not* 'give all the persons what they desire' or 'fill them with great joy'.[18]

A Midsummer Night's Dream, however, redresses the balance. It has never, so far as I am aware been put forward as such, but it might well be a contender for the title of the lost *Love's Labour's Won*. If weddings are required, there we shall find them in plenty. And there mistaken identities, if not yet the fully interiorized variety *Much Ado* will offer us, will yield a cornucopia of comic insights.

NOTES

1 Ernest Becker, *The Denial of Death* (New York: Macmillan, 1973), p. 231.

2 Henry Peacham, *The Garden of Eloquence* (1577), quoted in Sister Miriam Joseph's excellent account of figures of rhetoric, *Shakespeare's Use of the Arts of Language* (New York: Columbia University Press, 1947), p. 303.

3 In the sense made famous by John L. Austin, *How To Do Things With Words* (Cambridge, Massachusetts: Harvard University Press, 1965).

4 Quoted by Sister Miriam Joseph, *Shakespeare's Use*, in her treatment of the vices, pp. 64–73 and 251–9 passim. *Pleonasmus* is redundancy; *Periergia* is superfluity resulting from over-labour 'to show himself fine in a light matter' according to Puttenham (p. 258) and is characteristic of Hoskins' 'schoolmaster, foaming out synonymies' (J. Hoskins, *Directions for Speech and Style*, ed. Hudson, Princeton University Press (1935), p. 24; *Cacozelia* is the coining of fine words out of Latin and the use of new fangled expressions to appear learned (p. 251), but according to Peacham the kind of misapplication called today malapropism; *Solecismus* is the ignorant misuse of cases, genders, tenses (p. 251): '*bone* for *bene*. Priscian a little scratched; 'twill serve' (v. i. 30) and *Tapinosis* is the diminishing and debasing of a high matter by the baseness of a word (p. 259).

5 Bertolt Brecht, *Puntila and his Hired Man* (1940).

6 Derek Traversi, *The Early Comedies* (London: Longmans Green, 1960), p. 31.

7 *Shakespeare's Festive Comedy* (New Jersey: Princeton University Press, 1959), p. 99.

8 M. C. Bradbrook, *Shakespeare and Elizabethan Poetry* (London: Chatto & Windus, 1951), p. 215.

9 Barber, *Shakespeare's Festive Comedy*, pp. 91–2.

10 Horace Howard Furness, editor of The New Variorum edn (reprinted 1904; New York: Dover Publications, 1964), p. xviii. See also William C. Carroll, *The Great Feast of Language* (Princeton University Press, 1976): ' "Let us once lose

our oaths and find ourselves" . . . rings true on the deepest
level, for the movement of the entire play has been towards
such a self-discovery. Yet it is also a self-justification, and to
some extent another self-deception: its sincerity is under-
mined by the over-elaborate patterning and repetition . . .'
(p. 152).

11 Carroll, *The Great Feast*, p. 217. But irreconcilable responses
are on record. To Thomas McFarland, *Shakespeare's Pastoral Comedy* (Chapel Hill: University of North Carolina
Press, 1972), p. 76, the songs are 'the sweetest and most
gardenlike of all the play's language'; to Dover Wilson, editor
of The New Shakespeare (Cambridge: Cambridge University
Press, 1923), p. 184, 'they burst upon us with exquisitely
ludicrous effect'. Robert G. Hunter, 'The Function of the
Songs at the End of *Love's Labour's Lost*', *Shakespeare
Studies*, vol. VII (1974), pp. 55–63, says that the songs reaf-
firm cyclic return 'carnival time – circular, as round as Falstaff's belly' – despite 'Cormorant devouring Time', and finds
them 'moving, right and meaningful' (p. 55).

12 Both Carroll and S. K. Heninger, 'The Pattern of LLL', *Shakespeare Studies*, vol. VII (1974), find that the songs embody a
reconciliation of opposites which they take to be the play's
final thematic conclusion. Terence Hawkes, too, in *Shakespeare's Talking Animals* (London: Edward Arnold, 1973)
links the songs to a dialectic of the written, silent and book-
learned as opposed to the oral, resonant and unlettered; of
'rhyme against reason', sterile academia against fruitful
community.

13 G. B. Harrison, ed. *Complete Works* (New York: Harcourt
Brace, 1952), p. 394.

14 *Shakespeare and the Confines of Art* (London: Methuen,
1968), p. 37.

15 Cyrus Hoy takes this view, for instance, in '*Love's Labour
Lost* and the Nature of Comedy', *Shakespeare Quarterly*, vol.
XIII (1962).

16 Barber, *Shakespeare's Festive Comedy*, pp. 93–113. It is
worth noting that Shakespeare nowhere else forgoes his final
weddings. It is interesting, too, that Navarre's park, though

certainly a green and pleasant place does not make *Love's Labour's Lost* a green world comedy in Northrop Frye's valuable sense, in which the wild and recreative world of nature is set against a constraining and restraining world of culture. Sherman Hawkins, 'The Two Worlds of Shakespearean Comedy', *Shakespeare Studies*, vol. III (1967), goes so far as to classify it as a 'closed world' comedy, the category he finds antithetical to the comedies of the green world. Had the comedy ended differently, however, it would certainly have been received as a green world regeneration for the Platonic courtiers.

17 The New Shakespeare edn, pp. 117–24.
18 Willichius, ed. Terence's *Andria* (1550). See T. W. Baldwin, *Shakespeare's Five-Act Structure* (Urbana: University of Illinois Press, 1947), p. 232.

VI

FANCY'S IMAGES

'A *Midsummer Night's Dream* is best seen', says G. K. Hunter, 'as
a lyric divertissement . . . Shakespeare has lavished his art on the
separate excellencies of the different parts, but has not sought to
show them growing out of one another in a process analogous to
that of symphonic "development".'[1] I would claim, on the contrary, symphonic development of a particularly subtle kind; both
itself an impressive achievement in the unifying of complexities,
and a distinct conquest in the zig-zag progress towards Shakespeare's comic paradigm. This is a highly intellectual, highly
speculative comedy, like *Love's Labour's Lost* not the refashion-
ing of a previously-treated story or play but an original invention.
Through his basic comic structure of initial privation or perversity, comic device both deceptive and remedial, knots of errors
and final recognitions, Shakespeare has achieved not only a
benign resolution to the dialectic of folly and wisdom, but a
complex and witty exploration of the infirmities and frailties and
deficiencies and possibilities of the imaginative faculty itself.

The problem presented to Theseus four days before his wedding is a knotty one. From the point of view of the father, what is
required is that his daughter yield to his bidding and accept the
suitor he has approved. But this would please no one but himself
(and Demetrius). Theseus adopts the patriarchal view, naturally
enough. But suppose (in another age and another clime) the young

people had been left to choose their own mates? This procedure would not have solved the problem any more satisfactorily than the first, since the predicament we are asked to take in consists precisely of the asymmetry in the feelings of these four young people. The father's peremptoriness and the Duke's supportive edict lend urgency to their problem, but do not create it. The initial presentation of the situation invites us to perceive that while the tyrannical *senex* provides the outward and immediate obstacle to be surmounted, the root of the problem is elsewhere and within. The initiating recalcitrancy is the fact that two young men are competing with each other for one girl, when there is another available, and willing, to turn a triangle into a suitable set of couples. Two of both kinds makes up four, as Puck succinctly expresses it. And, it seems, some such arrangement had once been contemplated by these young Athenians themselves. Lysander (and later Helena) tells us that Demetrius made love to Helena before obtaining Egeus' consent to a match with Hermia. He deserted her then, it seems, for Hermia. But why? And when? 'This man', says Egeus (of Demetrius) 'hath my consent to marry her' (Hermia). 'This man' (of Lysander) 'hath bewitch'd the bosom of my child'. But it is impossible to determine the sequence of tenses. Did the bewitching occur before the consent, or since, or simultaneously? Was it perhaps some sudden new interest in Hermia on the part of Demetrius that stimulated Lysander's desire for her? Or could it possibly be a case of the other foot? Did Lysander's interest in Hermia deflect Demetrius' previous affection for Helena and draw it with magnetic attraction towards the object of Lysander's love?

The square-dance view of these proceedings is less helpful than it seems, mainly because it takes no account of the girls. 'The lovers are like dancers', says G. K. Hunter, 'who change partners in the middle of a figure; the point at which partners are exchanged is determined by the dance, the pattern, and not by the psychological state of the dancers.'[2] But we are asked to attend quite closely to 'the psychological state of the dancers', to the 'fierce vexations' of their dream. The girls, in point of fact, do not change partners at all. They are subjected to drastic changes in their lovers' attitudes, to which they bewilderedly respond, but their own attachments do not waver. Moreover, the play's peripeteia is a comic reversal which leaves in effect everything exactly where it was: Puck's mistake with the magic juice – designed by Oberon to rectify unrequited love – in fact compounds error and disturbance by causing the two young men to continue to be both in love with the same love object, though this time in the shape of the other girl. It is thus not a question of mistaken identity, or of disguise, those time-honoured sources of identity confusion in New Comedy plots. Nor is it quite true to say, though it is often said, that the lovers simply don't know what they want, are fickle, capricious and unreasonable, creatures of the senses, of the eye merely. It is worth attending to Helena's observations at the play's outset:

> How happy some o'er other some can be!
> Through Athens I am thought as fair as she.
> But what of that? Demetrius thinks not so;
> He will not know what all but he do know;
> And as he errs, doting on Hermia's eyes,
> So I, admiring of his qualities.
> Things base and vile, holding no quantity,
> Love can transpose to form and dignity.
> Love looks not with the eyes but with the mind;
> And therefore is wing'd Cupid painted blind.
> Nor hath Love's mind of any judgment taste;
> Wings, and no eyes, figure unheedy haste;
> And therefore is Love said to be a child,
> Because in choice he is so oft beguil'd.
> As waggish boys in game themselves forswear,
> So the boy Love is perjur'd every where;
> For ere Demetrius look'd on Hermia's eyne,
> He hail'd down oaths that he was only mine;
> And when this hail some heat from Hermia felt,
> So he dissolv'd, and show'rs of oaths did melt.
>   (I. i. 226–45)

If only Demetrius would use his eyes she says in effect, he would see that I am as fair as Hermia. If Demetrius' infected will did not betray him he would recognize this open and palpable truth. But if

Helena and Hermia are identical in this cardinal matter of their beauty, then there are no visual grounds for preference either way, and therefore there can be no question of errors in choice. Helena intelligently perceives this catch and she also perceives that what is sauce for the goose is sauce for the gander. 'So I' (err), she says, 'admiring in *his* qualities.' Helena announces with bitterness this insight concerning the total and wayward non-dependence of erotic preference upon visual perception: 'Love looks not with the eyes but with the mind;/And therefore is wing'd Cupid painted blind.'³ The comedy of the speech lies, of course, in Helena's assumption that 'eyes' offer a more objective basis for judgment in love than mind. Eyes don't indeed provide any security for love, nor any true representation of reality, as the woods prove; but then neither does (rational) mind. Later the bewitched Lysander's assertion that 'the will of man is by his reason sway'd;/And reason says you are the worthier maid' will be sufficient evidence of that. Helena's 'mind' is Desdemona's: 'I saw Othello's visage in his mind' (I. iii. 252) and Othello's: 'I therefore beg it not . . . But to be free and bounteous to her mind' (I. iii. 265). Only there (tragically) and here (comically) the mind, that subjective source of value, of form and of dignity, is subject to all kinds of disabilities and derangements. Mind, in its aspect as the image-making and image-perceiving faculty, is an errant faculty indeed, unstable, uncertain, wavering, and seeking anchorage among a welter of rival images and self-images. It is to these, I believe, that the opening of the play draws our attention.

What we are invited to perceive is a falling out among rivals, and what we are invited to infer is that, at a deeper psychic level than they are aware of, they do indeed know what they want: each wants what his brother-at-arms or rival has. We have the case of Proteus and Valentine for confirmation of Shakespeare's interest in the phenomenon. Says Proteus, with admirable candour:

> Even as one heat another heat expels,
> Or as one nail by strength drives out another,
> So the remembrance of my former love
> Is by a newer object quite forgotten.
> [Is it] mine [eye], or Valentinus' praise,

> Her true perfection, or my false transgression,
> That makes me, reasonless, to reason thus?
>
> (II. iv. 192–8)

Consider the extremely provoking nature of Lysander's remark to Demetrius:

> You have her father's love, Demetrius,
> Let me have Hermia's; do you marry *him* (my
> italics).   (I. i. 93–4)

Consider too the amplitude and intensity with which the sisterly affection between the two girls is treated:

> all the counsel that we two have shar'd,
> The sisters' vows, the hours that we have spent . . .
> All school-day's friendship, childhood innocence . . .
> Both on one sampler, sitting on one cushion,
> Both warbling of one song, both in one key . . .
>   So we grew together,
> Like to a double cherry . . .   (III. ii. 198–209 passim)

It furthermore transpires, as the play winds deeper into its conflicts in Act II, that Oberon and Titania are also at odds over a love object they both want. The competitive marital duel of this couple features antecedent jealousies, but at the moment in time the play dramatizes they are quarrelling over possession of the changeling child. We find immediate parodic confirmation of the incidence of this malady as early as Act I, scene ii, where the good Bottom, magnifier of folly, wants to play all the parts Peter Quince distributes to his cast – tyrants, lovers, ladies and lions – and is in his comic hubris convinced that he can do better at them all than any of his fellows.

Rivalry, then, fraternal or quasi-sibling, or marital is the comic disposition which the comic device exposes and exacerbates. It is also worth noting that the story of the night is set within a frame of *concordia discors* between erstwhile military rivals. Theseus wooed Hippolyta, we learn, with his sword, and won her love doing her injuries. This reconciliatory *concordia discors* is symbolized in the description of the hunt in Act IV, scene i, just before the royal pair discovers the one time 'rival enemies' now 'new in amity'. Theseus invites his Queen to the mountain top to

> mark the musical confusion
> Of hounds and echo in conjunction (IV. i. 110–11)

and she, remembering the hounds of Sparta, transforms his notion of dissonant confusion into the perception of a higher harmony:

> Never did I hear
> Such gallant chiding; for besides the groves,
> The skies, the fountains, every region near
> Seem all one mutual cry. I never heard
> So musical a discord, such sweet thunder.
>   (IV. i. 114–18)

Hippolyta is consistently Theseus' informant in the play and indeed Egeus might have done well to appeal to her judgment rather than his at the beginning. Fortunately, however, for what the play enables us to discover about rivalries, he did not. Rivalry is benign when it leads to differentiation, since concord requires distinct entities between which to exist; and harmful when it leads to the blurring of boundaries, to 'unnatural', imitative or confusing conjunctions. Hippolyta is no longer playing the role of a man–woman Amazon by this time. The play explores the comedy of mimicry in four different and complementary perspectives – that of the quasi-fraternal lovers, the quasi-sibling 'sisters', the Fairy Queen and her votaress, and the amateur comedians, the artisans of Athens, with the putative arch-mimic Bottom, who is never anything but himself, at their head.

Sibling rivalry takes the form of unconscious mimicry, an identification with the brother who must therefore be outdone in *his* sphere. I am as good as he. I am better than he. I must have what he has. 'I am, my lord as well deriv'd as he,/As well possess'd', says Lysander, and what is more, beloved of beauteous Hermia. And Demetrius later: 'I love thee more than he can do'. From the girls' side of the picture we have Helena: 'Through Athens I am thought as fair as she'. Sensible siblings fight their way into maturity by seeking, finding, exploiting, inventing if necessary, precisely those differences and distinctions between them which establish their individual identities, on the basis of which they can freely choose their mates. This is no doubt why identical twins are such a problem, and so disturbing we are told, to the primitive mind encountering sameness where difference is not only in order, is not only expected, but is indispensable to individuation. But identical twins are an accident of nature which the comic artist may exploit for errors, if he wishes. What we have in *Midsummer Night's Dream* is imagined identical twinship. It is just such an idealized childhood twinship that Helena invokes in her remonstrance to Hermia over the latter's treacherous confederacy (as she believes) with the men, both now in pursuit of her to mock her:

> Is all the counsel that we two have shar'd,
> The sisters' vows, the hours that we have spent,
> When we have chid the hasty-footed time
> For parting us – O, is all forgot?
> All school-days' friendship, childhood innocence?
> We, Hermia, like two artificial gods,
> Have with our needles created both one flower,
> Both on one sampler, sitting on one cushion,
> Both warbling of one song, both in one key,
> As if our hands, our sides, voices, and minds
> Had been incorporate. So we grew together,
> Like to a double cherry, seeming parted,
> But yet an union in partition,
> Two lovely berries moulded on one stem;
> So, with two seeming bodies, but one heart,
>
> And will you rent our ancient love asunder,
> To join with men in scorning your poor friend?
>
> (III. ii. 198–212; 215–16)

A replica of such an 'incorporation' at a later and more complex stage of a woman's life is Titania's relationship with her favourite votaress. Titania's account of her friendship with the boy's mother contains a wonderfully articulated image of imaginative mimicry:

> His mother was a vot'ress of my order,
> And in the spiced Indian air, by night,

Full often hath she gossip'd by my side,
And sat with me on Neptune's yellow sands,
Marking th' embarked traders on the flood;
When we have laugh'd to see the sails conceive
And grow big-bellied with the wanton wind;
Which she, with pretty and with swimming gait,
Following (her womb then rich with my young squire)
Would imitate, and sail upon the land
To fetch me trifles, and return again,
As from a voyage, rich with merchandise.

(II. i. 123–34)

Peter Quince's troupe literalize metaphors, too, but here the Indian maid's imitation of the big-bellied sails has a function other than *reductio ad absurdum*. The friends share the playful vision of the billowing sails as pregnant, which the expectant mother then playfully mimes, for the amusement and gratification of her companion. What is rendered here, we are invited to infer, is a vividly empathetic, imaginative sharing of the experience of pregnancy; and therefore when the mother dies it is no wonder that Titania's attachment to the child is more than the charitable rearing of an orphan. 'And for her sake do I rear up her boy:/And for her sake I will not part with him' has the ring of self-justification – she is claiming nothing for this adoption but an act of conventional piety – but what we see is that she has so identified herself with her votaress that the child has become her own. Oberon, furiously observing his exclusion from this relationship, wants to possess himself of the love object she is so wrapped up in, and, failing, will punish her by caricaturing her defection. She is to dote upon the first living creature she sees:

(Be it on lion, bear, or wolf, or bull,
On meddling monkey, or on busy ape),

(II. i. 180–1)

The animus, however, of

Set your heart at rest;
The fairy land buys not the child of me.

(II. i. 121–2)

invites us to infer (especially if we remember 'childing' autumn in her description of the disordered and distemperatured seasons) that Oberon might mend his marriage more effectively by getting Titania with child than by trying to get Titania without child. But rivalry and revenge (for previous peccadilloes real or imagined, with Theseus and Hippolyta)[4] is the order of the day at this stage – a midsummer madness – of the battle of the sexes, and at this stage of the comic development, which is the laying bare of the particular comic disposition dominant in the play.

The double plotting of *A Midsummer Night's Dream* is superb because it is so subtly related. Marital rivalry is more complex because double-decked: marriage partners must maintain their distinctive personalities, recognize each other's and enter into a new corporate personality, or transaction of personalities. But in this marriage on the rocks, with Titania playing the part of imagined twin to her votaress, and Oberon competing with her for possession of the Indian boy, rivalry has taken the place of reciprocity, competition of co-operation, and a riotous mimicry of clearly differentiated sexual roles.

We begin to perceive the nature of the comic infirmity in *A Midsummer Night's Dream*. It is that fluidity and instability of imagination which causes an individual to be either too identified or not identified enough; to resemble when to discriminate would be more politic and more appropriate; to represent reality in images generated by the desires of the mind.

Nature spirits that they are, these fairies, nature perfectly reflects their marital dissensions:

> Therefore the winds. . .
> As in revenge, have suck'd up from the sea
> Contagious fogs; which, falling in the land,
> Hath every pelting river made so proud
> That they have overborne their continents . . .
>   and the green corn
> Hath rotted ere his youth attain'd a beard . . .
> The nine men's morris is fill'd up with mud,
> And the quaint mazes in the wanton green,
> For lack of tread, are undistinguishable . . .

> hoary-headed frosts
> Fall in the fresh lap of the crimson rose,
> And on old Hiems' [thin] and icy crown
> An odorous chaplet of sweet summer buds
> Is, as in mockery, set; the spring, the summer,
> The childing autumn, angry winter, change
> Their wonted liveries; and the mazed world,
> By their increase, now knows not which is which.
>   (II. i. 88–114 passim)[5]

'Undistinguishability' and the wilder follies of not knowing which is which receive their richest comic gloss from the good artisans of Athens in their entanglement with the problems of dramatic representation – when a wall is a wall for example, or a lion Snug the Joiner; but the message of this *paysage moralisé* is quite clear: confusion, disorder, disarray, mock mimicry reign in the woods, and with all distinction gone, all relations are perverse or fruitless or unnatural. Puck's mischievous translation of Bottom literally embodies asininity. But it also reflects Titania's wrong-headed 'incorporation' of the Indian boy. It is a bonus for Oberon's punitive plan (he did not envisage monsters), while the metamorphosis and the coupling of Titania with this comic monster inflates the folly of misconceived images *ad absurdum*, revealing (but not to the victims) truth in motley.

The strategy of comedy is to maximalize error before matters will mend; the maximalizing indeed generates the mending. To Helena there does come a glimmer of liberating wisdom in the woods when she says: 'What wicked and dissembling glass of mine/Made me compare with Hermia's sphery eyne?' (II. ii. 98–9). This anticipates remedy but is as yet in too self-abasing a form.[6] The *processus turbarum*, with its cumulative and preposterous turbulence brings about for the lovers an intensification of folly to the point of giddying exhaustion; and discernment – the wisdom of discrimination, of getting images right – will emerge from the chaos, or de-composition of topsy-turvydom.

There should be no expounding of dreams, as Bottom knows, but the magic juice applied to sleeping eyes – the comic device – reveals in this play its fully Shakespearean iridescence. It is both delusive and applied in error and so causes the knot of errors and perturbations; but it is also the cause of ultimate reclamation and recognition. The magic at work operates therapeutically, cathartically, like dreams indeed.[7] It discovers, enlarging as in a distorting mirror, the shadowy wishes and fears of the mind, and by so doing enables the victims to enfranchize themselves from their obsessions. Shakespeare's moonlit wood, alive with trolls, grotesques and ambivalence is a potent symbol for the creative subconscious. And Puck, conveyor of dreams and potions, impish homogenizer, can be seen as a genius of comedy itself, mimicking (in the likeness of a filly foal, or a roasted crab), mocking, de-creating as he gives all nature's ingredients a great stir. As does Bottom, counterpoint Buffoon to Puck's Eiron (and unwitting Impostor as Titania's lover), giving all the theatre's ingredients a great stir:

> Nay; you must name his name, and half his face must be seen through the lion's neck, and he himself must speak through, saying thus, or to the same defect: . . . my life for yours. If you think I come hither as a lion, it were pity of my life . . .
>
> (III. i. 36–43)

Puck's error – to him all Athenians are alike – is homeopathic. It reflects the comic disposition of the play, exposes it, and is exactly what is required to exacerbate and exorcise it.

Thus, so far from the warblings of one song in one key, the fierce vexations of misprision in Act III bring about a positively inflamed consciousness of difference: '"Little" again? Nothing but "low" and "little"?' Abuse and vilification are not lacking on all sides: 'Thou cat, thou bur! Vile thing . . . tawny Tartar . . . loathed medicine' are a string of epithets from a sometime lover sufficient to draw from Hermia (to Helena) 'You juggler! You canker-blossom! You thief of love!' For which she gets as good as she gives with Helena's 'Fie, fie, you counterfeit, you puppet, you!' '"Puppet"?' shouts Hermia at this point:

> Ay, that way goes the game.
> Now I perceive that she hath made compare
> Between our statures: she hath urg'd her height,

And with her personage, her tall personage,
Her height, forsooth, she hath prevail'd with him.
And are you grown so high in his esteem,
Because I am so dwarfish and so low?
How low am I, thou painted maypole? Speak!
How low am I? I am not yet so low
But that my nails can reach unto thine eyes.
                                    (III. ii. 289–98)

'O, when she is angry', retorts a onetime part of an incorporate
double cherry,

                    she is keen and shrewd!
        She was a vixen when she went to school;
        And though she be but little, she is fierce.
                                    (III. ii. 323–5)

    This knot of errors is the world upside down, and Helena's
idyllic and lost childhood 'incorporation' is well and truly
mocked, as are Lysander's protestations of love to Hermia when
transposed to

                    Get you gone, you dwarf;
        You minimus, of hind'ring knot-grass made;
        You bead, you acorn.   (III. ii. 328–30)

At the same time these frenetic hyperboles are the fulfilment and
the acting out of everyone's deepest anxieties, misgivings and
obsessions. Hermia foresaw all and foresuffered all when she
dreamt of Lysander watching a serpent eating her heart away, and
Helena's masochism – her seeking to 'enrich her pain' – to cause
the pain she dreads and loves – has progressed from her embracing of the role of fawning and beaten spaniel (I. i. 246–51) to a
paroxysm of self-abasement: 'No, no; I am as ugly as a bear' (II. ii.
94). And this even before she becomes convinced of her victimiza-
tion at the hand of all.

    The *processus turbarum* of Act III, by intensifying aberration
and detonating hidden psychic dynamite discomposes, disorients
and disintegrates. They all collapse in the end, exhausted by these
traumas and by the hectic pursuit through the woods, and when

they awake they are tranquil and clear-seeing. Now that vision is improved they are able to look back upon their 'dream' experience as upon something distant and blurred. Hermia says: 'Methinks I see these things with parted eye,/When every thing seems double', and Helena concurs: 'So methinks;/And I have found Demetrius like a jewel,/Mine own, and not mine own' (IV. i. 189–92). These are pregnant sayings, these musings of the wondering and half-enlightened lovers. Perception and self-perception have passed through the alembic of dream and have been catalyzed. Demetrius, now seeing his love for Hermia as a childhood gaud and Helena as once again 'the object and the pleasure of (his) eye' speaks for all four when he says:

> These things seem small and undistinguishable,
> Like far-off mountains turned into clouds.
>
> (IV. i. 187–8)

It is an interesting word 'undistinguishable'. And it occurs only once again in Shakespeare: in Titania's description of confusion and disorder in nature already quoted.

The formal remedy, as Puck himself calls it, of the play is purely ophthalmic. Oberon's corrective juice causes the lovers when they awake from their sleep to sort themselves out into suitable couples – Jacks and Jills, as Puck puts it with benign contempt – and Titania to be released from her unsuitable coupling with sweet bully Bottom. But the whole question of corrected vision, of the tutored imagination, goes beyond the merely technical exigencies of plot. It is the essential mediator of the benign, non-disjunctive dialectic which conjures rejoicing out of mockery, and wisdom out of folly.

In the lovers' case errors of 'vision' are removed so that true relations can be re-discerned.[8] The lovers recuperate, literally, from their 'trip'. Lysander, it is now clear, fell into an infatuation with Helena when he was really in love with Hermia, and Demetrius fell into an infatuation with Hermia when he was really in love with Helena. But in the fairies' case, Titania, chastened by the onslaughts of the tender passion, relinquishes the child; and this yielding to Oberon's will produces in him the impulse of compassion required to melt hard-heartedness, soften anger and renounce retaliation. The passage is worth particular attention:

> Her dotage now I do begin to pity.
> For meeting her of late behind the wood,
> Seeking sweet favors for this hateful fool,
> I did upbraid her, and fall out with her.
> For she his hairy temples then had rounded
> With coronet of fresh and fragrant flowers;
> And that same dew which sometime on the buds
> Was wont to swell like round and orient pearls,
> Stood now within the pretty flouriets' eyes,
> Like tears that did their own disgrace bewail.
> When I had at my pleasure taunted her,
> And she in mild terms begg'd my patience,
> I then did ask of her her changeling child;
> Which straight she gave me, and her fairy sent
> To bear him to my bower in fairy land.
> And now I have the boy, I will undo
> This hateful imperfection of her eyes.
>
> (IV. i. 47–63)

In this recognition scene Oberon sees her, perhaps for the first time, certainly for the first time since 'Ill met by moonlight, proud Titania' in Act II, with detachment and tenderness.

Eyes are organs of visions; eyes (especially when starry) are beautiful objects of vision. But eyes are also vessels for tears. Titania's amorous fantasy as she orders Bottom led away to her bower will be recalled:

> The moon methinks looks with a wat'ry eye;
> And when she weeps, weeps every little flower,
> Lamenting some enforced chastity.
>
> (III. i. 198–200)

Drugs, potions, condiments alter vision and visibility, but the true transfigurations are those which take place invisibly at the heart. Bottom himself makes this point, as modestly as ever. When told by Peter Quince that Pyramus had been a lover 'that kills himself most gallant for love', 'That', remarks the sage Bottom, 'will ask some tears in the true performing of it. If I do it, let the audience look to their eyes'.

A *Midsummer Night's Dream* juggles conspicuously with multiple levels of representation, with plays-within-plays and visions within dreams. What is performed, what is meant, what is seen are often, as Theseus said of Peter Quince's prologue 'like a tangled chain; nothing impair'd, but all disorder'd' (v. i. 125–6). The Athenian lovers, Lysander and Hermia, fall asleep and dream (in Act II), fall asleep and wake (in Act IV), and what happens to them is ambiguously dream/reality, just as Oberon king of shadows, is ambiguously real/not real, visible to the audience but not to the lovers; and the 'angel' that wakes Titania 'from her flow'ry bed' (III. i. 129) is visible to her but not to the audience, who perceive only Nick Bottom assified. Puck stage-manages these 'transfigurations' for Oberon's delectation just as Peter Quince does for Theseus' and Shakespeare for ours.[9] And the audience is more than once pointedly invited to conflate these frames. When Theseus says 'The best in this kind are but shadows', his remark applies with equal validity to the artisans of Athens and the Lord Chamberlain's Men. By the same token Puck's 'shadows' in the epilogue ('if we shadows have offended') refers, intentionally, both to the fairies and the actors – the visible and the invisible.

Act V dazzlingly catches up and re-focuses the issues of the play, recapitulating its schooling of the imagination. When Theseus tempers Hippolyta's impatience with the mechanicals' efforts: 'This is the silliest stuff that ever I heard' (v. i. 210) with 'The best in this kind are but shadows; and the worst are no worse, if imagination amend them' (v. i. 211–12) he is retracting his previous repudiation of the imagination as the faculty which 'sees more devils than vast hell can hold', or 'Helen's beauty in a brow of Egypt', or some bringer of what is a merely 'apprehended' joy, or a bear in a bush on a dark night. The rationalistic and empirically minded duke has been more than cautious about the seething tricks of that fertile and moonstruck faculty; and it is in reply to his dismissal of the lovers' story as so much irrational and illusory dream stuff that Hippolyta enters her caveat concerning the story of the night:

FANCY'S IMAGES III

But all the story of the night told over,
And all their minds transfigur'd so together,
More witnesseth than fancy's images,
And grows to something of great constancy ...
(v. i. 23–6)

The ducal pair, as we have seen, are a model of *concordia discors* ('How shall we find the concord of this discord?' Theseus asks of the 'very tragical mirth' about to be presented by the artisans) and so it is fitting that they should conduct the dialectic of real and imaginary, meant and performed, visible and invisible towards a resolution for theatre-goers and lovers alike. When Hippolyta reflects upon the story of the night, she is inviting not only Theseus but the theatre audience as well to further reflection. She is inviting a retrospective reappraisal of all that has been enacted in the moonlit woods. Hippolyta's organic metaphor is interesting; cognition, it says, or re-cognition, grows in the mind in the process of recounting, re-telling. What the play celebrates as remedial, beneficent, recuperative it will have discovered by working its way through the fantastic follies the initial deficiencies or infirmities generated. These follies, reduced (or expanded) to absurdity, will prove to have been homeopathically therapeutic, if imagination amend them by making them intelligible. 'It must be your imagination then, not theirs', says wise Hippolyta, knowing that to stout bully Bottom nothing is invisible, not even a voice from behind a wall. So far as that parodic literalist of the imagination is concerned, moonlight cannot be better represented than by moonlight, shining in at the casement in all its factual actuality. And when a person is a wall, he must be well and truly plastered and roughcast. No fancy Brechtian placards will do for him, any more than he can conceive that anyone (of any size) called Mustardseed should not be instantly applied to roast beef.

Pyramus and Thisbe presents a tragedy of lovers' misprisions, and neutralizes disaster with its ludicrous comicality. It is irresistibly amusing in itself and needs no amending, by imagination or any other means; and it is also the vehicle of Shakespeare's most ironic private joke to *his* audience over the heads, so to speak, of Peter Quince and his. The latter possess the capacity to distinguish between walls and witty partitions, between run-on and end-stopped pentameters, between a lion and a goose and between a man and a moon. But they haven't always been so good at distinguishing. Their own follies have been, in their own way, no less de-constructive; but also no less recreative.

'Your play needs no excuse', says Theseus, amused, ironic and kind. 'Marry, if he that writ it had play'd Pyramus, and hang'd himself in Thisby's garter, it would have been a fine tragedy; and so it is truly, and very notably discharg'd' (v. i. 357–61). A great deal, and of great constancy, has been 'discharged' in this play. And not only Hippolyta, it has been suggested, has had an inkling that the fantasy of folly may grow into the wisdom of the imagination.

This resonant insight marks, at the level of overt theme, the dramatic growth in *A Midsummer Night's Dream* of the dramatist's capacity to conceive and render the interlacing of sexual and individual roles. Further growth will issue, in due course, in the achievement of a comic form completely adequate for the dialectical battle of sex and self, a form which will resolve the ambivalencies of that warfare's tamings and matings. Here the idea is still inchoate, for it lacks as yet the crystallizing force of the heroine protagonist in all the fullness of her virtuosity and her autonomy. Shakespeare's next comedy appears to present us, in Portia, with exactly such a missing link. But, as I shall hope immediately to show, the prime Shakespearean comic moment is not yet at hand. In *The Merchant of Venice* the conjunction between the dramatist's imagination and his story materials does not yield an unambiguously remedial comic structure. In this *The Merchant* resembles *Love's Labour's Lost*; both are disrupted or ruptured comic forms; and in neither is the role of the heroine-protagonist fully realized.

NOTES

1 G. K. Hunter, *The Later Comedies* (London: Longman Green, 1962), p. 4.
2 ibid., p. 5. A similar view is taken by Alexander Leggatt, *Shakespeare's Comedy of Love* (London: Methuen, 1974), p. 96.

3 Helena's exegesis of the blind Cupid commonplace does not merely repeat the platitudes of a received iconology. The medieval Cupid was blind because love was taken by medieval Christianity to be irrational, not seeing with the eyes of reason and judgment. The Renaissance Cupid was blind because love was taken by Florentine neo-Platonism to be intellectual, not seeing with a merely sensible organ. See Edgar Wind, *Pagan Mysteries of the Renaissance* (New Haven: Yale University Press, 1958), and Erwin Panovsky, *Studies in Iconology* (New York: Oxford University Press, 1939), ch. IV, pp. 95–9. We can make no sense of the logic of Helena's 'Nor hath' unless we see that it precludes a neo-Platonic 'mind', for it cannot be said of intellect that it 'hath not of any judgment taste'. Nor, however, can the denigratory medieval view of love as sensual appetite, a lust of the eyes, be made to sort with Helena's conception of love's capacity to transpose to form and dignity.cf. also Sonnet CXIII: 'Since I left you, mine eye is in my mind . . .'

4 See David P. Young, *Something of Great Constancy* (New Haven: Yale University Press, 1966), p. 139.

5 Thomas McFarland, *Shakespeare's Pastoral Comedy* (Chapel Hill: University of North Carolina Press, 1972), is misled by his determination to find an idealized pastoralism in Shakespeare's comedies to read this speech as an affirmation of 'the overwhelmingly ideal setting of *Midsummer Night's Dream*. Nothing could be less evil than the "progeny of evil" catalogued; it is in fact an account of paradise itself' (p. 84).

6 'The erotic instincts' as Freud said drily, in *Contributions to the Psychology of Love* (1910) 'are hard to mould; training of them achieves now too much, now too little.' The statement could serve as an epigraph to Shakespeare's collected comic works.

7 A similar view of dream in Shakespeare has been developed by Marjorie B. Garber, *Dreams in Shakespeare: From Metaphor to Metamorphosis* (New Haven: Yale University Press, 1974).

8 It is surely not true, as Larry Champion claims, in *The Evolution of Shakespeare's Comedy* (Cambridge, Massachusetts:

Harvard University Press, 1970) that 'their victimisation by whimsical passion is no less at the conclusion of the play than at the beginning' (p. 99).

9 See Anne Righter (Barton), *Shakespeare and the Idea of the Play* (Harmondsworth: Penguin, 1967), Philip Edwards, *Shakespeare and the Confines of Art* (London: Methuen, 1968), p. 46, and Leo Salingar, *Shakespeare and the Traditions of Comedy* (Cambridge: Cambridge University Press, 1974), pp. 277–82 passim, for suggestive comments on self-reflexive plays-within-plays.

VII

JESSICA'S MONKEY;
OR,
THE GOODWINS

In both Belmont and Venice there is treasure, and a treasure of a girl, locked up in a casket, or a locked and barred house, and liberated by a Prince Charming ready to take risks. Everybody in *The Merchant* takes risks, puts their fortunes to the hazard, whether these are business ventures (with lethal securities), or marital adventures for high stakes: a wealthy and beautiful wife or perpetual celibacy. Portia risks keeping her bond with her father's will; Jessica risks breaking hers. Shylock, too canny to take risks normally, for once casts caution to the winds and does so, joining, in his own macabre way, the Venetians' happy-go-lucky winner-take-all attitudes, which Launce parodies in one of his funniest speeches:

> Father, in. I cannot get a service, no, I have ne'er a tongue in my head, well! [*Looking on his palm.*] If any man in Italy have a fairer table, which doth offer to swear upon a book, I shall have good fortune. Go to, here's a simple line of life! Here's a small trifle of wives! Alas, fifteen wives is nothing! Aleven widows and nine maids is a simple coming-in for one man. And then to scape drowning thrice, and to be in peril of my life with the edge of a feather-bed, here are simple scapes. Well, if Fortune be a woman, she's a good wench for this gear. (II. ii. 156–67)

Each story has a 'provident' father, the ironic contrast in the nature of their 'providence' expanding metonymically into a contrast between two cultures or world-views: tight-fisted miserliness against open hearts and purses, sobriety against carnival carousing, getting and hoarding against getting and spending, bourgeois thrift against aristocratic negligence, mercenary self-interest against aesthetic disinterestedness. One of these fathers fathers the comic device – an apparent deception to reveal a truth: the triple test. The other is the father of a macabre parody of a comic device: the merry bond. It is ironically appropriate that the latter proposal – the flesh bond – is proposed in response to Antonio's lordly gesture of contempt for mere money bonds, between friends. One daughter is faithful to her bond, to 'the will of a dead father' in the locked caskets, and is rewarded by the acquisition of a handsome and courtly, but prodigal, young lover. The other, faithless to her filial bond, makes off, with another young prodigal, with her father's wealth in a locked casket.

The Venetians it seems are gamblers, but good, and win; Shylock is not a gambler, but also not good, and loses. This moral asymmetry calls into question any simple black-white, wicked-good, tight-free, shut-open antithetical reading of the plots, and makes for parody or parity at least. Some moral stock-taking is felt to be called for when the unearned gains of prodigality are thus set off against the undeserved losses of frugality. And any comic pleasure we derive from happy conclusions will certainly be less than unreserved. The playwright has taken risks, too, it seems. As Alexander Leggatt puts the matter: 'The gamble of wedding complex character to formalized action is exciting, but the combination is too volatile to allow more than a limited sense of harmony at the end'[1]

My alternative titles are meant to suggest the incompatibilities of this volatile mixture and to epitomize the two alternative, inconsistent and irreconcilable mental scenarios which *The Merchant of Venice* has produced in its readers at least since the mid-nineteenth century. It is this rupture of comic form which I wish to explore.

In Act III, scene i, Tubal tells Shylock that his apostate and runaway daughter, in addition to getting through four score ducats in one night in Genoa, has acquired an unusual pet to complement her elopement with her young blade.

> *Tubal*   One of them show'd me a ring that he had of your
> daughter for a monkey.
> *Shylock*   Out upon her! Thou torturest me, Tubal. It was my
> turkis, I had it of Leah when I was a bachelor. I would not
> have given it for a wilderness of monkeys.
>
> (III. i. 118–23)

It is a moment which has attracted attention. It is capable of arousing more than a spasm of compassion for Shylock and more than a touch of uneasiness regarding the manners and morals of his errant daughter. It is perhaps the germ from which burgeoned Irving's famous pathetic rendering of the Jew stumbling home alone in the dark to a shuttered and empty house.[2] What does this monkey mean? Is it a picturesque addition to the lady's accessories, which, because of its exotic unnecessariness effectively underlines the wild, inordinate nature of her new unrestraint? Are we to have sympathy for this trans-Appeninic shopping spree, recognizing the stifling, joyless, penurious existence she has led behind Shylock's shuttered windows? But if we recall Jessica's complaint to the 'merry devil' Launcelot Gobbo, her one companion, about the Jew's house being a hell (II. iii. 2), we might also remember with a qualm of (parental) uneasiness, the libertine cynicism of Gratiano as he and Salarino wait beneath the Jew's window, in the very next scene, for the meeting of Jessica and her lover:

> Who riseth from a feast
> With that keen appetite that he sits down?
>
> All things that are,
> Are with more spirit chased than enjoy'd.
> How like a younger or a prodigal
> The scarfed bark puts from her native bay,
> Hugg'd and embraced by the strumpet wind!
> How like the prodical doth she return,
> With over-weather'd ribs and ragged sails,
> Lean, rent, and beggar'd by the strumpet wind!
>
> (II. vi. 8–9; 12–19)

Are we (alternatively) piously to remember that we are enjoined not to lay up treasures on earth where the moth and rust corrupt, and that the conspicious waste of sordid ducats is certainly one way of not doing this; though the second half of the apostolic injunction has perhaps become somewhat obscured, possibly in the hugger-mugger of packing and moving? Or are we, *tout court*, to be revolted (as was Carnovsky)[3] by a callous little bitch, the disloyalty of whose apostacy is aggravated not only by her conscienceless 'gilding' of herself with her father's wealth in order to run off with an already gilded young gad-about, but by an utterly heartless disregard for any human feelings her father may be supposed to have if not for his only daughter, then at least for the memory of his late wife? What indeed are we to make of Jessica's flight? Is it from Hell to Grace? or is it merely from housekeeping, admittedly dull, to the charm of feckless, reckless, gracious living?

Renaissance iconology is not very helpful, it turns out, in deciphering monkeys. There is no conclusive opinion, in a neo-Platonic age when all symbols were reversible, all values transvaluable. We find that apes represent the lascivious or libidinous appetites (as they do for Othello, in his frenzy); or the primitive and unnurtured in man's development; or imitation – false, factitious, or mocking; or the poet, whose feigning brings us closer to Truth than mere reality does.[4] Does Jessica stand symbolically for one or more of these? I think myself that the sociology of monkeys, in a play as realistic as *The Merchant*, may well help us more than their iconology. In the Washington National Gallery there is a picture by Shakespeare's contemporary, van Dyck, of a grand lady with two accessories to wealth and status to keep her amused: a dwarf and a monkey.[5] The monkey there, it seems, is a pet; and a pet for the affluent and aristocratic. The effect in the play of this gratuitous, unexplained and unexpected detail is as stimulating to the imagination of reality as, painters always discover, figures portrayed from behind. Whatever affection-starved, companionship-starved impulse might be supposed to account for that sudden mad whim in Genoa, it is possible to perceive the whole of Jessica's dream of wealth and freedom caught, like a fly in amber, by Tubal's laconic report. And likewise, the extent and the degree of her father's pained incomprehension. If this is mockery of Shylock, it is cold ridicule indeed. And while conflict between the generations is inherent in New Comedy, this little episode (which I have entitled Jessica's Monkey) suggests an order and level of emotional investment for which Terentian solutions are hardly adequate. The loosening of the father's bond, the final knitting of the nuptial bond are the classic beginnings and endings of the inverted Oedipal plots of Roman comedies, in which youthful sex revolts against paternal injunction but is finally and victoriously reabsorbed in the paternal society.[6] Here, however, there is no reabsorption. And only if Tubal were mistaken could we hope for comic issues. But he is not.

So, alternatively, the Goodwins – the odd name of the narrow seas 'where the carcasses of many a full ship lies buried'. The Arden editor offers an exegesis: 'good friends', that is, Antonio is 'wrecked on the hidden shoals of friendship'; but the innocent ear, I believe, is caught in a more immediately effective way. It is at the opening of Act II, during which Antonio loses all, and Bassanio wins all, both having hazarded, gambled, trusted their luck. Immediate irony, then, is patent in terms of the play's double peripeteia. The play's further remedial reversal of fortune will, of course, reverse the irony: the Goodwins will signify the goodwinners after all and Belmont will celebrate 'Love's Wealth':[7] the transformation of the values of getting and spending into those of giving and forgiving, of the mercenary into the merciful, and of blind Fortune into beneficent Providence.

What one might call the main-line criticism of the play, seeking a reasonably unified reading, has plumped for an idyllic Belmont as dominant, and attempted in various ways to absorb or evade the realism of Venice in favour of 'The Goodwins'. One way of doing this is by idealization, all references in Belmont to commerce such as Portia's 'Since you are dear bought, I will love you dear' (III. ii. 313) being taken completely seriously as metaphors of the Spiritual life. Moreover, with Shylock a comic-monstrous ogre to be cast out, and Jessica an imprisoned maiden to be rescued, and the great central scene a scene of judgment, the magnetic attraction of Christian allegory has proved well-nigh irresistible and the world of fairy-tale transformations further transformed into a facsimile of Christian beatitude demonstrating the triumph of Grace over Law, love over revenge, mercy over justice and moonlight over money.[8] The verisimilitude of Shakespeare's realism, however, the naturalistic idiom of the Venetian scenes, makes it very difficult to entertain, without recourse to irony, a simple equivalence of spiritual and material wealth. Moreover, if we allow our twentieth-century imaginations, haunted by other scenes and other places, to colour our interpretation, we will inevitably take sides with the other side, see Shylock as the persecuted Jew of all the ages and the Christians exposed as triflers and hypocrites if not worse. And it is to be noted that as early as 1816 Hazlitt declared 'at least he [Shylock] is honest in his vices; they are hypocrites in their virtues', and observed that Shylock had become 'a half-favourite with the philosophical part of the audience who are disposed to think that Jewish revenge is at least as good as Christian injuries'.[9] Between the Scylla of a sentimentalized Belmont and the Charybdis of a sentimentalized Shylock, critical polemic has regularly oscillated, producing solutions, for the most part, by special pleading.

A. D. Moody argues for an 'ironic comedy' – a radically ironic exposé of mercantilism, disenchantedly urban, and as sceptical about noble and virtuous lovers as about wicked Pharisees.[10] For C. L. Barber on the other hand, it is one of the festive, restorative, 'green world' comedies.[11] Middleton Murry bravely plumped for 'tragi-comedy', Aristotle's plot of double issue in which the virtuous are rewarded and the wicked punished, and found it 'the finest example of the genre we possess'.[12] Salingar has recently proposed a classification of *The Merchant* with *Measure for Measure* and *All's Well* – traditionally 'dark' comedies – and *Much Ado*, on the grounds that in all four nuptials are interrupted so that tests and trials can take place.[13] These taxonomies, however, are based on surface similarities rather than on deep structures.

The following pages attempt to explore the deeper structures which have produced a play not only, as I have suggested, itself split, sundered, schizoid, but rich in the figuring of the estrangement, alienation and dismembering which are its obsessive themes. The homology is extremely impressive. I shall try to

suggest a reason for the play having, as comedy, run aground, like
its own 'wealthy Andrew', though it set out on its voyage, so to
speak, fully equipped for comedy. And, though my argument
dictates certain negative emphases I would like to insist that if
comedies as well as argosies can run aground, their riches, too,
may be detached and spread abroad, no less bewitching for the
fate that has overcome them. For the loss of momentum towards a
comic resolution is not necessarily also a loss of dramatic intensity, or of the hold a play has upon our imaginations.

On the face of it *The Merchant* is simply a variant of regular
New Comedy; all the ingredients seem to be present and are
marshalled and carried forward with admirable dramatic impetus
and force. The motivating privation is named by Bassanio the
moment he is alone with Antonio, to whom 'he owes the most in
money and in love'. The motivating privation is indeed what it
almost invariably has been: money and love.

> In Belmont is a lady richly left,
> And she is fair and, fairer than that word,
> Of wondrous virtues . . .
>
>   and her sunny locks
> Hang on her temples like a golden fleece,
> Which makes her seat of Belmont Colchis' strond,
> And many Jasons come in quest of her.
> O my Antonio, had I but the means
> To hold a rival place with one of them,
> I have a mind presages me such thrift
> That I should questionless be fortunate!
>
>   (I. i. 161–3; 169–76)

The follies of extravagant youth and the errors of older benefac-
tors, together with misfortune at sea and the ill will of a usurer tie
a knot of daunting legal intractability. A dazzling remedy is
discovered by Lady Bountiful herself, in disguise, thus synthesiz-
ing Fortune and Providence and enabling liberated and enlightened lovers to join in holy matrimony. But how liberated? Enlightened in what way? The comic device does not function to expose
and exacerbate the follies which are to be exorcized: on the

contrary, the comic device exposes the frailties of Arragon and Morocco, but the virtues of Bassanio, thus usurping the function of the remedial recognitions of the resolution and precluding the farcical enactment or working-out of folly which was Shakespeare's great comic discovery in earlier plays. That Bassanio's virtue in the caskets scene is precisely risk-taking – gambling – transformed into a Spartan virtue is exactly what would constitute a remedial recognition; while the rings episode is a displaced knot of errors and mistaken identities arriving, like a codicil, *after* the impossible choices of bond and trial have provided a *processus turbarum*, and too late to be effective.

Sherman Hawkins, in an admirably thought-provoking article distinguishes between what he calls

> the two worlds of Shakespearean comedy. The dramatic expression necessary to subdue or expel the anti-comic spirit seems to proceed on two principles. One is 'acting out' its latent impulses . . . [which] is expansive and cathartic . . . The second principle is 'fixing the blame' . . . [which] locates the general lunacy or evil in a criminal or scapegoat in whom it can be overpowered and driven out.[14]

If this is true, *The Merchant of Venice* must surely be seen to proceed on the second principle. But the trouble, I shall argue, is that for Shakespeare the scapegoat figure is germinal for tragedy and only the first principle generates, for him, truly comic forms. The plot Shakespeare is using is therefore at odds with the comic form he characteristically favours and the result is fracture, which he has compounded by an inversion at the level of ordination: the main plot – Portia's and Bassanio's – is subordinated to the plot which is causally dependent upon it. It is Portia's captivity, not Antonio's, which originates the story. She is the golden bait for the pursuit of which the impecunious Bassanio requires his friend's credit. Shakespeare has, to be sure, neatly interlocked the two bond stories, significantly changing his source story in order to do so.

In Ser Giovanni's *Il Pecorone*[15] the hero of the story is Giannetto. It is a single plot story in which the youngest of three sons is put to a test of (in effect) his virility, succeeding the third time, but too late to prevent his benefactor-uncle from becoming forfeit to the moneylender's bond. The pound-of-flesh bond is an episode in the success story of Giannetto with the Lady of Belmonte. It enables the lady (in disguise) to save the uncle, and to trap Giannetto with the ring stratagem, thus balancing *his* previous outwitting of her in the bed test. But Shakespeare, by giving the Shylock/Antonio story an independent weight and dynamic of its own, and by condensing the three tests of Giannetto into the triple choice for the suitors in the casket scene, has altered the whole ordonnance of the story and created the conditions for the disruption of his comic form. By throwing upon a scapegoat figure the whole burden of the comic exorcism he has frustrated his own comic intuitions. His was not the satiric mode of comedy which can make good punitive use of scapegoat exposures. What he does with his scapegoat, we find, is to convert him, by means of a confrontation with the impossible choice which structures disjunctive tragic forms, into a quasi-tragic protagonist.

Though *The Merchant* is superficially like the other dual location or green world comedies, its profound unlikeness in respect of the remedial comic principle is instructive. The 'other places' in Shakespeare's green world comedies create space within the play in which fantasy can function. The comic rhythm normally takes us from the represented real, through a preposterous or fantastic breakdown and recreation, back to a transfigured reality. But Belmont is not the recreative other place of dream, or play, or vacation, or magic, or nature from which the protagonists return transformed, having lost and found themselves. It is only Venice come into a windfall and relieved of sordid financial cares and a leech of a money lender.

The most powerful impression produced by the opening of *The Merchant* is that of estrangement. Whatever the cause of Antonio's mysterious melancholy may be, his companions are not capable of penetrating it. They live their own lives in those marvellously expressive first speeches, not his; they translate him into his wealth and fantasize about it, and when they cannot penetrate his mask, they, in a sense, disown him. Salarino, we are invited to infer, would dearly like to be

> Like signiors and rich burghers on the flood,
> Do overpeer the petty traffickers
> That cur'sy to them, do them reverence,
> As they fly by them with their woven wings.
>
> (I. i. 10; 12–14)

His vivid rendering of the anxieties of the rich:

> My wind cooling my broth
> Would blow me to an ague when I thought
> What harm a wind too great might do at sea.
>
> (I. i. 22–4)

while evoking the glamour and opulence of material possessions, is also at the same time a powerful image of disintegration:

> Should I go to church
> And see the holy edifice of stone,
> And not bethink me straight of dangerous rocks,
> Which touching but my gentle vessel's side
> Would scatter all her spices on the stream,
> Enrobe the roaring waters with my silks,
> And in a word, but even now worth this,
> And now worth nothing? (I. i. 29–36)

Antonio's dry asseveration of the wisdom of not putting all one's eggs in one basket produces Salanio's conjecture that love is the cause of his melancholy, and Antonio's repudiation of the very idea. Salanio abandons the attempt to understand Antonio with a verbal shrug of the shoulders:

> Now by two headed Janus,
> Nature hath fram'd strange fellows in her time:
>
> (I. i. 50–1)

and a pair of figures which dismember human physiognomy:

> Some that will evermore peep through their eyes,
> And laugh like parrots at a bagpiper;
> And other of such vinegar aspect
> That they'll not show their teeth in way of smile
> Though Nestor swear the jest be laughable.
>
> (I. i. 52–6)

Antonio is not worried about his merchandise, he is not in love, he is not the churlish malcontent Salanio decides to take him for, nor a fop affecting an air of grave profoundity as Gratiano presently suggests. Their attempts to pluck out the heart of his mystery only emphasize the degree to which they are divided from him, or he from them, much as the ocean, uniting lands and capital cities in the intercourse of commerce, also divides them from the vessels perilously carrying their merchandise. The suggestion of an absence of communion between these Venetians is confirmed by the exchange which follows their meeting. Salarino, seeing Bassanio and his companions approach, says

> I would have stay'd till I had made you merry,
> If worthier friends had not prevented me.
>
> (I. i. 60–1)

Whereupon Antonio takes a quiet revenge upon the spite or envy he perceives in Salarino's remark by calling the latter's scarcely concealed bluff:

> Your worth is very dear in my regard.
> I take it your own business calls on you,
> And you embrace th' occasion to depart.
>
> (I. i. 62–4)

These impressions are immediately reinforced by Bassanio's appeal:

> Good signiors both, when shall we laugh? say, when?
> You grow exceeding strange. Must it be so?
>
> (I. i. 66–7)

and by the contempt he expresses for Gratiano's 'infinite deal of nothing' (I. i. 114). If the initiating privation in Venice is the want of a wealthy and beautiful wife, or the want of means for the courting of one, the city's comic disposition, we perceive, is an unusual degree of alienation and divisiveness.

Matters are not otherwise in Belmont. Portia, who is piously scolded by Nerissa for being (like Antonio) so miserable when she is so well off, entertains the latter for the length of a scene with thumb-nail sketches of the strangers seeking her hand. Portia's protest against her situation, in which 'the will of a living daughter is curbed by the will of a dead father', and the degree of her rebelliousness, is indicated by her vehement declaration to Nerissa: 'The brain may devise laws for the blood, but a hot temper leaps o'er a cold decree – such a hare is madness the youth, to skip o'er the meshes of good counsel the cripple' (I. ii. 18–21). This again, be it noted, dismembers, and is neatly parodied a little later by Launcelot Gobbo. 'My conscience', that ingenious warrior informs us,

> hanging about the neck of my heart, says very wisely to me, 'My honest friend Launcelot, being an honest man's son – or rather an honest woman's son, for indeed my father did something smack, something grow to, he had a kind of taste – well, my conscience says, 'Launcelot, bouge not'. (II. ii. 13–19)

But if strangeness and fragmentation are everywhere, in both Venice and Belmont, the condition is essentialized in Shylock, the Venetian Jew. He is the epitome of the alien, and thus curiously becomes an epitome, an emanation, of their own self-alienation. He is socially bound to them, and they to him, and separated by that very fact. His membership in the Venetian community is vouched for by language, by livelihood, by citizenship. Yet he is divided from them by impassable barriers. Their common language yields opposing meanings (Antonio is a 'good' man for instance); the money that passes between them connotes contrary values. The encounter between these opponents invites us to perceive not only temperamental but ideological antinomies: the opposition between good value and good faith, between increase and consumption, between self-preservation and self-sacrifice, between a Providence which helps those who help themselves, and a Providence which protects those who cast their bread upon the waters. The superb dramatic propriety we register is the result of the consonance of temperament and value throughout, in characteristic language, in characteristic actions. The Jew locks up, binds fast, shuts in, is fiercely continent (see his scorn for bagpipe fans, IV. i. 50), hates music, hates masquerade. The Christians unlock purses and hearts, disport themselves, enjoy themselves, squander. Their devotion to the useless, the beautiful, the aesthetic, is set against his utilitarianism, his interest, his usance – words, interestingly enough, only just acquiring their economic connotations in this early phase of the new acquisitive society which is emerging out of the older feudal forms.

The power of the first scene of contest lies in the sardonic mental acuity of the Jew. He is a formidable opponent, and not to be fobbed off. 'Be assur'd you may (take Antonio's bond)' says Bassanio with a lordly air. 'I will be assur'd I may; and that I may be assured, I will bethink me.' (I. iii. 28–9) is Shylock's ironic reply. Again, to Antonio's sarcastic

> Was this inserted to make interest good?
> Or is your gold and silver ewes and rams?
>
> (I. iii. 94–5)

he replies with his own sardonic irony:

> I cannot tell, I make it breed as fast.   (I. iii. 96)

which galvanizes the old Aristotelian argument against usury and sets Antonio's gentlemanly teeth on edge. Functioning as Eiron, Shylock makes them seem fatuous. Totally without niceties, of the earth earthy, he makes them appear posturers. In this context of sardonic counterperspectives the story of Jacob and Laban sets up sequential circles of irony. In complete antithetical opposition to Bassanio's parable of the arrows:

> In my school-days, when I had lost one shaft,
> I shot his fellow of the self-same flight
> The self-same way with more advised watch
> To find the other forth, and by adventuring both
> I oft found both.   (I. i. 140–4)

it also suggests an antithesis in the matter of courtship. Jacob, it will be remembered, was herding his uncle's sheep as payment for the younger daughter of whom he had been cheated. But Bassanio who, to be sure, has cheated no Esau of his birthright, is asking to be enabled to court his way to a fortune. Jacob toiled fourteen long years for the bride of his choice. The text is a mirror in which each of the two contenders sees himself in his world and his orientation to fortune and enterprise:

This was a way to thrive, and he was blest;

(I. iii. 89)

This was a venture, sir, that Jacob serv'd for,
A thing not in his power to bring to pass,

Was this inserted to make interest good?

(I. iii. 91–3; 94)

Interest, use – the key words in the new mercantilism – are anathema to the gentiles who cultivate aristocratic disinterest (if not feckless dilettantism) in matters amatory as well as commercial. Hence Antonio's reply

If thou wilt lend this money, lend it not
As to thy friends, for when did friendship take
A breed for barren metal of his friend?
But lend it rather to thine enemy,   (I. iii. 132–5)

Friendship is for those who possess beautiful sentiments, in Antonio's view.

Most modern discussions of Shylock have understandably turned upon or implied the question whether Shakespeare was anti-Semitic, whether and to what degree he shared the anti-Semitic stereotypes of folk-lore and popular culture.

It would seem to me as hard to prove from the text of *The Merchant* that Shakespeare was anti-Semitic as it would be to prove him a republican on the grounds that his kings are not always all they should be. It would seem to me possible on the grounds of what Coleridge called the 'omni-humanity' of his imagination, as well as the power of his intellect, to dismiss the case out of court. But we are not therefore to suppose him incapable of creating an anti-Semite. The 'rush from word to world',[16] from character to author, obscures a vital distinction. Shakespeare may not have been an anti-Semite, but Antonio certainly is – undisputedly, and by self-confession. And one will go far to find in any literature a representation of the dynamic tension of the relation between anti-Semite and Jew more profound and comprehensive than this.

The Jew, says Sartre

finds arraigned against him the irrational powers of tradition, of race, of national destiny, of instinct . . . values accessible only to intuition . . . the Jew demands proof for everything that his adversary advances because thus he proves himself. He distrusts intuition because it is not open to discussion and because, in consequence, it ends by separating men. If he reasons and disputes with his adversary, it is to establish the unity of intelligence.[17]

The parable has been, in a sense, Shylock's bid 'to establish the unity of intelligence'. In a moment of expansion he makes a bid for friendship, for social recognition at least, for confirmation of himself as a person through an appeal to a shared scripture. There is a certain intimacy in his view of the biblical patriarchs and he is inviting Antonio's participation in it. When this is repudiated he is deeply offended, and thrown back as ever into his own defensive-aggressive postures. Hence his famous outburst:

> Signior Antonio, many a time and oft
> In the Rialto you have rated me
> About my moneys and my usances.
>
> (I. iii. 106–9)

'The merry bond', half ingratiating, half menacing is preposterous, absurd, improbable in the highest degree. But there is bitter enmity between the Merchant and the Usurer and Antonio is too ready to trust his luck. The bond encapsulates the antagonism between these two, the alienation which characterizes their relations. And there is a displaced eroticism in

> an equal pound
> Of your fair flesh, to be cut off and taken
> In what part of your body pleaseth me.
>
> (I. iii. 149–51)

The Jew, if he cannot be at one in love with these others, will devour them. Thus he himself feeds fat not only the ancient grudge he bears them, but also that figment of their own ancient blood-libel paranoia that he is. They reciprocally reinforce each other's antagonism in a self-perpetuating spiral. Where the one sees a fawning Jew, the other sees a fawning publican, and each is determined his view shall prevail. To this ancient contention, however, Shakespeare adds the vividly realized, specific motivation of betrayal, bereavement and revenge, and thereby definitively forecloses comic possibilities by actualizing the very human harm, the human suffering, which comedy exists to circumvent.

Shylock's response already quoted to Jessica's flight, – to Jessica's monkey – in Act III, scene i, is significant and expressive in the highest degree. The fury, the outrage, the pain, the incomprehension are rendered with that command of nuance, of rhythm, of immediacy which marks a totally imagined individual utterance. It is truly 'language in action', as Burkhardt has defined dramatic speech,[18] and it completes and fills out one of the scenes on which we ground our perception of the dynamic realism of *The Merchant of Venice*. This is important. For if Shylock is seen as craftily, and stereotypically, planning the death of Antonio from the start it will be easier to assimilate the play to its fairytale pole. But this is precluded by the realism of the portrayal. Consider the whole scene which follows Jessica's flight; the whole painful exchange with the Venetians. For instance, 'My own flesh and blood to rebel', mutters Shylock. 'Out upon it, old carrion, rebels it at these years?' (III. i. 36) is the contribution of the wit Salanio. And Shylock, dogged, obdurate: 'I say, my daughter is my flesh and my blood' (III. i. 37). As they bait him and he snarls back, and as he oscillates between fury and exasperation, lamentation and self-pity, grief and vindictive rejoicing at Antonio's losses, and renewed anguish at his own 'loss upon loss'; and as this tumult of emotion crystallizes upon the dream of revenge and the taste of power – 'Let him look to his bond' – we, who come to this play from the timeless universe of the whole Shakespearean canon, may well hear echoes from the lives and deaths of other fathers and other daughters: 'According to my bond' . . . 'a carbuncle in my blood' . . . 'these pelican daughters' . . . .[19] Be this as it may, it is the father's grief that is presented as engendering the thirst for revenge, the determination to *seek* revenge. Palmer[20] and many others have seized upon Jessica's words at Belmont as proof that Shylock had such an intention all along:

When I was with him I have heard him swear
To Tubal and to Chus, his countrymen,
That he would rather have Antonio's flesh
Than twenty times the value of the sum
That he did owe him ...   (III. ii. 284–8)

But, even leaving aside the question of the reliability of Jessica as reporter, these critics surely overlook the optative mode of this reported speech. A desire, wishful thinking, a dream, is different from an action, even from a plan. And it is worth noting in this connection that Launcelot Gobbo's parodic function appears to be mainly directed to underscoring the desertion of Shylock the father.

He first appears, with his conscience and *his* father, immediately after Morocco's arrival in Belmont and immediately before the domestic scene between Shylock and Jessica. His burlesque conflict of conscience anticipates that of both the daughters – the faithful and the faithless; but where he leaves the rich Jew for the poor but noble Bassanio, thus vindicating by implication Portia's intuitive choice of suitor, he also debases in anticipation the abandonment of Shylock by Jessica, not for a poor Bassanio, but for a Lorenzo enriched by stolen goods. Launcelot counts his future blessings with comic gusto, but old Gobbo's affection, and unintentional ironies from Launcelot like 'it is a wise father that knows his own child', together with expressions of disenchantment like Gratiano's on the 'strumpet wind' (II. vi. 19), all draw together as by magnetic attraction to foreground and enhance the father's loss, rather than the daughter's escape. It is the father's point of view which is given dominance, and which is directly expressed in Act III, scene i. Jessica's flight therefore presents itself as betrayal in contrast with the other daughter's good choice. And Launcelot is again choric commentator upon her defection when he announces that her one hope of not being damned is that she may be a bastard and not the Jew's daughter at all. And if that casts an aspersion upon her mother (as Jessica points out) why truly then, Launcelot fears 'she is gone both ways'. For when he shuns Scylla her father, 'he falls into Charybdis her mother' and so she is damned by both (III. v. 15–17).

Moreover, there is the impact of the Jew himself. In the climax of the scene between Shylock and the Christians after Jessica's desertion, when Shylock makes his famous plea for consideration as a member of the human race, it will be noticed that he, as it were, dismembers himself to do so:

> Hath not a Jew eyes? Hath not a Jew hands, organs, dimensions, senses, affections, passions; fed with the same food, hurt with the same weapons, subject to the same diseases, heal'd by the same means, warm'd and cool'd by the same winter and summer, as a Christian is?   (III. i. 59–64)

And as the speech reaches its end it is as if he consolidates his disintegrated, fragmented self upon the will to revenge. In this he will better his instruction, outdo them even at their own game of hate. If we do not see the weight Shakespeare is giving the birth and growth of this obsession in Shylock we will lose a large part of the dramatic agon of the trial scene; just as we will if we do not give due weight to a further inference we are invited to make: that Antonio's melancholy is triggered and exacerbated by Bassanio's determination to woo Portia, and to win thereby both a wealthy wife and clearance of his debt to Antonio.

Three wills are in asymmetrical conflict in that great scene. Shylock's, Antonio's, and Portia's, and the amazingly dramatic thing is that the wills of Shylock and Antonio are not opposed in the matter of the bond but secretly consonant. This perception has been carefully prepared for, particularly by the parallel reports from Salanio and Solarino of the Jew's discovery of Jessica's flight and of Antonio's parting from Bassanio. From the one we have the burlesquing of Shylock's outcry:

> My daughter! O my ducats! O my daughter!
> Fled with a Christian! O my Christian ducats!
>   (II. viii. 15–16)

What we have at first hand, be it noted, in Act III, scene i, is subtly but significantly different.

> The curse never fell upon our nation till now, I never felt it till now. Two thousand ducats in that, and other precious, preci-

ous jewels. I would my daughter were dead at my foot, and the jewels in her ear! Would she were hears'd at my foot, and the ducats in her coffin! No news of them? Why, so – and I know not what's spent in the search. Why, thou loss upon loss! the thief gone with so much, and so much to find the thief, and no satisfaction, no revenge, nor no ill luck stirring but what lights a' my shoulders, no sighs but a' my breathing, no tears but a' my shedding.   (III. i. 85–96)

This is Lamentations itself, a 'woe is me', a curse, a Jeremiad which consigns both thief and theft – all that was precious – to the grave in a transport of grief at the 'loss upon loss' that has befallen him.

On the other hand, there is the account of Antonio's farewell, which must surely strike us as excessively sentimental. It is before there is any real danger, remember:

> And for the Jew's bond which he hath of me,
> Let it not enter in your mind of love.

> And even there, his eye being big with tears,
> Turning his face, he put his hand behind him,
> And with affection wondrous sensible
> He wrung Bassanio's hand, and so they parted.
>   (II. viii. 41–2; 46–9)

If the Jew is in love with his daughter/ducats, Antonio it seems, is in love with Bassanio. Beautiful feelings, beautiful sentiments, are pitched against mercenary and demeaning utilities. So the Venetians view it. And we are invited to bring the same perspective to the trial scene.

Antonio expresses a disinterested, fastidious altruism:

> I do beseech you
> Make no more offers, use no farther means,
> But with all brief and plain conveniency
> Let me have judgment and the Jew his will.
>   (IV. i. 80–3)

But his exhibitionistic desire (expressed in his letter in III. ii.

315–22) for Bassanio to witness his self-sacrificial death is again made manifest in

> when the tale is told, bid her be judge
> Whether Bassanio had not once a love.
>
> (IV. i. 276–7)

He is driven by a positive compulsion to self-immolation. Antonio's *imitatio dei* is the ultimate aestheticizing of his protest at the loss of Bassanio's exclusive love. The strange 'I am a tainted wether of the flock,/Meetest for death;' (IV. i. 114–15) thus acquires a further meaning. He will be martyred sacrifice and high priest of magnanimity, and so legitimize and even enhance his love for Bassanio.[21] Thus not only is Antonio's life at stake, but his self-esteem in his own eyes, the worth or value he holds himself to possess.

No less is this true of Shylock. The Jew exhibits an absorbing and undissimulated passion. 'Do all men kill the things they do not love?' asks Bassanio and Shylock flashes back, 'Hates any man the thing he would not kill?' But not only his revenge is at stake. The Jew's demand for law has a validity of its own and an inner compulsion of its own. This is why his argument is so trenchant on the one hand – the argument from slavery, for instance – and so defiantly, perversely arbitrary on the other:

> But say it is my humor, is it answer'd?
> What if my house be troubled with a rat,
> And I be pleas'd to give ten thousand ducats
> To have it ban'd? What, are you answer'd yet?
>
> So can I give no reason, nor I will not,
>
> (IV. i. 43–6; 59)

His rage to have his own back is a burning need to be recognized as a man more sinned against than sinning, as an aggrieved victim of injustice and betrayal. By his demand for justice he will force them to recognize his humanity, coerce the Venetian polity into accepting his membership of it. He will prove his claim to dignity, worth and value, thrust it down their throats, so to speak, in all its maddened extremity.

What judgment shall I dread, doing no wrong?
The pound of flesh which I demand of him
Is dearly bought as mine, and I will have it.
If you deny me, fie upon your law!

(IV. i. 89; 99–101)

His cry of joy when he thinks that Portia endorses his bond: 'A
Daniel come to judgment' is, it will be noticed, not the Daniel of
the lion's den, but the Daniel – defender and justifier – of the
wronged and libelled Susanna. For both contenders the fulfilment of the bond is a desperate act of self-assertion.

To these violent compulsions Portia's speech is tangential,
irrelevant; but it lifts the issues at stake onto an impersonal plane
where they can be resolved, as Pauline doctrine demands they be
resolved, in terms of the age-old debate between the Christian and
the Pharisee, the New and the Old Law, mercy and justice, spirit
and letter. In this context the pound of flesh acquires still further
symbolic power. Shylock's 'pound of flesh' is the letter of the old
law. The blood, the invisible blood he may not spill, is the free-
flowing, transcendent and unquenchable life of the spirit. 'Blood'
has already acquired related connotations in Morocco's boast:

Bring me the fairest creature northward born,
Where Phoebus' fire scarce thaws the icicles,
And let us make incision of your love,
To prove whose blood is reddest, his or mine.

(II. i. 4–7)

and Bassanio's courtship:

Only my blood speaks to you in my veins,

            all the wealth I had
Ran in my veins . . .   (III. ii. 176; 254–5)

Portia's *coup de théâtre* is of course a triumph – casuistry
against casuistry in the name of equity. The Pharisee is crushed.[22]
And Portia drives her point home. He shall have justice and
nothing but justice. As he undoes step by step his previous repudi-
ations of all their offers in lieu of the forfeiture, he is exposed,

stripped, dispossessed and ridiculed. His humiliation is complete. Finally his life and all his possessions lie at their mercy and it is graciously forthcoming: his fine reduced by half, the other half in trust for his daughter, provided he become a Christian and leave all in his will to his son-in-law and daughter. The Venetian world of commerce is purged of its mercenary demon and redeemed by its merciful angels. The antinomy between beauty and utility dissolves in grace embodied in the gracious Portia. And the inner meaning of her magnificent remedy – that the spirit giveth life – will be played out again in the ring episode, where final recognitions are brought about, actions are reversible, and giving and taking transformed into giving and forgiving.

What could be a more triumphant comic resolution? Evil has not only been exorcized, it has been seen to have been exorcized, positively, literally, in the scapegoat figure. And it has been writ large, since he is offered redeeming baptism, that what is cast out is his carnal and vindictive sinful self, a sin-offering for all Venice. And so, indeed, the play has been taken by its apologizers, with the moonlit ending as lyric and festive dénouement. But we must truncate our imaginations in order to collaborate with this view.

Because there are two Shylocks in *The Merchant of Venice*. The burlesque ogre – paradigm of a comic *pharmakos* – and the human being possessing a gloomy and savage dignity. The two alternate bewilderingly and never cohere. They are distinguishable and inseparable, two incompatible images held in solution; yet another (perhaps the chief) evidence of the self-division, the self-alienation of the play. The older, naive, personified vice or humour level of the characterization gives us the stereotype figure about whom everything is known. It is also the figure others tell Shylock he is, and it is what he finally becomes, defeated in his desperate self-assertive effort to circumvent their reduction of him, even if it must be as one even more villainous than they think him. The other Shylock, the product of Shakespeare's histrionic imagination, of what Keats called his negative capability, unfolds, is unpredictable, responds in unforeseen ways to circumstances. And being a person, he has the dignity of human personality, the dignity that is grounded in pain and passion, irrespective of virtue or vice, of good or evil. The benign offer of conversation is the ultimate cruelty of alienation, of denial of that essential being which has just made itself so palpably manifest. Therefore it is counterfeit mercy.

By the same token, a *pharmakos*, if he is really to carry away his community's sins, must not stand there jeering at his sacrificers, must not disconcert them with the trenchant rationality of his argument, or challenge and defy them. Nor must he have a scamp of a faithless servant, and a runaway daughter whom he mourns with an exacerbated, irascible, impatient and totally undissimulated grief. He must not, in short, if we are to rejoice at his casting forth, impose upon us his alien and alienated vision in language which is uniquely, inviolably, uncompromisingly his own. Shakespearean comedy is not reducible to ritual comic origins. Shakespeare has trained us, and continually invites us, through the web of language and the play of depth and surface, to expect real recognitions rather than ritual gestures. Shylock the scapegoat may leave the stage as he will – totter or shuffle or creep – his experience, his exposure, seen as it has been seen, from within, precludes all possibility of *comic* exorcism and throws a long shadow across the moonlit garden of Belmont in Act V.

In Shakespeare's other dual-location comedies, *A Midsummer Night's Dream*, for instance, or *As You Like It*, or *The Shrew*, the benign comic dialectic of wisdom and folly dissolves in mockery the antinomies and disjunctions and impossible choices which generate tragedy. What is finally celebrated in them is a right seeing which is born of the lived-through delirium of wrong seeing; or wisdom bred of the experiencing of some liberating and remedial folly. And these saving higher follies are exactly what they are: figments of an imagination irradiated by its adventures in another, but available, realm of the psyche where extravagant, irrational, lunatic or preposterous possibilities are entertained. Bassanio's choice does partake of the nature of a higher folly, as does Shylock's of the preposterous, but Belmont is no such realm of transformation; only of an uneasy evangelicalism.

Morocco, Aristotle's magnanimous man – 'a golden mind stoops not to shows of dross' (II. vii. 20) – chooses gold because 'never so rich a gem/Was set in worse than gold' (II. vii. 54–5). Aragon, the fastidious, who

> will not choose what many men desire,
> Because I will not jump with common spirits,
> And rank me with the barbarous multitudes.
>
> (II. ix. 31–3)

chooses silver for its motto – 'Who chooseth me shall get as much as he deserves' – as an emblem of 'the stamp of merit'. While to Bassanio goes the prize for his refusal to be 'deceived by ornament': specious rhetoric, decorous piety, outward marks of virtue, artificial cosmetics; in other words for his choice of '-plainness' rather than eloquence, of a higher utility before an apparent beauty.

> Therefore then, thou gaudy gold,
> Hard food for Midas, I will none of thee;
> Nor none of thee, thou pale and common drudge
> 'Tween man and man; but thou, thou meagre lead,
> Which rather threaten'st than dost promise aught,
> Thy paleness moves me more than eloquence,
>
> (III ii. 101–6)[23]

This choice is in accordance with the evangelical role the figure in the casket is to play, but the casket choice exhausts too soon the function of a comic device to precipitate and exacerbate follies, errors, or fantasies, the exhibition of which will generate remedy in the therapeutic comic process of enlightenment. What it boils down to is that there is no true comic device. Shakespeare has tossed away this trump card, so that the maskings and unmaskings and reconciliations of the rings episode become mere comedy-game flourishes upon the theme of letter and spirit, inner meaning and outer manifestation. He has left the living to be done, in another world, by his scapegoat.

The Belmont of Act V is the way the Christians would like to see themselves – rid now of vulgar money cares. We do not feel that they are wiser than they were. Only that they have what they wanted. Portia's disguise has not been a device whereby her own self-discovery was extended, a means whereby she can be herself and not, or more than, herself at once and, we believe, for ever. Bellario vanishes, and the recognitions of Act V are merely technical.

According to the intuitions of inherited wealth, because these Venetians are beautiful, because they have beautiful feelings, they are also good. And happy. Belmont magnetizes all of the play's aestheticism, isolating Shylock as 'the man that hath no music in himself,/Nor is not moved with concord of sweet sounds'; and is therefore 'fit for treasons, stratagems and spoils'. But the moonlit lovers' duet 'On such a night', though it subdues to what it works in its remembered tales of tragic women, treacherous or betrayed – Cressida, Dido, Thisbe, Medea – echoes ominously. Though Jessica is carefully distinguished from her father, and saved for Belmont music lovers by her 'attentive' spirits, the motions of *his* spirit, Lorenzo tells us, 'are dull as night,/And his affections dark as [Erebus]' (v. i. 86–7). But this time, the story of the night is irremediably troubling.

Once again at the end, for closure, Antonio stands surety for Bassanio, for good behaviour this time, not hard cash. He offers his 'soul' as forfeit for Bassanio's good faith where once his body had been forfeit for Bassanio's 'wealth' (v. i. 249ff). The duplication emphasizes the duality arising from the uneasy split between the two *topoi*. The play remains dichotomized between its two places, their polarity unresolved, its comic potential unfulfilled.

Shakespeare abandons formal comedy at this point, for a while. His prodigious creative energies find expression in the paired *Henry IV* plays and *Henry V*. I shall argue that the twin histories and their comic counterpart, *The Merry Wives*, articulate Shakespeare's further explorations in the problem of comic scapegoats, and precipitate, even make possible, the masterpieces of romantic comedy which immediately follow.

NOTES

1 Alexander Leggatt, *Shakespeare's Comedy of Love* (London: Methuen, 1974), p. 150.
2 For the stage history, see John Russell Brown, introduction to the Arden edn (London: Methuen, 1955), pp. xxxii–xxxvi.
3 Morris Carnowsky, 'Mirror of Shylock', *Tulane Drama Review*, vol III (1958).

4 Horst Woldemar Janson, *Apes and Ape Lore in the Middle Ages and the Renaissance* (London: Warburg Institute, University of London, 1952).

5 Van Dyck, *Queen Henrietta Maria with her Dwarf and Monkey*, Samuel H. Kress Collection, No. 1118.

6 Martin Grotjahn, *Beyond Laughter* (New York: McGraw Hill, 1957), p. 260, speaks of the 'psychodynamics of comedy' as a kind of 'reversed Oedipal situation' in which 'the son plays the role of the victorious father with sexual freedom and achievement, while the father is cast into the role of the frustrated onlooker'.

7 The title of the chapter on *The Merchant* in J. Russell Brown, *Shakespeare and his Comedies* (London: Methuen, 1957).

8 Two recent instances are R. F. Hill, 'The Merchant of Venice and the Pattern of Romantic Comedy', *Shakespeare Studies*, vol. 28 (1975) and Ruth M. Levitski, 'Shylock as Unregenerate Man', *Shakespeare Quarterly*, vol. 28 (1977).

9 William Hazlitt, *A View of the English Stage* (1821), and *Characters of Shakespeare's Plays* (1817).

10 A. D. Moody, 'An Ironic Comedy', in *Twentieth Century Interpretations*. ed. Sylvan Barnet (New Jersey: Prentice Hall, 1970).

11 C. L. Barber, *Shakespeare's Festive Comedy* (New Jersey: Princeton University Press, 1959).

12 J. Middleton Murry, *Shakespeare* (1954; reprinted London: Jonathan Cape, 1961).

13 Leo Salingar, *Shakespeare and the Traditions of Comedy* (Cambridge: Cambridge University Press, 1974), pp. 301ff.

14 Sherman Hawkins, 'The Two Worlds of Shakespearean Comedy', *Shakespeare Studies*, vol. III (1967), p. 71.

15 See G. Bullough, *Narrative and Dramatic Sources of Shakespeare* (London: Routledge and Kegan Paul, 1957).

16 The pithy phrase is Jonathan Culler's in *Structuralist Poetics* (London: Routledge & Kegan Paul, 1975).

17 Jean-Paul Sartre, *Anti-Semite and Jew* (1948), trans. George J. Becker (New York: Schocken, 1948), pp. 112–14. Sartre's brilliant analysis is worth comparing at many points with Shakespeare's dramatization; see particularly pp. 126–9.

18 Sigurd Burckhardt, '*The Merchant of Venice*: The Gentle Bond', *ELH*, vol. XXIX (1962).

19 It is worth recalling that Freud, too, emphasizes the father theme when he links the three caskets with Lear's choice. Interestingly enough, the *Gesta Romanorum* has the lady the chooser: see Bullough, *Narrative and Dramatic Sources*, vol. I. Leslie A. Fiedler, *The Stranger in Shakespeare* (New York: Stein & Day, 1972), detects, in a Jungian exposition, subterranean links between Shylock as a monster-father, Antonio as surrogate father and Shakespeare himself as the lover of the Sonnets, and regards the play as a 'projection of the author's private distress'.

20 John Palmer, *Political and Comic Characters of Shakespeare* (1946; reprinted London: Macmillan, 1965), p. 429.

21 Graham Midgley, '*The Merchant of Venice*: A Reconsideration'. *Essays in Criticism*, vol. X (April 1960), comes to a similar conclusion. Shylock's defeat he says, is his defeat, too, for 'it has deprived him of the one great gesture of love which would have ended his loneliness and crowned his love with one splendid exit' (p. 131).

22 As Marc Parrott, *Shakespearean Comedy* (New York: 1949) pointed out: 'In Portia's decision, we see the triumph of the spirit over the letter, of equity over legalism' (p. 139). But the extra-literary irony is that Portia, so far from representing New Testament spirit against Old Testament letter is behaving exactly like a Pharisee. For it is Pharisaical (later Rabbinic) practice to seek loopholes in the letter of the law which will save both law and (according to supreme injunction) life. But such knowledge was hidden from Shakespeare by the inheritance of Pauline Christianity which had requisitioned the morality of the Old Law, leaving the latter, ostensibly, in possession of the mere empty husks of legal precept.

23 The word 'paleness' has aroused conjecture and emendation. Theobald proposed 'plainness' on account of the implied contrast with ornament. Russell Brown, who opposes the emendation, nevertheless points out that 'paleness', too, might be contrasted with 'coloured eloquence' (Arden edn, p. 83).

VIII

THE CASE
OF FALSTAFF
AND THE
MERRY WIVES

It is surely odd that the greatest of the Shakespearean comic
characters did not begin his career in a comedy at all, but in what
might be classed as a political satire; while the great Shakespearean achievement of romantic comedy features no such
character at all (even the distant cousin Sir Toby does not really
qualify), but has given the world its most dazzling comedy
heroines. To point out that Shakespeare in his lifetime mastered
not one but both of the basic forms of comedy – the Aristophanic
and the Menandrine – is perhaps only another way of talking of
the range and power and originality of the great dramatist's art.
But it is rare for both Old and New Comedy to have reached new
peaks in one man's work, and I believe there is a vital connection
to be uncovered between these two manifestations of the comic
impulse in Shakespeare. The brilliance, the charm, the freedom
and the wit of the heroines of his mature comedies, Beatrice,
Rosalind, Viola, is so familiar a phenomenon, so generally recognized, so much a part of our literary landscape as hardly to
occasion remark. The death of the heart-struck Falstaff, on the
other hand, has occasioned not only remark but passionate dispu-
tation: indignant outrage on the one hand and morally righteous
justification of Hal's rejection of the old rogue on the other. It will
be the argument of the following pages that the first phenomenon
is indeed most worthy of remark, and that the second is intimately

related to it, and that the two together can be examined from a developmental point of view and will provide a host of insights into the nature and growth of the Shakespearean comic imagination.

*

The points to be noted first are the following:

In the early comedies, up to 1597, the women, as we have seen, do not play protagonist roles though there are intimations of an inclination in this direction.

By the turn of the century the full flowering of the comic protagonist as romantic heroine has been achieved, and indeed, consummated, in *Much Ado, As You Like It* and *Twelfth Night*.

The watershed period therefore is 1597–1600, the period which, present scholarship is agreed,[1] saw the composition of the *Henry IV* plays, *Henry V* and *The Merry Wives*, as well as *Much Ado* and *As You Like It*.

The transfer of the comic initiative from the male to the female figures is effectuated both symbolically and practically, in *The Merry Wives*.

The life and death of Falstaff, therefore, is a central issue, made intriguingly crucial in any case by the fact that this great comic character appears in a comedy only, we are told, by virtue of special royal request, and is summarily despatched (with consequences mortal to himself and nearly so to the sentimental reputation of Prince Hal) from the history he officially inhabits.

The old tradition (dating from 1702) that the Queen requested a play of Falstaff in love because his shenanigans in *1 Henry IV*, had pleased her so, and that Falstaff was therefore resurrected by Shakespeare, presumably from his Elysian 'green fields' and transported to Elizabethan Windsor around 1602 (the date of the Quarto printing of *The Merry Wives*) is no longer accepted in its entirety. H. J. Oliver of the New Arden is prepared to believe that the Queen asked for the play after she had seen Part 1 of *Henry IV* in 1596 and before the completion of Part 2. The complex textual and topical reasons for Oliver's support of Hotson's theory that *The Merry Wives* was written for the Garter Feast of 1597 are given in his Introduction to the New Arden edition. He further makes the cogent point that the Queen would hardly have requested Falstaff in love *after* the Doll Tearsheet scenes in Part 2, generally thought to date from late 1598; Doll's lavish petting, he feels, should have been enough. Oliver's dating therefore is: the playing of *1 Henry IV* before the Queen – 1596; the composition of *The Merry Wives* on request, and *2 Henry IV* (the material of Part 1 having proved too large for a single play)[2] – 1597; the playing of *The Merry Wives* – 1597; the playing of *2 Henry IV* – 1598; *Henry V* (in which it has been conjectured Falstaff was originally to appear and was removed on second thoughts) – 1598–9.[3]

I shall presently return to the case of *The Merry Wives*. But first it is worth considering the first part of *Henry IV sub specie comoediae*. Since there is no truly distinctive 'historical form', the chronicles can all be said to exhibit or to be subject to the gravitational pull, as it were, of tragedy or comedy. *Richard II* and *Richard III* are very clearly proto-tragic in form. *Henry V* collaterally comic – with filial-parental conflict displaced onto the battlefield of Agincourt, and 'many a fair French city' as dowry for Hal's fair French bride; *2 Henry IV* is another question, to which I shall presently return. *1 Henry IV* is unquestionably assimilable to the comic form. But to which of the two alternative comic scenarios that can be seen to be immanent in the material?

If it is New Comedy, and Hal the protagonist, the defect or privation of the outset in *Henry IV* would be the King's lack of an heir well-behaved enough to be 'the theme of honour's tongue'. The choice of a marriage partner is not in question and its place neatly taken by the bone of contention between father and son provided by the Prince's choice of tavern companion. As in other Shakespearean versions of New Comedy, strife is engendered both between and within generations. The father's yearning for the other, better son:

> O that it could be prov'd
> That some night-tripping fairy had exchang'd
> In cradle-clothes our children where they lay,
>
> (I. i. 86–8)

makes a kind of sibling rivalry provide an emotional undercurrent, but still within a practically all-male world. Hotspur's Kate,

spirited, affectionate and long-suffering as she notably is, appears
on the scene only to be banished her battle-hungry husband's
bed:

> Away, you trifler! Love, I love thee not,
> I care not for thee, Kate. This is no world
> To play with mammets and to tilt with lips.
> We must have bloody noses and crack'd
> crowns. (II. iii. 89–93)

Hal's chosen milieu is the tavern as opposed to the council
chamber, but both are distinctly male domains.
Hal disguises himself, imitating the sun

> Who doth permit the base contagious clouds
> To smother up his beauty from the world,
> That when he please again to be himself,
> Being wanted, he may be more wond'red at.
> (I. ii. 198–201)

Thus he upholds 'the unyok'd humor of (their) idleness' (the
comic disposition of the tavern) while he tries and tests himself,
and discovers his true identity in a sequence of episodes designed
to unmask the braggart amoralist with whom he consorts. Act I
forewarns us of the unmasking, but if Hal's 'disguise' is a species of
deceptive comic device which will reveal the truth it allows a
modicum, at least, of candour right from the start:

> Falstaff Shall I? O rare! By the Lord, I'll be a brave judge.
> Prince Thou judgest false already. I mean thou shalt have
> the hanging of the thieves, and so become a rare hangman.
> (I. ii. 64–8)

In Act II Gad's Hill and the play-within-the-play expulsion of
Falstaff provide the maximalization of the comic disposition to
'idleness' with the audience in the know regarding the Prince's
comic device. Act III brings the garboils in the State to the point of
eruption and Hal to his turning-point decision. Act IV is ominous
and fraught with all kinds of dangers: Falstaff's press gang on the
one hand, dissension in the rebels' ranks on the other. But the
Prince is preparing for battle, and the victory at Shrewsbury in

Act V remedies the dynasty's ills temporarily at least. Hal's magnanimity towards Falstaff's misdemeanours:

> For my part, if a lie may do thee grace,
> I'll gild it with the happiest terms I have.
>
> (V. iv. 157–8)

ensures the continuation of his companionship with the fat knight. Hal will continue to be amused while Falstaff is nevertheless put in his place. Nothing is more characteristic of the pleasure of comedy than its allowing us, in defiance of the laws of nature and of nations, to have our cake and eat it.

On this reading of the play, Hal is the comic protagonist who comes into his inheritance at the end, and the comic device is the moral deception practised by Hal upon Falstaff and his tavern companions (indeed upon the whole world) which encourages them in their follies. By the same token Hal's role-playing is not only a comic device but an exploratory imaginative enterprise. In Act II, scene iv, in the drawer scene, when Hal self-abasingly confesses to having 'sounded the very base string of humility' with a fellow who has fewer words than a parrot, and then – with sudden ellipsis which demands interpretation – insists:

> I am not yet of Percy's mind, the Hotspur of the north, he that kills me some six or seven dozen of Scots at a breakfast, washes his hands, and says to his wife, 'Fie upon this quiet life! I want work.'   (II. iv. 101–5)

it is clear that the role playing is as much as anything an expression of a divided mind. The comic device thus brings out Hal's own deficiency or imperfection as much as it brings out and aggravates the riotous goings-on of the tavern. It thus enables him to face his self-division, to enact it, consciously to experience it, to suffer the encroachment of the rival whose life is a standing reproach to him, and by out-doing him, to exorcize it. And the exhaustion of the device occurs at Shrewsbury when Falstaff offers Hal a flask instead of a sword and is faced with his angry question, 'Is it a time to jest and dally now?'

The only trouble with Hal's comic device is that it exposes him to the comic devices of an adversary he didn't, so to speak, quite bargain for. Hal as Eiron exposing the arch-impostor Falstaff falls into the clutches of an Eiron greater than he, a hedonist whose comic device is the (deceptive?) temptation of the pleasure principle itself. It is Old Comedy phallic abandon which is, we perceive, embodied in and transmitted by the old rapscallion Falstaff, in a most disinhibitory, anarchic, preposterous, amoral and liberating form. Pleasure, indeed, is the issue in *Henry IV*. Single-minded Hotspur has no time to play with mammots or to tilt with lips. It is worth noting, however, for the veracity and density and poignance of the representation that Hotspur is no mere stock emblem of chivalric honour. He has humour and imagination and high animal spirits as his pantomimic Theophrastian sketches of fops on battlefields and myth-mystified Welshmen, and his teasing of Kate, show. And it is not through lack of a capacity for tenderness that he bullies poor Kate even about her too lady-like oaths. That very scene, incidentally, effectively dramatizes the exclusivist masculinity of his animation, his vitality.

Not yours, in good sooth! Heart, you swear like a comfit-maker's wife: 'Not you, in good sooth,' and 'as true as I live', and 'as God shall mend me'. . .

> Swear me, Kate, like a lady as thou art,
> A good mouth-filling oath, and leave 'in sooth',
> And such protest of pepper-gingerbread,
> To velvet guards and Sunday citizens.
>
> (III. i. 247–49; 253–6)

If he has no time for pleasure, his antithetical counterpart, Falstaff, clearly has no time for honour. And if he is single-minded, and Hal of divided mind, Falstaff is above all myriad-minded: Lord of misrule, impersonator, rogue, mimic, jester and wit. One may know where to have the good Mrs Quickly, but does one ever know quite where to have Jack Falstaff? He is, not to put too fine a point on it, lazy, greedy, lecherous, good-for-nothing, thievish and a liar, as cunning as he is unscrupulous, and as unable (or unwilling) to control his appetites as his expenditure on sack and his girth suggest. Having more flesh than another he has therefore more frailty but, impostor though he be, this he does not disguise. And it is the unabashed frankness of his infantile egoism which disarms. Even in the very act of playing the arch-hypocrite, he miraculously contrives never to pretend not to be what he is. Ultimately there is nothing to expose since he will pretend anything, and pretends to nothing.

> I was as virtuously given as a gentleman need to be, virtuous enough: swore little, dic'd not above seven times – a week, went to a bawdy-house not above once in a quarter – of an hour, paid money that I borrow'd – three or four times, liv'd well and in good compass . . .   (III. iii. 14–19)

Therefore the sheer histrionic virtuosity of his impersonations become a source of pleasure. Monsier Remorse:

> Thou has done much harm upon me, Hal, God forgive thee for it! Before I knew thee, Hal, I knew nothing, and now am I, if a man should speak truly, little better than one of the wicked. I must give over this life, and I will give it over.
>   (I. ii. 91–6)

modulates into Mister Hard-done-by: 'A plague of sighing and grief, it blows a man up like a bladder' (II. iv. 331–3). Mock piety gives way to mock indignation:

> I am accurs'd to rob in that thieve's company. The rascal hath remov'd my horse, and tied him I know not where. If I travel but four foot by the squire further afoot, I shall break my wind. Well, I doubt not but to die a fair death for all this, if I scape hanging for killing that rogue. . . . I'll starve ere I'll rob a foot further. And 'twere not as good a deed as drink to turn man and to leave these rogues, I am the veriest varlet that ever chew'd with a tooth.   (II. ii. 10–24)

Mock indignation reaches Jeremiad proportions:

> There is nothing but roguery to be found in villainous man, yet a coward is worse than a cup of sack with lime in it. A villainous coward! Go thy ways, old Jack, die when thou wilt: if manhood, good manhood, be not forgot upon the face of the earth, then am I a shotten herring. There live not three good men

unhang'd in England, and one of them is fat and grows old, God help the while! a bad world, I say. I would I were a weaver, I could sing psalms, or anything. A plague of all cowards, I say still.   (II. iv. 124–34)

And the bonhomie of self-gratulation 'Out, ye rogue, play out the play, I have much to say in the behalf of that Falstaff' (II. iv. 484–5) embraces both a squire-at-ease and Robin Hood on the warpath: 'Strike! down with them! cut the villains' throats! Ah, whoreson caterpillars! bacon-fed knaves! they hate us youth. Down with them! fleece them!' (II. ii. 83–5).

There are rich sources of enjoyment in the vivacity of his abusive and preposterous hyperbole, in the hair-breadth stratagems (reasons upon compulsion for instance, or cowardice upon instinct) whereby he eludes the Prince's ambushes; or the effrontery with which he forgives Dame Quickly for having accused her of theft. If he is a Prince of Libido, he is also, hilariously, *homo ludens*, revelling in mimetic impersonations, lightning improvization, uninhibited fantasy. He gets out of all scrapes. Hal will never corner him. He is witty intelligence itself in all its agility, speed, versatility and resourcefulness. He cannot be victimized, and this is what is irresistible. It carries us through the counterfeit death, through the counterfeit triumph, through the press-gang. It is why he has us on his side in the honour speech. Falstaff's bedrock vote for survival is irrefutable. He may play the role of an Alazon exposed on the stage, but to the theatre audience he is an Eiron mocking all cramping rule and order, old father Antic the law himself. And Hal recognizes the sap of vitality in this Hallowe'en spring and gladly responds to it. There cannot be many sources of primary comic pleasure Falstaff does not harness to his rollicking euphoria. But there is one; and one can only salute the sagacity of the first Elizabeth (or the legend) for demanding, in the case of this one missing pleasure, an acid test: Falstaff in love.

The decline of Falstaff in Part 2 is a commonplace of criticism, but I believe it to be special pleading in an attempt to justify his rejection. Falstaff, not only witty himself but the cause that wit is in other men, is not less witty in Part 2. It remains true that 'The brain of this foolish-compounded clay, man, is not able to invent anything that intends to laughter more than I invent or is invented on me' (I. ii. 7–9). The effortless rapidity of his opportunism is superb. One recalls his contempt of 'security', his evading the Chief Justice's servant with a pantomime of indignation out of the Puritan work ethic: 'What? A young knave, and begging?' (I. ii. 72), or his trumping of the Chief Justice's contempt with a *tour de force* of mock self-righteousness:

> There is not a dangerous action can peep out his head but I am thrust upon it. Well, I cannot last ever, but it was alway yet the trick of our English nation, if they have a good thing, to make it too common. If ye will needs say I am an old man, you should give me rest. I would to God my name were not so terrible to the enemy as it is. I were better to be eaten to death with a rust than to be scour'd to nothing with perpetual motion.
>
> (I. ii. 212–20)

Or of mock much-tried-virtue in his claim to have captured John Colevile of the Dale:

> I would be sorry, my lord, but it should be thus. I never knew yet but rebuke and check was the reward of valor. Do you think me a swallow, an arrow, or a bullet? Have I, in my poor and old motion, the expenditure of thought? I have speeded hither with the very extremest inch of possibility; I have found'red nine-score and odd posts, and here, travel-tainted as I am, have, in my pure and immaculate valor, taken Sir John Colevile of the Dale, a most furious knight and valorous enemy. But what of that? He saw me, and yielded, that I may justly say, with the hook-nos'd fellow of Rome, 'There, cousin, I came, saw, and over-came'. (IV. iii. 30–42)

His preposterous fantasy is at its ebullient best:

> I do remember him at Clement's Inn, like a man made after supper of a cheese-paring. When 'a was naked, he was for all the world like a fork'd redish, with a head fantastically carv'd upon it with a knife. (III. ii. 308–12)

Nor is his repartee ever nimbler than in the parrying of the Chief Justice's accusation regarding his great waste and his slender

means: 'I would my means were greater and my waist [slenderer]'
(I. ii. 142–3). Or his agility in killing two birds with one stone:
'My lord, this is a poor [mad] soul, and she says up and down the
town that her eldest son is like you' (II. i. 104–6).
It is true, and has been much remarked, that his happy corpu-
lence is now more heavily shadowed by whispers of mortality; it is
not only his purse which suffers consumption: 'A man can no
more separate age and covetousness than 'a can part young limbs
and lechery; but the gout galls the one, and the pox pinches the
other, and so both the degrees prevent my curses' (I. ii. 228–32).
But he has always been, to put it mildly, short-winded, and he
makes peace with and commodity out of disease as he will out of
every other contingency, seeing no reason, in the law of nature 'If
the young dace be a bait for the old pike . . . but I may snap at him'
(III. ii. 330–2). Even his miniscule page has 'profited' by contamination as the Prince points out (II. ii. 84). It is as much the
commonwealth that is diseased as Falstaff, from the sick king
down to Mouldy and Wart. And Falstaff in the wasteland is not
only master of what pleasures are available but of a wry self-
knowledge: 'Peace, good Doll, do not speak like a death's-head,
do not bid me remember mine end' (II. iv. 234–5).
   Moreover there is a self-propelling quality about Falstaff's
amusements in Part 2. They are only marginally engineered by
Hal, now not a habitué but a commuter in Eastcheap. And in the
eavesdropping scene Falstaff is barely disconcerted by his
unmasking at the hand of the Prince and Poins (II. iv). He is in fact
as 'apprehensive, quick, forgetive, full of nimble, fiery and delect-
able shapes' as ever, and far more so than anyone else; and only
where he is is there good cheer in England.
   The change that has come over him can best be described as
domestication. The scenes in which he appears are indeed extraordinarily domestic. He is cosily ensconced in Mrs Quickly's
establishment;[4] and Pistol's fateful announcement interrupts a
hardly less cosy post-prandial occasion in Shallow's 'goodly dwell-
ing'. But if it is domestication it is on an imperial scale. It is not
that he is tamed by the world, but that the world is absorbed by
him – town and country, war and peace. Sack is the volatile,
invigorating soul of all, and he its embodiment. Falstaff in Part 2

contains 'all the world' he claimed as his own in Part 1. The paean
to sack is a Dionysian dithyramb; a good sherris-sack 'ascends me
into the brain . . . warms the blood . . . and makes it course from
the inwards to the parts extreme':

> So that skill in the weapon is nothing without sack (for that sets
> it a-work) and learning a mere hoard of gold kept by a devil, till
> sack commences it and sets it in act and use. Hereof comes it
> that Prince Harry is valiant, for the cold blood he did naturally
> inherit of his father, he hath, like lean, sterile, and bare land,
> manur'd, husbanded, and till'd with excellent endeavor of
> drinking good and good store of fertile sherris, that he is
> become very hot and valiant. If I had a thousand sons, the first
> humane principle I would teach them should be, to foreswear
> thin potations and to addict themselves to sack.
>
> (IV. iii. 113–25)

There are orchards and wheat fields outside Shallow's house.
'Some pigeons, Davy, a couple of short-legg'd hens, a joint of
mutton, and any pretty little tiny kickshaws' have made up the
repast. Falstaff looks forward to rich pickings in the country and
rich laughter at court. He will devise matter enough out of this
Shallow to keep Prince Harry in continual laughter 'till his face be
like a wet cloak ill laid up'. There is a sense in which his im-
perialism of the belly appears benign, a country spirit. One speaks
of fat fields as well as fat knights. And the nostalgia so pervasive in
the latter part of Part 2 is perhaps not so much for the chimes of
midnight Falstaff produces for Shallow's benefit, as for an expan-
siveness of pleasuring which the cold fish Hal will banish his
kingdom. The play tantalizes with its intimations of a festive close
but we anticipate the outcome; we have our glimpse of buxom
Doll, hustled away by a 'thin thing, an atomy, a blue-bottle rogue,
a filthy famish'd correctioner', and the too sanguine premature
rejoicing of Falstaff: 'Blessed are they that have been my friends:
and woe unto my Lord Chief Justice!' (v. iii. 137–8). But the
repudiation when it comes is devastating:

> I know thee not, old man, fall to thy prayers.
> How ill white hairs becomes a fool and jester!

I have long dreamt of such a kind of man,
So surfeit-swell'd, so old, and so profane;
But being awak'd, I do despise my dream.
Make less thy body (hence) and more thy grace,
Leave gormandizing, know the grave doth gape
For thee thrice wider than for other men.
Reply not to me with a fool-born jest,
Presume not that I am the thing I was,
For God doth know, so shall the world perceive,
That I have turn'd away my former self;
So will I those that kept me company.

(V. V. 47–59)

In terms of Policy, Falstaff must go. He is a demon of jest, subversive to the State. No custom, no institution is safe from him. He will absorb or undermine all. The commonwealth casts its scapegoat forth; can find no way to accommodate his anti-moral counter-morality of candid hedonism, before which no pretence of virtue, no ideal counterfeit can stand. Shakespeare, who understands Hal, politics and reality, understands that his Falstaff is leading him along a royal road to a radical and anarchic non-conformism; he is nevertheless (or possibly therefore) reluctant to let him go, and thus to renounce that bewitching compost of comic pleasures made up of fantasy and freedom, witty mocking intelligence, improvization and ventriloquist dexterity.

The great discovery which is mediated by *The Merry Wives* is that these can be preserved, transformed and metamorphosed, in romance. Comic heroines, it will transpire, may even better their instruction, in a comic mode that nurtures, and remedies, preposterous fancies. But the feminization of comic pleasure entails the curtailing of Falstaff's male monopoly of the field of the comic. The domestication of bacchic comedy, the transfer of comic energies to the women, requires the emasculation of Falstaff. And that is precisely what happens in *The Merry Wives*, the only play in the canon, incidentally, where a man is ridiculed in the disguise of a woman.

Moreover there has already been an insistent feminization of his genius:

I have a whole school of tongues in this belly of mine, and not a tongue of them all speaks any other word but my name. And I had but a belly of any indifferency, I were simply the most active fellow in Europe. My womb, my womb, my womb undoes me.   (2 *Henry IV*, IV. iii. 18–22)

It is not without interest to observe that the roast Manningtree ox with the pudding in his belly of Part 1 becomes the sow who has overwhelmed all her litter but one in Part 2. In the final scene there is an almost lover-like appeal in 'My King, my Jove! I speak to thee, my heart'; and in his anxiety about making the right impression (Falstaff worried about making the right impression!) upon his Jove: 'But to stand stain'd with travel, and sweating with desire to see him, thinking of nothing else, putting all affairs else in oblivion, as if there were nothing else to be done but to see him' (2 *Henry IV*, V. v. 24–7).

In 2 *Henry IV* a mythic Silenus appears to be in confinement with the whole world. In *The Merry Wives* he is 'confined' indeed in buckbasket, killhole, press, coffer, chest, trunk, well, foxhole. Jeanne Roberts, in a perceptive essay on *Merry Wives* goes so far as to suggest that the fairy Masque in Act V 'masks' a symbolic castration – the 'dis-horning' of 'Fall-staff'.[5] That romantic love is the one source of comic pleasure Falstaff cannot experience and so is beaten and pinched and humiliated by revengeful Maenads may be another legitimate perspective. At all events according to Roberts, 'the sex drive is not so much punished as rechannelled: the merry wives defend social order against uncontrolled sex' while Ann Page 'moves with all the cool clear-sightedness of Shaw's life force to select her mate' (p. 48).[6]

In what sense, however, can the representation of romantic love be construed as comic pleasure save in its aspect as ludicrous enslavement or affectation, *vide* Speed, Moth, Mercutio and Puck upon the various objects of their observations? In its courtly manifestations, at least, it had been far more a matter of dolours and anguish, self-castigation and the idealization of non-consummation. Romeo and Juliet, Shakespeare's first full-fledged romantic lovers, affirm the joy of romantic passion, but they are caught in the terror of a no-exit plot, tragically deadlocked,

without remedy, without providential escape, though it would
not have taken more than one tricky Italian *zanni* with a disguise
or a bed trick, or Dogberry from nearby Messina, to turn *Romeo
and Juliet* into a standard Italianate New Comedy, with the fathers
outwitted by nimble lovers, helpful friars, and cheerful old bawds
of Dame Quickly's persuasion. But romantic love has not
appeared to sort well with the comic, in Susanne Langer's valuable sense of 'the vital rhythm of self-preservation'.[7]

For the metamorphosis of romantic love from object of comedy
to subject of comedy to occur, the life and death of Falstaff, I
suggest, like that of the wine-god himself, had to be enacted. And
this is what I shall presently attempt to show.

The degradation of Falstaff in *The Merry Wives* has been fertile
ground for critical disappointment with that play; but it is worth
examining closely to see just what is involved. The difference
between Falstaff of *1 Henry IV* and *The Merry Wives* is that in the
former he is a Prince's companion and treads circumspectly for all
his privileged audacity. In the latter, he lords it over these provin-
cial burghers and attempts to brazen out his impecunious circumstances with his restive retainers. The difference is a tribute to
Shakespeare's verisimilitude just as is the objection of bourgeois
Master Page to his daughter's marrying 'above her'. But the
character of Falstaff has not changed. The craft, the shrewdness,
the brass, the zest are all there. The very accents and rhythms, the
vivid similes, the puns, the preposterous hyperboles, the loving
ingenuity with which he enlarges upon his monstrous girth:

> If it should come to the ear of the court, how I have been
> transform'd, and how my transformation hath been wash'd
> and cudgell'd, they would melt me out of my fat drop by drop,
> and liquor fishermen's boots with me. I warrant they would
> whip me with their fine wits till I were as crestfall'n as a dried
> pear.   (*Merry Wives*, IV. v. 94–100)

> you may know by my size that I have a kind of alacrity in
> sinking; [and] the bottom were as deep as hell, I should down. I
> had been drown'd, but that the shore was shelvy and shallow –

> a death that I abhor; for the water swells a man; and what a
> thing should I have been when I had been swell'd! I should have
> been a mountain of mummy. (III. v. 11–18)

> a man of my kidney. Think of that – that am a subject to heat as
> butter; a man of continual dissolution and thaw. It was a
> miracle to scape suffocation. And in the height of this bath
> (when I was more than half stew'd in grease, like a Dutch dish)
> to be thrown into the Thames, and cool'd, glowing-hot, in that
> surge, like a horse-shoe; think of that – hissing-hot – think of
> that, Master [Brook]. (III. v. 114–22)

Once again, while righteous indignation is a pose, complacent
narcissism is as ingenuous as ever. The one occasion, often
noticed, when a speech will not consort with the verbal physiognomy of Falstaff:

> And these are not fairies? I was three or four times in the
> thought they were not fairies, and yet the guiltiness of my mind,
> the sudden surprise of my powers, drove the grossness of the
> foppery into a receiv'd belief, in despite of the teeth of all rhyme
> and reason, that they were fairies. See now how wit may be
> made a Jack-a-Lent, when 'tis upon ill employment! (v. v. 121–8)

is accounted for by Dover Wilson's conjecture of the remnant of
an earlier play.[8] Falstaff is no more changed in his essential
lineaments than a lead character in any reasonably good televi-
sion serial, give or take a variation or two due to plot circumstance and accompanying cast. But he is radically changed in his
comic role.

In Part 1, Hal is the author of the play's comic device designed
to unmask Falstaff's bravado, but Falstaff is the master of comic
device at a deeper and older level of the comic impulse – the
antinomian pleasure principle which will expose Hal as impostor.
And, supreme escape artist that he is, he is never trapped. In *The
Merry Wives* the comic device, originally his, becomes the pre-
rogative of the merry wives and Falstaff is the impostor who will
be trapped. The comic device is their counterplot against his

scheme – characteristically prodigal – both mercenary and amorous, and with both available wives. Ford's own counterplot revolves in its orbit, so to speak.

In the Gad's Hill episode the fun lay in the exhibition of boasting and prevaricating which he predictably put on when his bluff was called. A double pleasure was to be derived from this. Chastisement for a grandiloquent braggart and the escape of a very wily cony-catcher from the trap. A principle of double indemnity is at work in *1 Henry IV*, whereby Falstaff is both fooled (for his vices) and therefore foil to Hal's superiority, and victor (by virtue of his wit) and thus parodist of royal prevarications. It is no wonder Falstaff is so infallible a mirth producer, since there is double collusion: between these tricksters, and between trickster and audience. Thus the audience is gratified both by Hal's triumph, and by Falstaff's escapades.

In *The Merry Wives* double indemnity operates too, for the wives, and for the audience; only not for Falstaff. In Act II, scene ii, for example, the contrast between the suspicion of the disguised jealous husband and the unsuspectingness of lover, his cuckolder-to-be, is made deliciously ludicrous for the audience by the chagrin of the one and the complacency of the other mutually reinforcing each other; but Falstaff is unaware of the identity of his interlocutor. It is the wives who can't lose now, since both jealous husband and impertinent lover will get their deserts; and it is the impostor upon whom the tables will be turned. No trick, no device, no starting hole can he find now, to hide him from open and apparent shame, save the infelicities of laundry baskets and the indignities of fat witch disguises.

The comic device admirably educes and enlarges comic dispositions. Ford's jealousy, for example, the particular nature of which is perhaps best described by Keats' famous phrase: 'an irritable reaching after fact and reason':

Has Page any brains? Hath he any eyes? Hath he any thinking? Sure they sleep, he hath no use of them. Why, this boy will carry a letter twenty mile, as easy as a cannon will shoot point-blank twelve score. He pieces out his wive's inclination; he gives her folly motion and advantage; and now she's going to my wife,

and Falstaff's boy with her. A man may hear this show'r sing in
the wind. And Falstaff's boy with her! Good plots . . .

(III. ii. 30–8)

'The clock gives me my cue, and my assurance bids me search –
there I shall find Falstaff. I shall be rather prais'd for this than
mock'd; for it is as positive as the earth is firm that Falstaff is
there' (III. ii. 45–9). He is tormented not so much by the thought
of his wife's possible infidelity as by the wealth of irresistible
opportunities provided by a malicious universe. It is as if it would
be irrational not to seize them and even more irrational not to
suppose, exultingly, that they were being seized. It is an auto-
intoxication as well as an absurd logic that is expressed in his
'heaven be praised for my jealousy'.

What the comic device brings out is the absurdity of both
wanton and censor: one is too loose, and conceited to boot, the
other too tight and a busybody to boot. The buffoons, busy about
their own and everybody else's affairs, gloss these absurdities with
their own milder pretensions, and their own sets of complementary excesses and defects. Both the irascibly knowing Caius and
the unfathomably idiotic Slender have pretensions to Anne's
hand; and the parson Evans to the general management and cure
of souls in Windsor. Falstaff's gang, Pistol and Nym, and the
compleat go-between Mrs Quickly, have pretensions to the
book-learned culture in the tattered shreds of which they variously
strut, making 'fritters' of English at a great rate. The bringing of
doctor and parson, with Slender in tow piping 'sweet Ann Page',
to the brink of a duel of which they are both terrified is redone,
with advantages, in *Twelfth Night*; and there, as here, a remedy
must be found not only for the tangles of the *processus turbarum*
but for the mismatching of the 'pretty virginity' Anne Page.

It will be noticed that this remedy is mediated by the final
'dishorning' of the buck in the forest scene when the vain knave is
pinched, mocked and exposed; but the bourgeois stratagems of
prudence and forethought and marriage settlements also collapse
in the masque of fairies, ouphs, elves, hobgoblins and Fenton's
elopement with Anne. It is perhaps hard to be persuaded that the
genial good sense of Master and Mistress Page could ever have

conceived of such a match as Caius or Slender for their daughter, but at least the madcap woodland elopement is a piece of 'folly' which the outwitted parents have the wisdom to embrace with a good grace.

As for Anne Page herself, she has very little room for manoeuvre in *The Merry Wives*. Energies are elsewhere engaged. But she motivates one half of Shakespeare's double plot and, in terms of the play's initial postulate, the courting of worthy Page's daughter – 'Seven hundred and possibilities, is goot gifts', as canny Evans puts it – and its final resolution, hers is the framing story. Her young man, though he speaks holiday, capers, dances, has eyes of youth, writes verses, and smells April and May according to the good host, is badly scanted, no doubt for reasons of haste. But the one meeting between these two is extremely interesting for its bald statement of a proposition which provides a thematic and formal mainspring in Shakespeare's major comedies:

> Why, thou must be thyself.
> He doth object I am too great of birth,
> And that my state being gall'd with my expense,
> I seek to heal it only by his wealth.
> Besides these, other bars he lays before me,
> My riots past, my wild societies,
> And tells me 'tis a thing impossible
> I should love thee but as a property.
>
> (III. iv. 3–10)

Anne's reply: 'Maybe he tells you true' is interestingly and teasingly non-committal. Shakespeare's mature comedy dramatizes at large just such a young woman: capable of being separately 'herself', of standing up for herself, of being independent and adventurous and not a mere accessory or 'property'. She it is who will become the subject of comic plots, not the object.

It is a process germinal in Luciana, in Julia, in the ladies of *Love's Labour's Lost*. Julia's defiance of categorical impossibilities, Rosaline's challenging realism, Hippolyta's defence of intuitionism and the imagination, are all milestones in the correction of masculine follies. So is the releasing of Katherina from the prison of her thwarted aspirations a milestone. But it is not until

the turning point of *The Merry Wives* that the great transformations of *Much Ado*, *As You Like It*, and *Twelfth Night* are
realized and the heroines are liberated to take their share – even a
lion's share – in the pleasure of comic remedies.[9]

For Jonson, Ornstein tells us, 'wit was masculine and calculat-
ing; for Shakespeare, in the comedies, it was feminine and intuitive'.[10] But he forgets that this was not always so. The transmis-
sion to the woman of a masculine comic energy, of racy wit and
high spirits, of irony and improvization, of the uninhibited zest
for mockery which were the prerogatives of maverick and adventurous males was a gradual process. It is a process whose primeval
analogue is to be found at the *fons et origo* of comedy itself, in
what Kerenyi has called one of 'the most miraculous events in the
history of European cultures'.[11] 'The world of the Old Comedy',
he writes, 'was a world without limits', rooted in the intoxication
of the Komos, in the undifferentiation of men and women, or of
men and animals. 'Male choruses dress as women, or . . . play
roles of women disguised as men, or disguise themselves as
women to mingle with women who are themselves men disguised'
(p. 341). But 'the universality of comic unrestraint burst like a
soap bubble and was gone . . .' (p. 343). Instead we encounter in
Menander 'a universality of *philanthropeia*, human sympathy. . . . The resulting transformation of comedy is among the
most miraculous events in the history of European culture. There
the religion of Dionysos disclosed its finest, most human possibility' (p. 348).

It is, I submit, a replica of this transformation that we watch
enacted through the progress of Shakespeare's career as comic
dramatist, so that Kerenyi's claim can be adapted to Shakespeare's case. In Shakespearean comedy the culture of Christian
Europe disclosed its finest, most human possibility. That possibility is a dynamic synthesis: Shakespeare's New Comedy inverts
traditional feminine roles, thus transforming a male-oriented,
male-dominated perspective into its antithetical opposite. And it
is this transformation, grafted upon his remedial, exorcist, dialectical comic plot that yields, in place of the disjunctive alternatives
of polarization, new sexual identities, new resolutions and new
horizons. It is to these that we now turn.

NOTES

1 The scholarly information is thoroughly and excellently set out by H. J. Oliver in his introduction to the New Arden edn (London: Methuen, 1971).

2 As Harold Jenkins has argued in *The Structural Problem in Shakespeare's Henry the Fourth* (London: Methuen, 1956).

3 New Arden edn, p. xivi.

4 Cf. Leonard Dean's engaging account of Falstaff as social outsider 'acting his way into an openly theatrical version of the lower middle class . . . at a farewell dinner party for Falstaff before he leaves for the front', *SEL*, vol. XVI, no. 2 (1976), pp. 268–70.

5 Jeanne Addison Roberts, '*The Merry Wives*: Suitably Shallow, But Neither Simple nor Slender', *Shakespeare Studies*, vol. VI (1970), p. 110.

6 ibid. Or, according to Northrop Frye's witticism: 'Falstaff must have felt that after being thrown into the water, dressed up as a witch and beaten out of a house with curses, and finally supplied with a beast's head and singed with candles, he had done about all that could reasonably have been expected of any fertility spirit' (*The Anatomy of Criticism*, New Jersey: Princeton University Press, 1957), p. 183.

7 Susanne Langer, *Feeling and Form* (New York: Charles Scribner's, 1953), p. 351.

8 J. Dover Wilson, editor of The New Shakespeare edn (Cambridge: Cambridge University Press, 1921), p. xxx.

9 Ralph Berry, *Shakespeare's Comedies* (New Jersey: Princeton University Press, 1972), takes a diametrically opposed view of *The Merry Wives*. The play does not, he feels, 'appear to contribute organically to Shakespeare's development' (p. 146).

10 Robert Ornstein, 'Shakespearean and Jonsonian Comedy', *Shakespeare Survey*, vol. 22 (1969), p. 45.

11 C. Kerenyi, *Dionysos: Archetypal Image of Indestructible Life* (New Jersey: Princeton University Press, 1976), pp. 341–8 passim.

IX

'BETTER THAN
REPORTINGLY'

Much Ado About Nothing contrasts notably with the early
Shrew, which is similarly structured in terms of antithetical
couples, not only in its greater elegance of composition and
expression, but in its placing of the comic initiative in the hands of
its vivacious heroine Beatrice. In both plays, as indeed in all of the
comedies, courtly love conventions and natural passion, affectation and spontaneity, romance and realism, or style and substance, saying and believing, simulation and dissimulation interlock; while the dual or agonistic structure of courtship allows for
reversals, exchanges and chiastic re-positionings of these contraries during the dynamic progress of the plots. In *Much Ado*,
moreover, Shakespeare modifies his usual multiple-plot practice.
He normally has a sub- or mid-plot which functions as a distorting mirror for the main plot, exaggerating to a degree of positive
aberration the deficiencies adumbrated in the latter, while the
lower-order fools provide at once a ridiculing parody of the
middle characters and a foil for the higher recognitions of the
higher ones. As Salingar points out, 'it appears to be necessary for
the lovers to act out their fantasies, and to meet living images or
parodies of themselves before they can rid themselves of their
affectations and impulsive mistakes'.[1] Here, however, as in *The
Shrew*, it is at first blush hard to tell which is model and which
parody. Beatrice and Benedick's unorthodox views on marriage

are a parody of normal conventions and so confirm Hero and Claudio in their soberer ways. Only later do we perceive that it is the conventionality, and subsequent frailty, of the Hero/Claudio relationship that provides a flattering reflector for the freewheeling, impulsive, individualist demands of Beatrice and Benedick.

That it is the authenticity of the sub-plot Beatrice-Benedick relationship which is finally paramount is vouched for by the response of audiences. From its earliest appearances[2] the play was received as the story of Beatrice and Benedick – Charles I himself is a royal witness. But this again does not do justice to the whole. D. P. Young would have us 'stop speaking of plot and sub-plot in Shakespearean comedy' altogether, finding the 'uniqueness of the form' in the mirroring of themes in all the strands of action.[3] But it is the specific equilibrium of the two plots in Much Ado, with Hero and Claudio remaining insistently, and not only formally, the official main protagonists, and Beatrice and Benedick challenging their monopoly of attention, which buttresses our perception of the dialectic of contraries the play embodies. As Alexander Leggatt has skilfully argued, in opposition to those who tend to ignore Hero and Claudio, or to find them insipid or pasteboard figures:

> The love affair of Beatrice and Benedick, so naturalistically conceived, so determined by individual character, is seen, at bottom, as a matter of convention. In praising its psychological reality we should not overlook how much the pleasure it gives depends on the essential, impersonal rhythm it shares with the other story.[4]

Benedick and Beatrice are the latest in a line of heretics and mockers and the most complex. In the earlier comedies the lover is perceived as the absurd and predictable victim of his love-longing and his lady's imperious aloofness, and is mocked by impudent individualists like Speed and Moth. Shakespeare's dialogue with the courtly lover has advanced in stages, and by the constant locating and re-locating of couples in dynamic opposition to each other. In The Comedy of Errors it is the Antipholus twins who are opposing doubles: one the worried, married man – a realist; the other the ardent and idealistic courtly lover. In The Shrew there is a neat reversal of oppositions which foreshadows *Much Ado*: the anti-romantic couple find love-in-marriage, the apparently ardent lovers find cold comfort in theirs. In *The Two Gentlemen* doubles appear again, more complexly, in Valentine the devoted ex-heretic, and Proteus the treacherous ex-votary of courtly love. The deadlocking of these extremities is resolved only by the substantial presence of the loving Julia. In *Love's Labour's Lost* all the men – initially heretics – become courtly-love romantics, while all the women play the role of satirical realists. Berowne, who mocks love, both style and substance, becomes an advocate and acolyte of the very *dolce stil nuovo* he formerly disdained. But he can still be fooled by a reliance on rhetoric which lacks real substance, as Rosaline points out. The conventions and the substance of courtly love are turned upside-down for the doubled couples in *A Midsummer Night's Dream*, but balance is restored through the 'cure' of the married lovers. Anne Page and Fenton, those honest bourgeois lovers, have no romantic style, over-shadowed as they are by the matrimonial problems of the stout matrons of Windsor; but they sensibly make off, leaving their worthy parents to patch up their marriages as best they may. Now Benedick and Beatrice, forewarned apparently, disavow love, placing no faith in its conventional vows and protestations, but are very much affected by the substance of the passion; while for Claudio and the compliant Hero the courtly love conventions camouflage a courtship of convenience, the substance of which will be tested and found wanting. Further turns are to come. Rosalind, deeper in love than there are fathoms to measure it, becomes a pert Moth herself, mocks her sonneteer lover, and exposes the conventional style of the quasi-courtly lovers Phebe and Silvius as very cold Pastoral and quite empty of substance; while Orsino, the very impersonation of the courtly-love style, is liberated from its insubstantiality by the substantial discovery of a girl in his personable young page's clothes. And there the dialectic rests, a romantic heroine having been created whose various follies, acted out, prove transcendently beneficial, and whose self-assured wit can contain even what Leggatt calls 'the comically unoriginal situation of being in love'.[5]

What is wanting at the outset of *Much Ado* is a match for

Claudio, and a match for the high spirited Lady Beatrice – the two 'matches' are poised against each other in double antithesis. Claudio, back from the wars and eager to 'drive liking to the name of love', replies gratefully and decorously to the Duke's offer of intercession:

> How sweetly you do minister to love,
> That know love's grief by his complexion!
>
> (I. i. 312–13)

But already in Act I, scene i, Claudio's 'Hath Leonato any son, my Lord?' alerts us to the substance behind the rhetoric of 'Can the world buy such a jewel?' 'Seven hundred pounds, and possibilities, is a goot gift' as Evans sensibly put it in *The Merry Wives*. Matchmaking is afoot and Claudio has a weather eye for material circumstances. 'Love's griefs, and passions' are perfunctory, the accepted, conventional, romantic rhetoric which masks a relation essentially impersonal. Claudio is asking 'Who is Hero, what is she? but his enquiries it will be noticed, are about others' opinions of her, with which to endorse her value for him. And the Prince's agreement to act proxy suitor for him is both further endorsement that the match is desirable, and further indication of the absence of need on Claudio's part for the direct challenges and intimacies of courtship. He does, when he feels himself cheated, bitterly exclaim:

> Therefore all hearts in love use their own tongues.
> Let every eye negotiate for itself,
> And trust no agent; for beauty is a witch
> Against whose charms faith melteth into blood.
>
> (II. i. 177–80)

But his eye is on the treachery of the proxy suitor, not on the object of his attentions.

Nothing could be more appropriate than that such a relationship should be vulnerable to the slightest breath of scandal. Nor that in the church scene Claudio should utter the contemptuous

> There, Leonato, take her back again.
> Give not this rotten orange to your friend,
>
> (IV. i. 31–2)

He is accusing a business associate of bad faith in the conveyance of shoddy goods, and blatantly violating all accepted convention to do so. But he also thereby gives expression to the animosity latent behind the chivalric mask. Poor Hero faints away under the shock, as well she might. For this is her world upside-down – a nightmare of hostility, a midsummer night's dream without benefit of magic, and a revelation of the hollowness and inauthenticity of their relationship.

The match has been counterfeit; its romantic rhetoric camouflage for purely practical proprieties and proprietorships; and it is consonant with the exquisite symmetry of this play that Claudio's second wedding, formally reversing the ill effects of the first, is with an anonymous and unknown – a camouflaged – bride. It is her anonymity, however, that turns out to be, mercifully, counterfeit. Unreconstructed aggressiveness has been exorcized in the church scene and the ritual expiation makes possible a second chance.

Against this pair, stand Beatrice and Benedick. These would-be lords and owners of their faces are sturdily non-conformist. 'I had rather hear my dog bark at a crow than a man swear he loves me' (I. i. 131–2). Thus Beatrice, and Benedick is of a similar mind: 'God keep your ladyship still in that mind! so some gentleman or other shall scape a predestinate scratched face (I. i. 133–5). Benedick is a professed tyrant to the opposite sex, an 'obstinate heretic in the despite of beauty' (I. i. 234–5), and Beatrice, too, a confirmed 'batchelor':

> For hear me, Hero: wooing, wedding, and repenting, is as a Scotch jig, a measure, and a cinquepace; the first suit is hot and hasty, like a Scotch jig, and full as fantastical; the wedding, mannerly-modest, as a measure, full of state and ancientry; and then comes repentance, and with his bad legs falls into the cinquepace faster and faster, till he sink into his grave.
>
> (II. i. 72–80)

In these two hostility is not latent but flagrantly proclaimed. They give each other no quarter in the merry war. Benedick is a braggart, a stuffed man, little wiser than a horse, as fickle as fashion itself, caught like a disease, the Prince's jester, a dull fool; it is a dear happiness to women that he loves none. Beatrice is Lady Disdain, Lady Tongue, a parrot teacher, a chatterer, a harpy; he will go to the world's end rather than hold three words with her. However, though they maintain loudly that they cannot stand each other it does not require superhuman powers of perception to observe the marked interest, little short of obsession, they take in each other.

It is no other than Signior Mountanto that Beatrice enquires about, and no other than Beatrice who occurs to Benedick as the model with which to compare Hero, to the latter's disadvantage: 'There's her cousin, and she were not possess'd with a fury, exceeds her as much in beauty as the first of May doth the last of December' (I. i. 190–2). Their anti-romantic posture is therefore also a mask, as has frequently been noted, aggressive-defensive and designed to forestall the very pain it inflicts. For example, 'I wonder that you will still be talking, Signior Benedick, nobody marks you.' (I. i. 116–17) is an interesting opening ploy. It translates into a whole set of messages. First of all, someone does. She does. Clearly she has, provocatively, caught his attention, when (we infer) he was ostentatiously *not* marking her. Then, I wish no one *did* mark you, you great fool, *not* being marked being the greatest punishment possible to a boaster like yourself, and therefore a good revenge. Revenge for what? Not for your not having marked me, certainly. Don't imagine that I mark you, or that you are the least important to me, or that I in the least care whether you mark, marked, or will mark me. 'What, my dear Lady Disdain! Are you yet living?' (I. i. 118–19). And they are off.

What came between these two in the past is half concealed and half revealed. One infers a quarrel: 'In our last conflict four of his five wits went halting off, and now is the whole man govern'd with one; so that if he have wit enough to keep himself warm, let him bear it for a difference between himself and his horse' (I. i. 65–70). One infers a roving eye on Benedick's part: 'He set up his bills here in Messina and challeng'd Cupid at the flight' (I. i. 39–40) and 'He wears his faith but as the fashion of his hat: it ever changes with the next block' (I. i. 75–7). Later, we hear explicitly: 'Indeed, my lord, he lent it [his heart] me awhile, and I gave him use for it, a double heart for his single one. Marry, once before he won it of me with false dice, therefore your Grace may well say I have lost it' (II. i. 278–82).

Benedick's protestations too, partly conventionalized caution against cuckoldry, smack of the once bitten, who now demonstratively projects an image of invulnerability: 'Prove that ever I lose more blood with love than I will get again with drinking, pick out mine eyes with a ballad-maker's pen, and hang me up at the door of a brothel-house for the sign of blind Cupid' (I. i. 250–4). 'Alas, poor hurt fowl! Now will he creep into sedges.' (II. i. 202–3) says Benedick of Claudio, whose proxy wooer has stolen his girl, it seems; and immediately reverts to his own affront: 'But that my Lady Beatrice should know me, and not know me!' (II. i. 203–4). A similar image appears again, significantly, just before the gulling of Beatrice:

> For look where Beatrice like a lapwing runs
> Close by the ground, to hear our conference.
>
> (III. i. 24–5)

One infers wounded susceptibilities on both sides and one therefore perceives that where Claudio's idealization of love-and-marriage is the packaging he and his milieu regard as suitable for an eminently practical and profitable marriage arrangement, these others de-idealize love and marriage as an insurance against a recurrence of loss.[6]

At the masked ball the comic disposition of Messina is paradigmatically dramatized. Hearsay and conjecture dominate. That the Prince woos for himself is assumed by all, and how can one know with so much rumour about? The point about the limitations of knowledge and the tendency to jump to conclusions is made graphically by the masked ball itself. Pedro and Hero evidently recognize each other. Margaret and Balthasar (possibly) don't; Ursula knows Antonio, whom she recognized by the wagging of his head and whom she flatters upon his excellent wit, though he swears he counterfeits. What of Beatrice and Benedick? Who is pretending? Does Benedick, recognizing her, take the opportunity of a gibe about her having her wit out of the *Hundred Merry Tales*? Does Beatrice, as he evidently believes, not recognize him and therefore speak from the heart when she calls him 'the Prince's jester'? Or is this taunt her knowing revenge for Benedick's gibe about the *Hundred Merry Tales*? Which possibility is confirmed by Benedick's soliloquy after the ball: 'But that my Lady Beatrice should know me, and not know me'? Does he mean at the ball specifically, or in general? Is he angry at not being recognized, or at not being appreciated? These two take particular pride in their wit, it will be noticed, and no affront will be less easily forgiven than disparagement on that score. Whether both now assume that the other really means the wounding things he or she says, or both know that the other was intentionally meaning to wound, a new turn is given to the warfare between them. We no longer witness the reflection of an old quarrel but the quick of a new one. There is no reason, however, why the spiral should ever stop since the dynamics of self-defence will ensure that the more they pretend to ignore each other the more they will fail, *and* the more wounded their self-esteem will become. It is a knot too hard for them to untie, but fortunately there are plotters at hand.

The comic disposition of Messina is thus to be taken in: to dissimulate, or simulate, to be deceived by appearance, or by rumours. The sophisticates go further. They do not believe what they really want to believe, or do believe what they perversely do not want to believe. 'I should think this a gull, but that the white-bearded fellow speaks it. Knavery cannot sure hide himself in such reverence' (II. iii. 118–20). Or, for that matter, they believe what they really do not want to believe, like Leonato, who says in the church scene

> Would the two princes lie, and Claudio lie,
> Who lov'd her so, that speaking of her foulness,
> Wash'd it with tears?   (IV. i. 152–4)

It is, indeed, precisely the last of the logical possibilities that the remedy in this play must bring about, causing both couples, reassured, really to believe what they really want to believe without recourse to defence or counter-defence maskings.

Even the good Dogberry masks his ineptitude with liberal borrowings from the learned languages but – a tertiary irony –

when he most desires that Borachio's aspersion of assdom be recorded, so that the mockery of the law it implies be made public, all that he succeeds in making public is the open and palpable truth of the aspersion. Masking in this play is a fertile generator of dialectical ironies.

Only Don John, who despises 'flattering honest men', cannot hide what he is. He would rather 'be disdain'd of all than to fashion a carriage to rob love from any', and boasts of not wearing a mask – he is a plain-dealing villain, he says. But this is *his* illusion, of course, since in his plot to defame Hero he does precisely 'fashion a carriage', and it is only that sharp lot, the constabulary, who capture the deformed thief Fashion wearing 'a key in his ear and a lock hanging by it' (v. i. 308–9) – a piece of creatively significant nonsense – that save the day.

The comic device – both eavesdropping tricks – ironically both deception and source of truth, is perfectly adapted to mesh with, exacerbate and finally exorcize this comic disposition. One eavesdropping stratagem is benignly plotted by the well-meaning Duke who aims to bring Signior Benedick and the Lady Beatrice into a mountain of affection 'th' one with th' other', the other malignly staged by Don John who aims to cross the marriage his brother has arranged; and both are marvellously counterpointed by the inadvertent overhearings of those stalwart guardians of the law and the city – Dogberry's watch. It is worth noticing that when the first plot of Don John fails he at once sets about devising another, any marriage his legitimate brother arranges being grist to his mill; and the failed plot at the masked ball deftly gives us advance notice of the play's modalities of masking and mistaking, of tests and testimonies.

Don Pedro's plot provides the plotters with the opportunity to tease their victims with some home-truths real or imagined. On the men's side:

> *Don Pedro*   She doth well. If she should make tender of her love, 'tis very possible he'll scorn it, for the man (as you know all) hath a contemptible spirit.
> *Claudio*   He is a very proper man.
> *Don Pedro*   He hath indeed a good outward happiness.

Claudio   Before God, and in my mind, very wise.
Don Pedro   He doth indeed show some sparks that are like wit.
Claudio   And I take him to be valiant.
Don Pedro   As Hector, I assure you, and in the managing of quarrels you may say he is wise, for either he avoids them with great discretion, or undertakes them with a most Christian-like fear.   (II. iii. 178–90)

And the women's:

Hero   But nature never fram'd a woman's heart
Of prouder stuff than that of Beatrice.
Disdain and scorn ride sparkling in her eyes,
Misprising what they look on, and her wit
Values itself so highly that to her
All matter else seems weak. She cannot love,
Nor take no shape nor project of affection,
She is so self-endeared.   (III. i. 49–56)

But the cream of the jest in the eavesdropping scenes is that those who speak the truth believe that they are inventing it.

Beatrice and Benedick are thus equivocally provided with apparently 'objective' testimony concerning the real state of the other's affections, and the defensive strategy each adopted becomes supererogatory. Benedick, abandoning his armour, contrives to preserve some semblance of a complacent self-image:

happy are they that hear their detractions, and can put them to mending. . . . I may chance have some odd quirks and remnants of wit broken on me, because I have rail'd so long against marriage; but doth not the appetite alter? A man loves the meat in his youth that he cannot endure in his age. Shall quips and sentences and these paper bullets of the brain awe a man from the career of his humor? No, the world must be peopled. When I said I would die a bachelor, I did not think I should live till I were married.   (II. iii. 229–44)

But Beatrice abandons hers with an immediate generous contrition:

Can this be true?
Stand I condemn'd for pride and scorn so much?
Contempt, farewell, and maiden pride, adieu!
No glory lives behind the back of such.
And, Benedick, love on, I will requite thee,
Taming my wild heart to thy loving hand.
(III. i. 107–12)

Whether Beatrice and Benedick were hiding their real selves until reassurances of reciprocity overcame psychological barriers, or whether they were caused to suffer love by the magic of knowing themselves recipients of affection, they both abandon themselves to the fantasy of love. Their status, however, as objects of comic mockery is skilfully preserved by the necessary time-lag of the contrivance. When Benedick is convinced that he is loved while Beatrice is still her old self, the folly of rationalization displays itself at large before our very eyes. Benedick's response to Beatrice's as yet untransformed scorn is ingenuity itself, at work upon most unpromising material:

Ha! 'Against my will I am sent to bid you come in to dinner' – there's a double meaning in that. 'I took no more pains for those thanks than you took pains to thank me' – that's as much as to say, 'Any pains that I take for you is as easy as thanks'. (II. iii. 257–62)

And when each in his or her transformed state – transformed be it noted into the very style of suffering love they originally ridiculed – when each meets his or her friends, each undergoes the teasing equivalent of the scorn they once poured upon lovers, and survives!

The benignly staged eavesdropping releases undissimulated feeling in Beatrice and Benedick by apparently disclosing the feelings of the other. It is paralleled by the malignly staged eavesdropping, which apparently exposes Hero to Claudio by its sham disclosure of her dissimulation, and releases the passion in which Claudio will destroy (temporarily) his own happiness, and a lovely lady, in the church 'unmasking'.

The point I wish to emphasize is the consummate realization of the Shakespearean comic therapy which these symmetries produce. Both plottings bring out, in diametrically opposed ways, the implications of the protagonists' masks; both trigger an acting out of what was hidden and latent: the joyous dream of love proved and requited – a homeopathic *remedia amoris* – in the case of Beatrice and Benedick; a nightmare fantasia of enmity in the case of Claudio and Hero.

Don John, says Anne Barton, 'a plot mechanism more than a complex character in his own right, appears in the play as a kind of anti-comic force, the official enemy of all happy endings'. It is a striking insight, for it is not by chance that the malign plotter sets off a malign, potentially tragic dialectic of either/or, while the benign plotter releases a benign dialectic of both/and – the comic resolving principle itself. *Much Ado* achieves what the double plot of *The Merchant* fails to achieve: exorcism without a scapegoat, and comic metamorphoses in which the fooled outwit, in their folly, the wisdom of the foolers.

In addition to the admirable ordering of affairs in the higher stratum of society the burlesque eavesdropping of the watch is a *tour de force* of comic sub-plot strategy. Unstaged and inadvertent, it discloses counterfeit and exposes truth without the vessels of this providential occurrence having for one moment the dimmest conception of what is afoot. It is therefore ironic foil to the benign fooling of the good plotters and their victims who do know, at least partly, what they are about, and ironic parody of the folly of the malignant plotters and theirs.

Dogberry's anxiety to be star performer at the enquiry occurs just as Leonato is hurrying off to the wedding and cannot, understandably, take the time clearly required to get to the bottom of Dogberry's dream.

A good old man, sir, he will be talking; as they say 'When the age is in, the wit is out.' God help us, it is a world to see! Well said, i'faith, neighbor Verges. Well, God's a good man; and two men ride of a horse, one must ride behind. An honest soul, i'faith, sir, by my troth he is, as ever broke bread; but God is to be worshipp'd; all men are not alike, alas, good neighbor!

(III. v. 33–40)

This anxiety culminates only in disappointment at not having been written down an ass, but he does succeed in exposing the crafty Borachio and Conrade for the wrongdoers they are.

Dogberry's comic hybris or 'delusion of vanity', his blithe confidence in the 'gifts that God gives', thus mocks that of all his betters. He is the fulcrum upon which the wit-folly dialectic turns, in a riot of ironic misprisions. He is also the cause of the play's double peripeteia: the climactic church scene, which he could have prevented, and the confession of Borachio, which he nearly does prevent. This double peripeteia marks the final exhaustion of the comic device. Both plots, the benign and the malevolent, have succeeded. Beatrice and Benedick have been tricked into love, Claudio and Hero tricked out of it. The apparently deceitful Hero is unmasked, and this precipitates the unmasking to each other of Beatrice and Benedick, each knowing the other indirectly, by hearsay, rumour and opinion, and only presently to know each other through direct confrontation.

When they reveal themselves to each other, Benedick boldly and Beatrice now hesitant, their knowledge is unmediated either by others, or by their own self-induced obliquities. Now they will really believe what they really want to believe, and have in practice already believed 'better than reportingly'. But the repudiation of Hero presents them with a further acid test. It is a test of trust, which is as different from belief as knowledge from opinion. 'Kill Claudio' is Beatrice's demand that he trust absolutely her absolute trust in her cousin's innocence. It is a dangerous moment. Beatrice plays for high stakes – her lover for her cousin. And if he agrees he will wager beloved against friend. It is the moment of incipient disaster for which the fortunes of comedy produce providential remedies – in this case the voice of that sterling citizen, Dogberry, uncovering the thief Fashion – 'flat burglary as ever was committed' – in the next scene. Beatrice puts the reluctant Benedick to the oldest of chivalric tests – to kill the monster and rescue the lady, thus proving his valour and his love. It is a fantasy of knight errantry, and his commitment to this mission, in response to her fierceness, transforms the whole flimsy romance convention into the deadly seriousness of his challenge to

Claudio. This is a reversal of all expectations and roundly turns the tables upon the tricksters.

Beatrice's violence is more than passionate loyalty to her cousin. In the war of the sexes with Benedick, Beatrice's combativeness is self-defence, self-assertion, the armour of a vulnerable pride. But when she says 'Would it not grieve a woman to be overmaster'd with a piece of valiant dust? to make an account of her life to a cold of wayward marl?' (II. i. 60–3); or replies to Pedro's 'Will you have me lady?' with 'No, my lord, unless I might have another for working-days. Your Grace is too costly to wear every day.' (II. i. 327–9), we are invited to perceive an added ingredient. She will not have a husband with a beard, or without one; she will not have a husband at all. St Peter will show her where the bachelors sit in heaven and there 'live we as merry as the day is long'. She will be no meek daughter like her cousin: 'But yet for all that, cousin, let him be a handsome fellow, or else make another cur'sy, and say, "Father, as it please me"' (II. i. 53–6). She will be won on her own terms or not at all.

It is a grave demand for independence she is making; and it is possible to infer from her mockery of Benedick's soldiership and from the significant touch of envy in the remark, 'he hath every month a new sworn brother' (I. i. 72–3), that it is at the circumscription of her feminine condition as much as anything that the Lady Beatrice chafes. She suffers, as we are to discover, love. But before she is love's sufferer she is love's suffragette. And when she says with passion

> You dare easier be friends with me than fight with mine enemy . . . O that I were a man . . . O God, that I were a man! I would eat his heart in the market place . . . or that I had any friend would be a man for my sake . . . I cannot be a man with wishing; therefore I will die a woman with grieving. (IV. i. 298–323 passim)

she is far from the acceptance of biological fact. And so Benedick's acceptance of her challenge, in love, and in trust, and in identification with her point of view, proves the very safety valve Beatrice's accumulated truculence requires. In *As You Like It* there is a reverse, though precisely equivalent moment when Rosalind faints at Oliver's story of Orlando's rescue and wounding, and the episode serves quite clearly as a safety valve for Rosalind's hidden and temporary stifled femininity. There, too, the episode marks the exhaustion of the device (the disguise) and precipitates recognitions.

What *Much Ado* invites us to understand about its comic remedies is only fully articulated by the end of the dénouement. Act V has to do with questions of the visible and the invisible, the seen and the unseen, upon which trust ultimately depends. There is no need for trust if all is open and palpable. Since, in human affairs, nothing is ever open and palpable, much ado about nothing or 'noting'[7] ensues. By noting of the lady, says the Friar

> I have mark'd
> A thousand blushing apparitions
> To start into her face, a thousand innocent shames
> In angel whiteness beat away those blushes,
> And in her eye there hath appear'd a fire
> To burn the errors that these princes hold
> Against her maiden truth. . . .   (IV. i. 158–64)

and his proposal is to allow time and the rehabilitating 'study of imagination' to bring

> every lovely organ of her life
> Shall come apparell'd in more precious habit,
> More moving, delicate, and full of life,
> Into the eye and prospect of his soul,
>   (IV. i. 226–9)

while Hero herself, given out as dead, be concealed from sight.

The theme is plentifully embodied in Act V. First in the further glimpse of the incipient tragic possibilities: the father's grief, which he refuses to hide, the young men's self-righteous callous arrogance. This is followed by the appearance of a Benedick, outwardly unchanged, inwardly transformed, outdaring his friend's baiting concerning 'Benedick the married man'. Finally, taking in that Benedick is in 'most profound earnest' for, Claudio is sure, the love of Beatrice, Don Pedro's contemptuous dismissal: 'What a pretty thing man is when he goes in his doublet and hose and leaves off his wit!' (v. i. 199–200). This immediately precedes Dogberry's entrance with the bound Borachio and the revealed truth. Borachio rubs it in: 'What your wisdoms could not discover, these shallow fools have brought to light . . .' (v. i. 232–4) but no new pieties about 'what men daily do, not knowing what they do' will bring Hero back. Claudio must clear his moral debt and he must be seen to do so. It is fitting that he do this by placing himself totally in Leonato's hands:

> O noble sir!
> Your overkindness doth wring tears from me.
> I do embrace your offer, and dispose
> For henceforth of poor Claudio.   (v. i. 292–5)

It is himself that he surrenders to Leonato and to his masked bride. And while Claudio thus places himself in trust with Leonato, Beatrice and Benedick flaunt their hidden trust with an outward show of their old defensive combativeness, and a mock denial, till their own letters give them away, of the love we have heard them confess.

> *Benedick* Come, I will have thee, but, by this light, I take thee for pity.
> *Beatrice* I would not deny you, but, by this good day, I yield upon great persuasion, and partly to save your life, for I was told you were in a consumption.   (v. iv. 92–6)

The masked wedding neatly symbolizes the antinomies of seeing and knowing. Benedick's kiss stops not only Beatrice's mouth, but the see-saw of hearsay and double talk, of convention and counter-convention.

The taming of Beatrice has been a more formidable undertaking than that of Katherina because she supplies more varied and imaginative occasions for the comic pleasure wit provides; and with no remedy will we be satisfied that denies us these. If humour and vivacity, individuality, resilience, spontaneity, fantasy and irony are to be the price of wedding bells, no marriage Komos will seem to us a celebration. But the Beauty of it is that comedy's double indemnity is triumphantly validated in the final teasing. We are to have our self-assertive witty cake and eat it, too, *con amore*; the remedy – this imagined possibility of remedy – for that suffering state not being such as to deprive us of the value of Beatrice's and Benedick's wit once its function as protective mask is rendered unnecessary. Head and heart, style and substance, convention and nature, are for once – man being a giddy thing – in consonance.

But if the battle of the sexes has thus been won to the satisfaction of both parties, as is comically proper, it is still, in *Much Ado*, by means of a heroine only half divested of her traditional feminine garb. Even 'Kill Claudio' is a command which reflects the immemorial dependence of lady upon knight, and, as we have seen, the lady Beatrice chafes at it. The next step, however, is presently to be made, in *As You Like It*, which also harks back to an earlier play. And just as the comparison between *Much Ado* and *The Shrew* (or *Love's Labour's Lost*) provided a measure not only of the scope and subtlety of Shakespeare's growing art but of the changes in its nature, so does comparison between the page disguise of the forlorn Julia and that of Rosalind.

NOTES

1 Leo Salingar, *Shakespeare and the Traditions of Comedy* (Cambridge: Cambridge University Press, 1974), p. 282. Salingar, however, is speaking here of *LLL* and *MSND*, and he does not distinguish between the middle and lower levels of parody.

2 See Furness, editor of The New Variorum edn (reprinted 1899; New York: Dover Publications, 1964), pp. xxii, and xxi for comment upon the 1613 record of a play called *Benedicte and Betteris*.

3 David P. Young, *Something of Great Constancy* (New Haven: Yale University Press, 1966), pp. 97–106.

4 Alexander Leggatt, *Shakespeare's Comedy of Love* (London: Methuen, 1974), p. 181.

5 Ibid., p. 182.

6 David L. Stevenson observes in the introduction to the Signet edn (New York: New American Library, 1964), p. xxvii: 'They are everywhere presented as completely aware of the

fact that they are playing roles with and for each other – Beatrice as shrew, Benedick as misogynist – and enjoying the playing. The subject matter of their game is a distaste for institutionalized romantic love leading to marriage, the precise kind of "love" that Claudio and Hero accept easily and without thought. . . . The subtle obstacle to the union of Benedick and Beatrice is that neither is ever sure of what he or she would like if they agreed to quit playing their respective roles.' But this does not seem quite right. The writer is apparently seduced by the exuberance of the playing into ignoring the depth of their need to play these roles. Muriel Bradbrook, *The Growth and Structure of Elizabethan Comedy* (London: Chatto & Windus, 1925), p. 181, sees them simply as flirting from the very beginning.

7 The possible pun was observed as early as 1733 by Theobald and confirmed by R. G. White on the basis of his studies of Elizabethan pronunciation. He interpreted the play as 'Much ado about watching, observing'. See the New Variorum, pp. 6, 113ff. Ralph Berry, *Shakespeare's Comedies* (New Jersey: Princeton University Press, 1972) adds a third layer to the near pun: note/know, and finds in it the mainspring of the play's thematic preoccupation.

X

EXISTENCE
IN ARDEN

The two great comedies composed during the last years of the sixteenth century share many features which place them in something of a class apart. One of these is the confident, even demonstrative nonchalance with which they relate to the Terentian tradition. It is as if Shakespeare reaches his majority in them, knows it, and would have us know it. It is almost as if we hear him indulging in a sly joke about the whole paternalistic New Comedy model when he has Rosalind, at some undramatized point, meet her father in the forest, where, as she later reports to Celia, she had much question with him: 'He ask'd me of what parentage I was. I told him of as good as he, so he laugh'd and let me go. But what talk we of fathers, when there is such a man as Orlando? (III. iv. 36–9). With no parental obstacles, no separating misprisions or vows or oaths, with no reason (as has often been pointed out) for Rosalind's continuing disguise once she is safe in the forest and the writer of the execrable verses identified, *As You Like It* is the only comedy in which the two chief protagonists fall in love not as victims of blind Cupid, or of plots of one kind and another, or against their own conscious will, but freely, open-eyed, reciprocally and as if in godsent fulfilment of their own deepest desires.

Their meeting is finely, appropriately rendered. Orlando is hesitant, disconcerted, incredulous, speechless; Rosalind responds with the immediate joyful, irrepressible spontaneity of her confession to Celia. Some of *her* speechlessness, she says, is 'for my child's father' (I. iii. 11). But this is a comic ending (or very near ending), rather than a comic beginning; and indeed the whole carriage of the play seems almost to set the comedy sequence on its head. The grave potential dangers are concentrated at the start, the tangle of mistaken identities occurs as late as the end of Act III.

'What', indeed, asks Barber, 'is the comedy in *As You Like It* about? What does Shakespeare ridicule? At times one gets the impression that it doesn't matter very much what the characters make fun of so long as they make fun.'[1] Sandwiched between *Much Ado* and *Twelfth Night*, Harold Jenkins notes:

> *As You Like It* is conspicuously lacking in comedy's more robust and boisterous elements – the pomps of Dogberry and the romps of Sir Toby . . . [and] it has nothing which answers to those bits of crucial trickery . . . which link events together by the logical intricacies of cause and effect. *As You Like It* takes Shakespearean comedy in one direction nearly as far as it could go before returning (in *Twelfth Night*) to a more orthodox scheme.[2]

The point is very well taken. The play exhibits not only a different direction but a markedly looser and more casual handling of the 'orthodox scheme', which I take to mean the Terentian formula; and it is this which makes inspired improvisation, the capacity to seize and make the most of one's opportunities, a key factor in the comic remedy itself. That which is therapeutic to the human condition is elicited here too by considerable anxiety and error, is winnowed clear of delusion and snatched by a hair's breadth from disaster. But what is prominently displayed, extruded, so to speak, as surface structure in *As You Like It* is the wisdom/folly dialectic of comedy itself, as antinomies are first exacerbated and then transcended. And what it embodies in its trickster heroine is comic pleasure itself, in practice and in action: a liberating playful fantasy, an expansive reconciliation of opposites of all kinds, enlivening and enchanting, to be enjoyed and rejoiced in; a heaven-sent euphoria. It is a play so self-assured as not to care whether we notice or not that it is talking about its own mode of being. It is a meta-comedy, in which the underlying principles of Shakespearean practice are drawn out for all to see and turned into the comic material itself.

The play polarizes harm and remedy in its initial catalogue of imperfections and deficiencies – the most dire we have yet encountered – and in the flight of its refugees. A youngest son seeks his proper place in the world. His elder brother keeps him rustically at home, like a peasant, breeds his horses better – they are not only fed but taught – allows him nothing but mere growth and, in short 'mines his gentility with his education'. For this servitude become unendurable. Orlando knows no wise remedy, and there begins his sadness. Elsewhere in the kingdom a duke is displaced by his younger brother and flees into exile, leaving his daughter mourning his absence. A thug is hired to dispatch the rebellious younger brother under cover of a court wrestling-match, and when the plan miscarries, the young man and his faithful retainer are unceremoniously turned out to make their way in the world as best they can. The usurping duke, unable to bear the accusing presence of his elder brother's daughter banishes her the court on pain of death. 'Thou art a fool', he says to his daughter, her friend, who entreats him to let her stay:

> She is too subtile for thee, and her smoothness,
> Her very silence, and her patience
> Speak to the people, and they pity her.
> Thou art a fool; she robs thee of thy name,
> And thou wilt show more bright and seem more virtuous
> When she is gone. . . .   (I. iii. 77–82)

His counterpart, Oliver, has a similar message concerning folly to deliver to his younger brother: 'What will you do, you fool', he says, in effect, 'when you have the meagre pittance your father left you? Beg when that is spent?'

This is the cold world of Edmund and Goneril in which there is no place for goodness and virtue, no room for undissimulated feeling; the tainted, radically corrupt world of court or city, of lust for gain and place, of craft and deceit. From wicked brother and wicked uncle there is no recourse for the oppressed but to take flight, which they do gladly. They go 'To liberty, and not to banishment.' (I. iii. 138), to 'some settled low content' (II. iii. 68) as they say in their worldly folly, and arrive by a providential coincidence in the same wood, with nothing but their natural loyalty and generosity, their foolish good nature, and love, contracted at the wrestling-match. Back home, cunning and treachery – called worldly wisdom – grow ever more manifest under the impetus of their own accumulation. This is rendered with a splendid acid brevity in Act III, scene i, when Oliver declares his kinship to Duke Frederick in the matter of affection for his wayward brother Orlando:

> *Oliver*   O that your Highness knew my heart in this!
> I never lov'd my brother in my life.
> *Duke Frederick*   More villain thou. Well, push him out of
>   doors,
> And let my officers of such a nature
> Make an extent upon his house and lands.
>   (III. i. 13–17)

The exposition of *As You Like It* presents a whole society in need of cure, not a temporary emergency, or lunacy, to be providentially set right.

Since this is the case, however, a good deal of manoeuvring is required to keep the play within the orbit of comedy. The source story in Lodge is far fiercer – there are several deaths; but even Shakespeare's toning down of the violence, and a reduction of the casualties to Charles' broken ribs is not sufficient to make the initiating circumstances mere harmless aberrations, or, at worst, aberrations which only an accumulation of mishaps and ill-fortune will render disastrous. To transform the Lodge story into comedy, therefore, necessitated a shift of gear, and the production of what one might call a second order set of follies from the realm not of the reprehensible but of the ridiculous; a modulation from vice to error, and potentially liberating error at that. It is the flight into the forest during the long second act which effects this transformation.

The flight into the forest draws upon the tradition of that other time and other place of the nostalgic imagination – the *locus amoenus* where the return to nature from corrupt civilization allows the truth, simplicity and humility of innocence to replace the treachery, craft and arrogance of worldly sophistication. But the audience, following the courtiers in their flight from usurpation, cruelty, artifice and deceit discover in the forest the usurpation of Corin, the boorish rusticity of Audrey and William and the factitious elegancies of imitation courtly love masking sexual tyranny in the shepherd lovers; while, before the story is over, the forest's lionesses and snakes will have revealed in it possibilities no less inhospitable, not to say predatory, than those of the vicious court.

What we perceive is a plethora of disjunctive contraries. The whole of Act II bandies views of the good life about between defendants of court and country respectively, in a battery of claims and counter-claims which turns each into its opposite, revealing the absurdity of polarized and partial solutions. Shakespeare erects a burlesque dialectic during which, at every point, assumptions are refuted by realities and opinions fooled by facts.

Amiens sings to whoever

> doth ambition shun,
> And loves to live i' th' sun,   (II. v. 38–9)

promising him no enemy but winter and rough weather. The disenchanted Jaques, whom there is no pleasing, caps Amiens' with another stanza (or stanzo – Jaques cares not for their names since they owe him nothing) pointing out that anyone who leaves his hearth and ease is an ass, and will find nothing but fools as gross as he in the greenwood. And Amiens' second song is less buoyant about winter and rough weather, not to mention friendship and loving, than the first.

Orlando, who has no illusions about 'the uncouth forest' swears to succour the fainting Adam: if there be anything living in the desert, he says, 'I will either be food for it, or bring it for food to thee'. It is as succinct a summary of nature red in tooth and claw as may be found, but oddly enough Orlando, who complained of the poverty of Nature, denied the benefits of Nurture, steeling himself for savagery, finds civility in the forest. 'Your gentleness shall force./More than your force move us to gentleness', says the Duke, his rhetorical chiasmus figuring the contraries. More precisely: figuring the contraries resolved in a way that is characteristic, as we shall see, of the Duke.

According to the melancholy Jaques that 'poor dappled fool' the deer, who has his 'round haunches gored' in his own native 'city' is a standing reproach to all seekers of the good life in the forest. But Jaques' bleak account of human ageing in the seven ages speech (II. vii. 139 ff.) is immediately refuted by Orlando's tender care for an old and venerable faithful servant. Jaques' various orations 'most invectively' pillory not only country, city and court, but 'this our life' in its entirety (II. i. 58). But Jaques' view that evil is universal and good an illusion is countered from yet another perspective by Touchstone's: that folly is universal and wisdom an illusion.

These two represent the play's opposing poles, but in asymmetrical opposition. They are a teasingly complex instance of Shakespeare's fools, referred to in Chapter I.

The meeting between them is reported exultantly by Jaques in Act II, scene vii, with much rejoicing, on the part of that arrogant nihilist, in the capacity for metaphysics of a mere fool. But the audience is quietly invited to perceive that there is an extraordinary similarity between Touchstone's oracular ripening and rotting and Jaques' own disenchanted rhetoric, and we are invited to wonder whether it is not after all the ironical fool who is mocking, by parody, the philosophical pretensions of the sentimental cynic. The scene plays handy dandy (like Lear) with the question most germane to comedy (as Lear's to tragedy): which is the Eiron, which the Alazon? Which is the mocker and which the mocked? Who is fooling and who is fooled?

What after all does Touchstone *not* mock? He dismantles, systematically and with detached amusement, the entire structure of syllogistic reasoning with which his betters occupy their minds:

> Truly shepherd, in respect of itself, it is a good life; but in respect that it is a shepherd's life, it is naught. In respect that it is solitary, I like it very well; but in respect that it is private, it is a very vild life. Now in respect it is in the fields, it pleaseth me

well; but in respect it is not in the court, it is tedious. As it is a
spare life (look you) it fits my humor well; but as there is no
more plenty in it, it goes much against my stomach. Hast any
philosophy in thee, shepherd?   (III. ii. 13–22)

A premise, to Touchstone is nothing but its own potential contrary, as he delights to demonstrate with his mock or anti-logic of
all's one:

That is another simple sin in you, to bring the ewes and the rams
together, and to offer to get your living by the copulation of
cattle; to be bawd to a bell-wether, and to betray a she-lamb of
a twelve-month to a crooked-pated old cuckoldly ram, out
of all reasonable match.   (III. ii. 78–83)

Nevertheless, Touchstone is a fool. Audrey is there to remind us of
that. And so what we come to see is that both monistic or
polarized solutions – that evil is universal and good an illusion,
and that folly is universal and wisdom an illusion are being
mocked.

However, the play makes it clear which it prefers,[3] which it
includes, finally. It finds a place – a key place, as we shall see – for
the mother wit which Touchstone demonstratively parades, and
parodies. It is Jaques, totally lacking in good humour, who is sent
packing. First by the Duke, in terms which are significant, in view
of comedy's concern with remedies for human ills. The Duke
checks Jaques' enthusiasm about cleansing with satire the foul
body of the infected world with the command, Physician, heal
thyself:

Most mischievous foul sin, in chiding sin:
For thou thyself hast been a libertine,
As sensual as the brutish sting itself;
And all th' embossed sores, and headed evils,
That thou with license of free foot hast caught,
Would'st thou disgorge into the general world.
                    (II. vii. 64–9)

And then by the lovers. 'I thank you for your company, but, good
faith, I had as lief have been myself alone' is Jaques' opening ploy

when he meets Orlando. He doesn't, it transpires, approve of Orlando's verse, of his love's name, of his 'pretty answers' (probably 'conn'd out of rings'), of his 'nimble wit' at which he learnedly sneers, of his being fool enough to be in love at all. What he would like to do, he says, is to sit down and 'rail against our mistress the world, and all our misery'. At the end of this dispiriting conversation Orlando sends him to seek the fool he was looking for in the brook (III. ii. 253–93 passim). And Rosalind, similarly tried by Jaques' disquisition on his own unique and inimitable brand of melancholy, would 'rather have a fool to make [her] merry than experience to make [her] sad – and travel for it too!' (IV. i. 28).

If (much virtue in 'if') – if we must choose between disjunctions, too cool a head is evidently preferable to too cold a heart. But must we choose? Certainly Act II (in particular) with its reiterated pastoral polemic, its multitude of syntactic, imagistic, situational figurations of either/or places us constantly in attitudes of indecision, or of quasi-dilemma. Nothing is happening, of course, so that these are not the impossible choices of tragic action; they are merely virtual. These constantly collapsing or exploding solutions of the greenwood constitute the comic disposition which the process of the play heightens and mocks. The characters all have answers to the question of the good life, but their answers keep being refuted; keep being invaded by aspects of reality they have not taken into account. Yet they continue tirelessly searching. Moreover, the comedy of this second act is an almost Chekovian dialogue of the deaf. Everybody is talking philosophically about life. Ah Life. But it is only themselves they really hear.[4] The Duke, who needs grist for his mill, loves, he tells us, to cope Jaques in his sullen fits, for 'then he's full of matter'. But Jaques, who has no patience with another's problems, has been trying all day to avoid him: 'He is too disputable for my company', says he, with sardonic derision. 'I think of as many matters as he, but I give heaven thanks, and make no boast of them' (II. v. 35–7).

If then disjunctive logic is the comic disposition in Arden (reflecting the disjunction of good and evil in the play's outer frame), any remedy will have to mediate or bridge the fissuring of human experience which is thus symbolized. It is the good Duke (meta-*senex* for a meta-comedy?) who points the way to such a resolution.

The Duke's stoicism is more than a brave show. His speech (II. i. 1–17) on the sweet uses of adversity and the preferability of biting winter winds to man's ingratitude and the ingratiation of court sycophancy is a profoundly dialectical *concordia discors*, transcending, with its paradoxes, diamectrical contraries. He is, it is to be noted, as aware as Jaques of the universality of evil. It is he who first notices the anomaly of the deer hunt, though it is Jaques who rubs it in. He does not say that Arden is a rose garden. He only says that he recognizes the penalty of Adam.[5] Duke Senior does not deny the icy fangs of the winter wind, the ugly venom of the toad. On the contrary, he welcomes them because they 'feelingly persuade him what he is'. The contraries: painted pomp and icy fangs; chiding and flattery; feeling and persuasion (intuition and reason, we would say); books and brooks; sermons and stones, are all resolved in his remedial vision of the good life to be found in the hard discipline of nature, not in her soft bosom; in the riches of deprivation, not in the poverty of prodigality. 'Happy is your Grace', says Amiens, 'That can translate the stubbornness of fortune/Into so quiet and so sweet a style' (II. i. 18–20).

This Duke is indeed wise enough to be Rosalind's father but his wisdom of retreat, his embracing of penury, does not nurture a comic economy which requires bonus and liberating excess. He is the ideologue of resolutions, not their protagonist. Nor is the virtue that he makes of dispossession entirely victorious. They are doing their best, these exiles, to keep their spirits up, and there are moments of greenwood merriment, to be sure, but it doesn't take much to set off in them a yearning for better days. When the young man rushes on with his drawn sword shouting for food, and meets the Duke's courteous welcome, he also poignantly reminds him of the privations of a purely private virtue:

> what e'er you are
> That in this desert inaccessible,
> Under the shade of melancholy boughs,
> Lose and neglect the creeping hours of time;
> If ever you have look'd on better days,

> If ever been where bells have knoll'd to church,
> If ever sate at any good man's feast,
> If ever from your eyelids wip'd a tear,
> And know what 'tis to pity, and be pitied,
>
> (II. vii. 109–17)

The Duke echoes his sentiments with enthusiasm, and invites him to a meal served with as ducal a propriety as circumstances permit. The Duke can do much, but *As You Like It* requires, for its proper centre, his daughter. Which brings us to the lovers.

*

While the veteran refugees are thinking of many matters, these newcomers are thinking of one alone. Orlando, so far from finding settled low content in the forest, finds a compulsion to dream of fair women and to publish his poetasting upon every tree; and Rosalind, who had seized the opportunity, while she was about it, to satisfy a girl's tomboy fantasies:

> Were it not better,
> Because that I am more than common tall,
> That I did suit me all points like a man?
> A gallant curtle-axe upon my thigh,
> A boar-spear in my hand, and – in my heart
> Lie there what hidden woman's fear there will –
> We'll have a swashing and a martial outside,
> As many other mannish cowards have
> That do outface it with their semblances.
>
> (I. iii. 114–22)

now finds an echo to her own thoughts in the love-lorn Silvius. 'Alas, poor shepherd searching of [thy wound],/I have by hard adventure found my own' is her sympathetic response to Silvius' plaint (II. iv. 44–5ff). The meeting precipitates the process of self-discovery which the comic device in Act II, the disguise whereby Rosalind both reveals and conceals her true identity, will infinitely advance.

'Arcadia', says Peter Marinelli (and the perceptive remark applies as well to Arden), 'is a middle country of the imagination

... a place of Becoming rather than Being, where an individual's potencies for the arts of life and love and poetry are explored and tested'.[6] Shakespeare's Arcadia offers a further turn: his comic heroine's own potencies for the arts of life and love and poetry are explored and tested by a variety of contingencies even while she is testing and exploring these same potencies in others.

Her initial absence of mind at the first encounter with Silvia is amusingly rendered by her failure to take in Touchstone's derisive parody of fancy shepherds:

> I remember when I was in love, I broke my sword upon a stone, and bid him take that for coming a-night to Jane Smile; and I remember the kissing of her batler and the cow's dugs that her pretty chopp'd hands had milk'd; and I remember the wooing of a peascod instead of her, from whom I took two cods, and giving her them again, said with weeping tears, 'Wear these for my sake'. (II. iv. 46–54)

All she hears, and that inattentively, is his epigrammatic ending: 'as all is mortal in nature, so is all nature in love mortal in folly'. Upon which she sagely replies, 'Thou speak'st wiser than thou art ware of', and misses again entirely the fool's ironic snub: 'Nay, I shall ne'er be ware of mine own wit till I break my shins against it' (II. iv. 58–9).

But this is the last time Rosalind is inattentive or absent-minded. Indeed it is her presence of mind which dominates and characterizes the middle acts.

From the moment when she finds herself trapped in her page role and exclaims in comic consternation, 'Alas the day, what shall I do with my doublet and hose?' to the moment of her unmasking, Ganymede releases in Rosalind her best powers of improvisation, intuition, and witty intelligence. Her quick wit transforms her page disguise into the play's grand comic device, and turns comic predicament to triumphant account. When she says to Celia: 'Good my complexion, doest thou think, though I am caparison'd like a man, I have a doublet and hose in my disposition? One inch of delay more is a South-sea of discovery.' (III. ii. 194–7), her gift for comic hyperbole as well as her ironic self-awareness are delightfully in evidence. But the master invention of the play lies in 'the inch of delay more' which she cannily, deliberately, takes upon herself (though with a handsome young fellow like Orlando wandering about the forest scratching 'Rosalind' on every tree there is nothing that would please her more than to be revealed) and in the 'South-sea of discovery' it allows her to make. For if Orlando discovers culture – sonnets and banquets – in the forest, Rosalind discovers nature, and rejoices in the occasion for the expression of her own ebullient, versatile and polymorph energies. It is a superbly audacious idea, this saucy lackey cure for love, if she can bring it off:

> At which time would I, being but a moonish youth, grieve, be effeminate, changeable, longing and liking, proud, fantastical, apish, shallow, inconstant, full of tears, full of smiles; for every passion something, and for no passion truly any thing, as boys and women are for the most part cattle of this color; would now like him, now loathe him; then entertain him, then forswear him; now weep for him, then spit at him; . . . and this way will I take upon me to wash your liver as clean as a sound sheep's heart, that there shall not be one spot of love in't.
>
> (III. ii. 409–24)

And if she can bring it off, how can she lose? She is invisible. She is in control. She is master–mistress of the situation. She can discover not only what he is like, but what she is like; test his feelings, test her own; mock love and mask love and make love; provoke and bask in the attentions of the lover whose company she most desires, pretend to be the boy she always wanted, perhaps, to be, and permit herself extravagances everyday decorum would certainly preclude: 'Come, woo me, woo me; for now I am in a holiday humor, and like enough to consent. What would you say to me now, and I were your very very Rosalind?' (IV. i. 68–71).

It is no wonder the gaiety of this twinned character is infectious, the ebullience irrepressible, the high spirits inimitable. She/he is all things to all men and enjoys every moment of this androgynous ventriloquist's carnival, the more especially since, unlike her sisters in disguise, Julia and Viola, she has the relief of candid self-exposure to her confidante Celia as well: 'O coz, coz, coz, my pretty little coz, that thou didst know how many fathom deep I am in love! But it cannot be sounded; my affection hath an unknown bottom, like the bay of Portugal' (IV. i. 205–8). 'You have simply misus'd our sex in your love-prate', complains the soberer Celia, concerned for sexual solidarity. But what is sexual solidarity to her is to her chameleon cousin sexual solipsism and she will have none of it.

She provokes preposterously, and so exorcizes (in this a double for Orlando) the paranoia of male anti-feminism with her dire threat:

> I will be more jealous of thee than a Barbary cock-pigeon over his hen, more clamorous than a parrot against rain, more new-fangled than an ape, more giddy in my desires than a monkey. I will weep for nothing, like Diana in the fountain, and I will do that when you are disposed to be merry. I will laugh like a hyen, and that when you are inclin'd to sleep.
>
> (IV. i. 149–56)

only to reveal herself with utter if inadvertent candour the next moment: 'Alas, dear love, I cannot lack thee two hours' (IV. i. 178) and then, to cover her slip, immediately dissimulates again in the mock tirade of an abused and long-suffering wife: 'Ay, go your ways, go your ways; I knew what you would prove; my friends told me as much, and I thought no less. That flattering tongue of yours won me. 'Tis but one cast away, and so come death! Two a'clock is your hour?' (IV. i. 185–6).

Her double role is a triumph of characterization through impersonation, inconsistency, not consistency, being the key to dramatic versimilitude if a complex and dynamic individual is to be represented. More, Rosalind, the girl, in whom natural impulse is finely cultivated and worldly wisdom cohabits with a passionate nature, together with her own 'twin' Ganymede, in whom a youth's beauty and a youth's jaunty irreverence combine, provides the double indemnity of comedy with lavish generosity. The duality of her masculine and feminine roles – itself an abolition of disjunction – gratifies our craving both for pleasure and reality, satisfies a deep defensive need for intellectual scepticism as well as an equally deep need for impulsive and limitless abandon, provides at once for cerebration and celebration,[7] resolves the dichotomies of nature and culture, wisdom and folly, mockery and festivity.

I find in a recent study of what existential psychologists call 'peak experience', interesting confirmation of the theory of comic therapy Shakespeare's practice, particularly in this play, appears to support. 'Peak experiences', says Abraham H. Maslow, make characters in plays and their audiences more apt to feel 'that life in general is worth while, even if it is usually drab, pedestrian, painful or ungratifying, since beauty, excitement, honesty, play, goodness, truth, and meaningfulness have been demonstrated to him to exist. . . . Life itself is validated, and suicide and death wishing must become less likely.'[8]

Thus the make-believe courtship, invented on the pretext of furnishing a cure for Orlando's love melancholy (or at least for his versification!), provides Rosalind with a homeopathic *remedia amoris* for hers. Free to fantasize, explore, experiment, she confers upon the audience a vivid sense that the mortal coil might not be solely a curse, nor the working-day world of briars beyond transfiguring.

And even that is not all. Ganymede's undertaking to cure Orlando's love-longing passes the time entertainingly in the greenwood but it also runs Rosalind into difficulties with the native population, thus providing the canonical knot of errors through a mistaken identity, and Ganymede with more livers to wash as clean as a sound sheep's heart.

Phebe's high-handed scorn for her doleful lover's courtly style exposes the substance of her own callousness as well as the absurd affectations of courtly love:

'Tis pretty, sure, and very probable,
That eyes, that are the frail'st and softest things,
Who shut their coward gates on atomies,
Should be called tyrants, butchers, murtherers!
Now I do frown on thee with all my heart,
And if mine eyes can wound, now let them kill thee.
Now counterfeit to swound; why, now fall down,
Or if thou canst not, O, for shame, for shame,
Lie not, to say mine eyes are murtherers!

                                        (III. v. 11–19)

Rosalind, too, knows that 'these are all lies'; that 'men have died from time to time, and worms have eaten them, but not for love' (IV. i. 108), she, too, knows that 'men are April when they woo, December when they wed', and that maids 'are May when they are maids, but the sky changes when they are wives' (IV. i. 147–8). But her realism is of another order altogether than Phebe's callow literalism, and is vouched for by the vigour with which she scolds the pair of them, combining the swashbuckling gusto of Ganymede with the passionate sincerity of Rosalind, in a *nosce teipsum* totally free of illusion:

> 'Od's my little life,
> I think she means to tangle my eyes too!
> No, faith, proud mistress, hope not after it.
> 'Tis not your inky brows, your black silk hair,
> Your bugle eyeballs, nor your cheek of cream
> That can entame my spirits to your worship.
> You foolish shepherd, wherefore do you follow
>   her,
> Like foggy south, puffing with wind and rain?
> You are a thousand times a properer man
> Than she a woman. 'Tis such fools as you
> That make the world full of ill-favor'd children.
> 'Tis not her glass, but you that flatters her,
> And out of you she sees her self more proper
> Than any of her lineaments can show her.
> But, mistress, know yourself, down on your knees,
> And thank heaven, fasting, for a good man's love;
> For I must tell you friendly in your ear,
> Sell when you can, you are not for all markets.
>   (III. v. 43–60)

Ralph Berry takes a counter-view of *As You Like It*, and especially of this incident.[9] He finds unease, irritation and hostility – the groundswell of a power struggle latent or overt – to be the dominant motif of the play. This, however, is a view as over-selective as Jaques' seven ages speech. What it leaves out is the fun. But it is also not strictly accurate. Berry accounts, for instance, for the 'quite astonishing warmth' of Rosalind's diatribe – 'thirty odd lines of vulgar abuse' he calls it – in terms of Phebe appearing to Rosalind as a subtly threatening parallel or caricature of herself. 'Phebe is a domineering woman who . . . has mastered her man; so is Rosalind.' But when the incident occurs Rosalind has mastered no one. She has merely suggested to Orlando that they meet again. Phebe is, to be sure, the phantom Ganymede conjures to cure Orlando of just such love-longing as Silvius'. The caricature double surely provides a foil to the hidden Rosalind; and the comedy arising from the idea of Rosalind meeting a 'real' embodiment of Ganymede's fantasy is quite lost in Berry's reductive reading.[10]

It is no wonder that Phebe, whose dejected lover Silvius is clearly not manly enough for his imperious mistress, falls head over heels in love with this high-spirited outspokenness, thus hoisting Rosalind/Ganymede with his/her own epicene petard. Ganymede has in his face that which Phebe would feign call master, it seems, and this is a tangle not easy to untie. A remedy for deadlock, however, is provided by the very occurrence which virtually exhausts the Ganymede device. The arrival of Oliver, reformed by his experience of courtly treachery, with the tale of his brother's heroic rescue (a recapitulation of the native *virtu* of the wrestling exploit on a higher moral level) provides not only proof that Orlando is no tame snake like Silvius, but also a patrimony for him and a partner for Celia. The exhaustion of the comic device is neatly dramatized by the emotional collapse of Rosalind at the sight of the bloodied handkerchief, and there is now nothing in the world to prevent the trickster heroine from undoing the turmoil she has caused. Her power to do this is beautifully 'masqued' by the chiming quartet of Act V, scene ii: Love is 'to be made of sighs and tears' –

> *Silvius*   And so am I for Phebe.
> *Phebe*   And I for Ganymede.
> *Orlando*   And I for Rosalind.
> *Rosalind*   And I for no woman.   (v. ii. 85–93)

and so on, until Rosalind begs, 'Pray you no more of this, 'tis like the howling of Irish wolves against the moon' (v. ii. 109–10).

This is the ironic voice which ends the play with the classic plea for applause in the epilogue, and it is worth a moment's further reflection. That Rosalind is still dressed as Ganymede has been convincingly argued in terms of the scarcity of time available at that point for a boy to change into elaborate women's clothing.[11] But there is a cogent argument to be drawn from the play's own dialectical resolution. If she is still Ganymede in the epilogue, then 'If I were a woman' is spoken out of her saucy lackey role, as the man-of-the-world bawdy of 'that between you and the women the play may please' seems to suggest. She is thus drawing the audience, too, into her transvestite trickster's net, prolonging the duplicity of self-discovery and self-concealment, the enchanting game of both/and. But if she is dressed as Rosalind, then 'If I were a woman' is spoken over the heads, so to speak, of characters and play, by the boy-actor of Shakespeare's company, and this will *collapse* the dramatic illusion of 'real' make-believe from which the whole play draws its dynamic power. Shakespeare, I submit, is not calling attention to his play as play, as opposed to reality: he is calling attention to Rosalind's 'play' as a component reality would do well to absorb.

At the end of *As You Like It* dukes are restored to their dukedoms, sons to their inheritances. Wickedness has burst, like a boil, by some mysterious spontaneous combustion, leaving not a rack behind. But not all Jacks have their Jills. Jacques is unassimilated. But he is by nature a solitary and continues his travels, happily sucking melancholy out of all occasions as a weasel sucks eggs, on the outer edge of remedy.

There is also unaccommodated William at the marriage feast. But there's hope even there, if Touchstone's fidelity can be relied upon; Jaques gives him two months (v. iv. 192). For though 'wedlock', in the view of that philosopher of life's most minimal expectations, 'will be nibbling', what of it?

But what though? Courage! As horns are odious, they are necessary. It is said, 'Many a man knows no end of his goods'. Right! many a man has good horns and knows no end of them. Well, that is the dowry of his wife, 'tis none of his own getting. Horns? even so. Poor men alone? No, no, the noblest deer hath them as huge as the rascal. Is the single man therefore bless'd?

No, as a wall'd town is more worthier than a village, so is the
forehead of a married man more honorable than the bare brow
of a bachelor . . .   (III. iii. 51–61)

If this is a mockery of 'romance' it is also a mockery of 'reason'. A
protuberance is a protuberance, whether it be the bastion of a
walled town or the horned frontlet of a married man. To Touchstone, logic is a bagatelle. All is immaterially interchangeable:
court and country, culture and nature, fact and fiction, sense and
folly, wedlock and non-wedlock, for that matter, too. Earthly
things made even atone together in Touchstone's anti-logic as
well as in Hymen's conjuration. Touchstone's courtship has been
a mocking parody of the affectations of the mid-level characters
Phebe and Silvius; but he is also a mocking foil to Rosalind's
superior synthesis of culture and nature, just as his bawdy
'prick' song (If a hart do lack a hind [III. ii. 100–12]) is foil to her
own frank naturalism. In this matter she can give as good as she
gets, too, in Mercutio's very vein (III. ii. 117–20).

                                        *

'Rosalind, Viola, and, to a less extent Beatrice', says Charlton
(forgetting, however, Julia and Hippolyta),

> have entered into the possession of spiritual endowments
> which, if hitherto suspected to exist at all, had either been
> distrusted as dangerous or had become moribund through
> desuetude . . . they have claimed the intuitive, the subcon-
> scious, and the emotional as instruments by which personality
> may bring itself to a fuller consciousness of and a completer
> harmony with the realities of existence. They have left Theseus
> far behind; they have also outgrown Falstaff.[12]

It is perhaps, as I have tried to show, less a matter of outgrow-
ing Falstaff, than of replacing him, by a new combination: the Lady
and the Fool. Touchstone is a professional jester,[13] not a bumbling
village constable or a Bacchic life-force. He is not a merry fool,
either. He is too Ecclesiastes-wise; and besides his feet hurt. But
his burlesque fool's wisdom serves throughout most excellently to
mediate our recognition of the Erastian higher folly of his ebullient mistress. When Wylie Sypher speaks of 'the unruliness of the

flesh and its vitality', he characterizes the buffoon nature in all its manifestations. 'Comedy', Sypher continues, 'is essentially a carrying away of Death, a triumph over mortality by some absurd faith in rebirth, restoration, salvation.'[14] Perhaps we could say that Touchstone epitomizes the absurdity, and Rosalind the faith; and that it is the interlocking and paradoxical partnership of the two that characterizes this second, and second last of Shakespeare's post-Falstaffian comedies.

Shakespeare is not done with the wayward and unruly erotic passions. Nor will he be, needless to say, until the last word he contributes to *Two Noble Kinsmen*. But his romantic comedy treatment of them does come to an end with his next play *Twelfth Night*, in which the rivalries and duplicities, twinnings and doublings of the battle of the sexes are further extended into the ambivalent twinnings, duplicities and doublings within the lovers' own individual identities.

NOTES

1 C. L. Barber, 'The Use of Comedy in *As You Like It*', *PQ*, vol. xxi (1942), p. 353.

2 Harold Jenkins, '*As You Like It*', *Shakespeare Studies*, vol. 8 (1955), pp. 40–1.

3 Unless, of course, we choose to invert the play entirely, and make the solitary, melancholy Jaques our Diogenes, and the rest mere mortal, convivial fools.

4 As D. J. Palmer puts it in 'Art and Nature in *As You Like It*', *PQ*, vol. xlix (1970), pp. 33–5: 'the forest brings its inhabitants face to face with their own shadows everyone becomes more fully himself in the forest'. I find several of my observations anticipated by Palmer in this important essay, but his argument is meshed into discussion of the theme of Art and Nature and the bearing of his remarks therefore somewhat oblique to my own concerns.

5 Theobald emended 'not' to 'but': 'Here feel we but the penalty Adam,/The seasons' difference . . .' etc., and many editors follows the eminent good sense of the emendation.

6 Peter V. Marinelli, *Pastoral* (London: Methuen, 1971), p. 37.

7 The neat opposition comes from Michael McCanles' excellent account in *Dialectical Criticism and Renaissance Literature* (Los Angeles: University of California Press, 1975).

8 Abraham H. Maslow, *Towards a Psychology of Being* (New York: Van Nostrand Reinhold, 1968), pp. 101–2. Quoted by Michael Payne in *SRO*, edited by W. R. Elton, nos. 7–8 (1972/4), p. 76.

9 'No Exit from Arden', *Shakespeare's Comedies* (Princeton University Press, 1972), pp. 175–95.

10 Phebe and Silvius are a particularly fine example of the subtle effects Shakespeare derives from his middle-level mirror image characters. Richard Levin, *The Multiple Plot in English Renaissance Drama* (Chicago: Chicago University Press, 1971), has noted the social stratification in the play and points out that it is marked by appropriate emblematic animals: the stag for the courtiers, sheep for Phebe the shepherdess and the lowly goat for Audrey.

11 Maura Slattery Kuhn, 'Much Virtue in If', *Shakespeare Quarterly*, vol. 28 (Winter, 1977).

12 H. B. Charlton, *Shakespearean Comedy* (London: Methuen, 1938), p. 283.

13 Robert Armin had by this time replaced Will Kempe for the fool's roles in Shakespeare's company, a circumstance which no doubt played its part in the Shakespearean transformation here described.

14 Wylie Sypher, 'The Meaning of Comedy' in *Comedy* (New York: Doubleday, 1956), p. 220.

XI

NATURE'S BIAS

Twelfth Night has been called a 'masterpiece of recapitulation'.[1] Twins, reunions, rivalries, love's tamings and matings, mistakings and unmaskings, the ladder of language upon whose lower rungs ambitious nitwits bark their skinny shins, a (finally) domesticated Falstaffian rogue, an impostor whose posturing is an oblique and distorted mirror image of the protagonists' besetting deficiencies (even his name is a dark anagram of his mistress's), the page disguise, the partnership of lady and mocking fool. It is familiar Shakespeare country, and the Terentian itinerary is familiar, too,[2] save in one important respect. There are no interfering or match-making parents in *Twelfth Night*, as there are virtually none in *As You Like It* as well. Rosalind's father, important as he is, as we have seen, is not to be thought of while there are young men like Orlando about in the forest, and the father of the Illyrian twins provides no more than the canonical mole for identifications. Fathers will return, to be sure, in the tragedies and the romances, but they are at present in eclipse, leaving the field to the initiatives and the entanglements of their daughters, and when these are scarcely adequate, to great creating Nature herself. As Sebastian says:

> So come it, lady, you have been mistook;
> But Nature to her bias drew in that. (v. i. 259–60)

and truly a creative and providential musicianship is required to
compose the oceanic Illyrian eros, as Illyria's Duke intimates in
his very first speech:

> If music be the food of love, play on,
> Give me excess of it; that surfeiting,
> The appetite may sicken, and so die.
> That strain again, it had a dying fall;
> O, it came o'er my ear like the sweet sound
> That breathes upon a bank of violets,
> Stealing and giving odor. Enough, no more,
> 'Tis not so sweet now as it was before.
> O spirit of love, how quick and fresh art thou,
> That notwithstanding thy capacity
> Receiveth as the sea, nought enters there,
> Of what validity and pitch soe'er,
> But falls into abatement and low price
> Even in a minute. . . .   (I. i. 1–14)

Illyria, it will be remembered, is sea-girt. Not only are the twins
cast up out of the ocean, and the impression of a coastal town
maintained in the idiom of the inhabitants: 'Will you hoist sail,
sir?' says Maria, for instance, to the snubbed Viola (I. v. 202); we
also have two sea captains in assiduous attendance, and imagery
of the 'hungry sea' presenting itself constantly to the protagonists'
imaginations.

The first exchange between Orsino and his entourage advances
considerably our understanding of what is deficient, imperfect or
wanting in Illyria. Orsino is restless, dissatisfied, vacillating between moods, introspective to a degree, with a mind full of
shapes, but without an object upon which his mind can rest and
with which his desire can engage. And Curio, whose name is
significant, as is Valentine's – we note that the names of these two
servitors of Orsino's suggest connoisseurship in what the Vic-
torians called the tender passion – provides our next clue.

Curio   Will you go hunt, my lord?
Duke   What, Curio?
Curio   The hart.

Duke Why, so I do, the noblest that I have.
O, when mine eyes did see Olivia first,
Methought she purg'd the air of pestilence!
That instant was I turn'd into a hart,
And my desires, like fell and cruel hounds,
E'er since pursue me.   (I. i. 16–23)

The Duke's reply informs us of Olivia. But it also informs us of Orsino's self-image. Before the hunting metaphor is over, it is Orsino who is transformed into a pursued creature, not Olivia. He is Actaeon, turned into a stag and pursued by the hounds of his desire. 'How will she love', sighs Orsino, 'when the rich golden shaft/Hath kill'd the flock of all affections else/That live in her;' (I. i. 34). This is an image which neatly joins the double face of venery, phallic and predatory. But it is to sweet beds of flowers that the Duke returns, to be alone in the delicious auto-eroticism of love thoughts and the high fantastical images they generate.

It is common in the criticism to hear of the malaise of Illyria as having to do with sentimentality, affectation, infatuation, narcissism. It is, says Jon S. Lawry 'a land transfixed in self love'.[3] 'Orsino glories in the proper fickleness and moodiness' of the love-sick swain, and is 'unaware that he is in love with love rather than with a person'.[4] Olivia is in similar case, and only in Viola and Sebastian do we find 'a love as honest and spring-like as Illyria's is affected and wintry'.[5] Jan Kott on the other hand, takes an antithetical view which stresses the symbolic import of the sex-disguise. 'The real theme of Illyria', as of the Sonnets, he says, 'is erotic delirium, or the metamorphoses of sex . . . the impossibility of choice between the youth and the woman, the fragile boundary between friendship and love . . . the universality of desire which cannot be contained in or limited to one sex'.[6]

I wish to argue for a *via media* between these two views, grounded in the discovery of Shakespeare's unfolding comic form which analysis of his early comedies allows us to make. The formula which comes closest to the theory of Shakespeare's deep structure which I have been pressing in these pages is Barber's 'through release to clarification', but oddly enough his own chapter on *Twelfth Night* – 'Testing Courtesy and Humanity'[7] does not seem to me to grapple with the central issues of the play. A closer examination of the comic process of imbalance and excess, of preposterous fantasy, of disinhibition and of re-equilibrium is required.

Before the first act is over we shall have been given striking insights into the comic disposition in Illyria, which subsequent events will bear out.

'How will she love', sighs Orsino, 'when the rich golden/shaft/ Hath kill'd the flock of all affections else/That live in her' (I. i. 34). As has been noted, it is a truculent, masculine, predatory image. But when he sends his proxy page to pay court on his behalf, it is, strangely, on account of the page's youthful nubility, his harmless tenderness of aspect. One might well have expected an amatory ambassador to be more self-assertive than his client, not less. But Cesario will be a suitable suppliant, Orsino feels:

> For they shall yet belie thy happy years,
> That say thou art a man. Diana's lip
> Is not more smooth and rubious; thy small pipe
> Is as the maiden's organ, shrill and sound,
> And all is semblative a woman's part.
>
> (I. iv. 30–4)

The speech tells us much: of the way Orsino conceives of the role of suitor; of what he imagines the wishes of the lady he is wooing to be; and of those features of his new page which have caught his eye and noticeably advanced the page in his affections.

It is the femininity of his young page which appeals to him, but not, I submit, in narcissistic attraction to a quality his own nature shares. As has already been observed, Orsino is Shakespeare's latest embodiment of the courtly-love convention. He is conducting his amorous affairs in the style of woeful and love-lorn Petrarchanism which had been the target of the satirical mockery of Speed, Moth and Ganymede himself. He is Silvius in *As You Like It* writ large. He is, it will be noticed, conservative in his tastes, nostalgic for the old age, and scornful of these 'most brisk and giddy-paced times' (II. iv. 6). He is, in a way, a Don Quixote as out of joint with his times as that good Knight was with the very same times. Or, as was the doting and chivalric Don Armado, who did not enjoy any noticeable success with Jacquenetta. In the realistically conceived Elizabethan milieu of *Twelfth Night* the suppliant posture is easily made to appear ineffectual and even effeminate. In *As You Like It*, too, it will be remembered, the meek entreaties of Silvius did not fare well with the high-handed Phebe, who, for her part, promptly fell in love with the swashbuckling airs and demonstratively non-feminine demeanour of Ganymede. Shakespeare, it seems, is using the outworn Petrarchan postures that Orsino strikes to characterize the deficiency in him, at any rate *vis-à-vis* Olivia, of a sufficiently masculine self-assertiveness.

The portrait of Orsino is subtly drawn; as subtly as is that of Olivia. They are both in unstable tension with themselves, Olivia through the exigencies of her circumstances, Orsino through a degree of self-delusion or misguidedness regarding his own nature and his role as lover.

Fatherless and brotherless, Olivia is the sole mistress of her household. She is its source of authority, and her unruly house guests are there to show that she is able to take command, though the turbulence below stairs under Sir Toby's aegis indicates that her control is not impregnable. She leans upon her steward in her lonely eminence, and not only to ward off a suit from the count (I. v. 109). But her even-handed distribution of remonstrance and consolation to the former shows her not inconsiderable capacity for mastery:

> *Olivia* O, you are sick of self-love Malvolio, and taste with a distemper'd appetite. To be generous, guiltless, and of free disposition, is to take those things for bird-bolts that you deem cannon-bullets. There is no slander in an allowed fool, though he do nothing but rail; nor no railing in a known discreet man, though he do nothing but reprove.
>
> (I. v. 90–6)

Interestingly enough, Sebastian later argues for her sanity in an apparently mad world on the grounds that otherwise

> She could not sway her house, command her followers,
> Take and give back affairs, and their dispatch,
> With such a smooth, discreet, and stable bearing
> As I perceive she does. . . .   (IV. iii. 17–20)

But that this is not the sole dedication of her life is perhaps indicated by the shrewd Feste's ironically appreciative acknowledgement of her defence of fools, in the form of an off-hand blessing upon his madonna's future maternity:[8] 'Thou has spoke for us, madonna, as if thy eldest son should be a fool; whose skull Jove cram with brains! for – here he comes – one of thy kin has a most weak *pia mater*' (I. v. 112–15).

Moreover, 'She'll none o' th' Count', Toby tells Andrew. 'She'll not match above her degree, neither in estate, years, nor wit; I have heard her swear't. Tut, there's life in't, man' (I. iii. 109–11). No word here of the mourning. True, the rich jest here lies in Toby's poker-faced encouragement of Andrew's hopes for a match with his wealthy niece, a matter in which Toby has no small stake. But throughout the early scenes our impression grows that the cloistering of Olivia is just possibly a mourning of convenience to ward off an unwelcome suitor. And is it any wonder indeed, that this lady, gallantly and graciously and not without difficulty performing a man's role in her household, cannot fall in love with a Duke in whom the balance of the masculine and feminine is diametrically discordant to her own? She supposes him virtuous, knows him noble, of great estate, of fresh and stainless youth, good reputation, free, learned, valiant and handsome (II. i. 258–62). Yet she cannot love him.

Viola's arrival upon the coast of Illyria reveals, however, a degree of ambivalence in her behaviour as well as in Olivia's. 'O that I served that lady', she exclaims when she hears of the latter's loss of father and brother. But she does not fly to the Countess Olivia for succour, woman to woman, despite her sympathy for a fellow-mourner. Instead she chooses to be adventurously epicene in the Duke's entourage. Viola escapes her feminine state but at the cost of a (symbolic) castration: it is as a eunuch (to account for her voice) that she will 'sing/And speak to him in many sorts of music' (I. ii. 57); Olivia, cloistered for a dead brother's love, suffers a real incarceration.

The play thus invites us to perceive a degree of instability or volatility in the perception of themselves of all these three protagonists. This being so, no play of Shakespeare's is launched with greater dispatch into its vortex of truth-discovering deceptions than this. Act I, scene iv, already finds the disguised Viola a reluctant ambassador, on behalf of her deceived employer:

> I'll do my best
> To woo your lady. [*Aside*] Yet a barful strife!
> Whoe'er I woo, myself would be his wife.
>
> (I. iv. 40–2)

The great embassy scene in Act I is prepared for by Malvolio's acidulous reply to Olivia's question concerning the stubborn messenger:

> *Olivia*   Of what personage and years is he?
> *Malvolio*   Not yet old enough for a man, nor young enough for a boy; as a squash is before 'tis a peascod, or a codling when 'tis almost an apple. 'Tis with him in standing water, between boy and man. He is very well-favor'd, and he speaks very shrewishly. One would think his mother's milk were scarce out of him.   (I. v. 155–62)

And presently we observe that he speaks very shrewishly indeed, and with a blend of urbane irony, provocative impertinence and taut vulnerability which might well catch attention harder to catch than that of the Lady Olivia. Both ladies are veiled in the encounter and the drama therefore takes place in the audience's mind on two distinct levels. What we watch is a wit combat in which each side gives as good as she gets. The text of Orsino's bosom provides a prolegomenon, the unveiled picture of Olivia's face the centrepiece. 'Excellently done, if God did all', says Viola (I. v. 236), the impudence a mask, we infer, for a pang at the heart. Olivia's coolly unperturbed reply, ' 'Tis in grain, sir, 'twill endure wind and weather' (I. v. 237) produces the genuine, and generous, compliment of

> 'Tis beauty truly blent, whose red and white
> Nature's own sweet and cunning hand laid on.
> Lady, you are the cruell'st she alive
> If you will lead these graces to the grave,
> And leave the world no copy.   (I. v. 239–44)

Nothing could be less like the courtly hyperboles of Orsino's complaints to his disdainful beauty. This unaffected candour transcends finesses of courtship diplomacy. We know why: this really is woman to woman. But to Olivia's ears, we may suppose, the words of the new ambassador must possess a ring of undissimulated, disinterested, unconventionalized frankness totally new to her. The Lady Olivia retains her own urbane self-possession, however:

> O, sir, I will not be so hard-hearted; I will give out divers schedules of my beauty. It shall be inventoried, and every particle and utensil labell'd to my will: as, *item*, two lips, indifferent red; *item* two grey eyes, with lids to them; *item*, one neck, one chin, and so forth. Were you sent hither to praise me?   (I. v. 244–9)

until a reminder of Orsino's Petrarchan ardours – 'adorations, fertile tears . . . groans that thunder love . . . sighs of fire' (I. v. 255–6) causes her to reveal for a moment a chink in her armour. Her description of Orsino (I. v. 258–63) (honey, no doubt, in the ears of his ambassador) is accompanied by the puzzlement, even the distress of 'I cannot love him . . . But yet, I cannot love him'. What does he lack, that, strangely enough, his cheeky ambassador apparently possesses, since the sisterly mourning ritual is cast aside in a trice after their first encounter?

It is her adventurous, plucky, give-as-good-as-you-get braggartry, we are invited to infer, that not only gains her entrance to the Lady Olivia, but captures the lady's heart. The touch of reckless forthrightness, the spirit, the candour, the imaginative panache with which the willow cabin fantasy is described and courtly compliment revivified in the loyal cantons of condemned love in which Cesario would 'Hallow your name to the reverberate hills,/And make the babbling gossip of the air/Cry out "Olivia"!' (I. v. 272–4) – these are surely precisely the self-assertive, masculine qualities which have been lacking in Orsino and which promptly bring out the womanly Olivia, a 'bringing out' in which discretion becomes impetuosity and composure disintegrates in distracted doting upon the Duke's peevish messenger.

But if the embassy thus brings about a speedy Nemesis upon Viola's hermaphrodite adventure, it also provides a rich source of information concerning her master's fluctuating self-image and with beautifully designed symmetry the undisguisable femininity of Cesario/Viola brings out in Orsino a new, mature and manly good sense.

It is a scene of intimate man-to-man confidences, during which Orsino advises his young companion regarding the desirable age of a wife. The latter's choice, 'About your years, my Lord', would be

> Too old, by heaven. Let still the woman take
> An elder than herself, so wears she to him;
> So sways she level in her husband's heart.
> For, boy, however we do praise ourselves,
> Our fancies are more giddy and unfirm,
> More longing, wavering, sooner lost and worn,
> Than women's are.   (II. iv. 29–35)

But it is a moment only. Orsino is in unstable equilibrium in his views of women, and sways from the normal male sex-object chauvinism of

> For women are as roses, whose fair flow'r
> Being once display'd doth fall that very hour.
>   (II. iv. 38–9)

to an inflated and self-regarding tirade in which he casts himself in the role of neo-Platonic courtier saint, and sweeps aside the claim made by Cesario for the integrity of the lady's affections in the case:

> There is no woman's sides
> Can bide the beating of so strong a passion
> As love doth give my heart; no woman's heart
> So big, to hold so much; they lack retention.
> Alas, their love may be call'd appetite,
> No motion of the liver, but the palate,
> That suffer surfeit, cloyment, and revolt,
> But mine is all as hungry as the sea,
> And can digest as much. . . .   (II. iv. 93–101)

The Duke's mind, as Feste says, is a very opal-changeable taffeta. But the changes can be charted. The encounters between the Duke and his page offer rich material for inference. When Orsino responds to Cesario's tale of a sister who pined for love with a green and yellow melancholy, smiling at grief, with the question: 'But died thy sister of her love my boy?' it is not in mere curiosity or sudden sympathetic interest in the tale that I believe he speaks. It is a pressing, triumphant rhetorical question, which still harps upon the superiority of men as martyrs to love. The song he requested, it will be remembered, and which spurred him to renewed beseechings to his sovereign cruelty, was the complaint of a sad true lover, slain by a fair cruel maid.

We begin to understand Orsino's self-delusion. Olivia represents to him the sonneteer's lady he believes himself in love with, while what his nature truly needs and responds to is the youthful, dependent, and devoted femininity of Viola which is scarcely veiled by the page disguise. What we are thus invited to perceive in each of these protagonists is not merely illusion, posture or attitudinizing. They are each in a state of disequilibrium regarding masculine and feminine roles and impulses which they themselves misassess. And it is precisely the comic device, the misapprehensions it entails, the *processus turbarum* of tumult and preposterous complication which serves to bring out, and even exacerbate their latent sexual identities. In no play of Shakespeare's is the effect of the comic device, source of error and truth, more aptly therapeutic. It plunges them into misprision, fools them to the top of their bent, ties a 'knot too hard for [Viola] to untie' but in the volatile process they are all released from the various traps – emotional or circumstantial – which prevent the benign fulfilment of their natures. For it is not that there is no consonance between temperament and self-image. Orsino is a touch effeminate, Olivia is masterful, Viola is headstrong. We have only to imagine characters dominated by these traits, growing fixed and embedded and compulsive in them, to be aware of the proximity of Jonsonian humours (in literature) or personality problems (in life) to this Illyrian fantasia.

But we do not need Jonson. We have Malvolio. Not to mention the feckless Andrew, who, though he has the back trick simply as strong as any man in Illyria, and was adored once, is perhaps as marvellously impenetrable to self-knowledge as any character in drama. The lower plot counterpoints the upper as in *A Midsummer Night's Dream* and *Love's Labour's Lost*, and its scenes are cunningly interspersed with those above stairs. Its practices are devised by the lively Maria, as witty a piece of Eve's flesh as any in Illyria, as the disguise stratagem was devised by Viola, and both in subtle ways, unmask.

When we first observe Malvolio alone, unaware that he is being watched, he is practising behaviour to his shadow, and fantasizing, in a way that brings Sir Toby near to apoplexy, a marriage with Olivia:

> *Malvolio* Having been three months married to her, sitting in my state –
> *Sir Toby* O, for a stone-bow, to hit him in the eye!
> *Malvolio* Calling my officers about me, in my branch'd velvet gown; having come from a day-bed, where I have left Olivia sleeping –
> *Sir Toby* Fire and brimstone!
> *Fabian* O, peace, peace!
> *Malvolio* And then to have the humor of state; and after a demure travel of regard – telling them I know my place as I would they should do theirs – to ask for my kinsman Toby –
> *Sir Toby* Bolts and shackles!
> *Fabian* O, peace, peace, peace! Now, now.
> *Malvolio* Seven of my people, with an obedient start, make out for him. I frown the while, and perchance wind up my watch, or play with my – some rich jewel. Toby approaches; curtsies there to me –
> *Sir Toby* Shall this fellow live?   (II. v. 44–62)

That place and power are his obsessive motivations is plain to be seen, and neatly dramatized by the fingering of his steward's badge of office, which fantasy transforms to 'some rich jewel'. If the main protagonists are confused or in unstable equilibrium about their sexual identities, Malvolio can hardly be said to possess a *sexual* identity at all. It is surely not by chance that Maria's maxim,

'Some are born great, some achieve greatness, and some have
greatness thrust upon them' parodies the Gospel according to
Matthew on the subject of marriage: 'For there are some eunuchs,
which were so born from their mother's womb; and there are
some eunuchs, which were made eunuchs of men: and there be
eunuchs, which have made themselves eunuchs for the kingdom
of heaven's sake' (Matt. XIX. 12). And Malvolio strutting and
preening and being unctuously coy in yellow stockings and cross
garters is doubly ludicrous to the extent that he is doubly
deluded.

> *Olivia*   Why, how dost thou, man? What is the matter with
>   thee?
> *Malvolio*   Not black in my mind, though yellow in my legs. It
>   did come to his hands, and commands shall be executed. I
>   think we do know the sweet Roman hand.
> *Olivia*   Wilt thou go to bed, Malvolio?
> *Malvolio*   To bed? Ay, sweet heart, and I'll come to thee.
> *Olivia*   God comfort thee! Why dost thou smile so, and kiss
>   thy hand so oft?   (III. iv. 24–33)

This caricature of a self-image totally unconsonant with the
facts is repeated in the idiotic Aguecheek, who, though occasion-
ally capable of regretting his over-expenditure of time in fenc-
ing, dancing and bear-baiting rather than in the arts, is never
less than complacent about his achievements. His Nemesis will
be the duel; Malvolio's the exorcism rites of Sir Topaz, in which
Feste's elegantly learned fooling and his pantomimic virtuosity
magically create the madness imputed to the imprisoned
steward:

> *Malvolio*   I am not mad, Sir Topaz, I say to you this house is
>   dark.
> *Clown*   Madman, thou errest. I say there is no darkness but
>   ignorance, in which thou art more puzzled than the Egyp-
>   tians in their fog.
> *Malvolio*   I say this house is as dark as ignorance, though
>   ignorance were as dark as hell; and I say there was never man
>   thus abus'd. . . .   (IV. ii. 40–7)

It is customary in Shakespeare's comic tumults for things to get worse before they can get better. Impulses released must spin out of control, become preposterous or excessive before the system can reject or properly harmonize them. Thus Olivia hurls discretion to the winds in her pursuit of Cesario and in her precipitous marriage, which, added to Cesario's smooth and rubious lip brings out an excess of masculine aggressiveness in Orsino. The speech in Act V, scene i, in which this is expressed is as packed and as menacing as anything in the tragedies still to be written:

> But this your minion, whom I know you love,
> And whom, by heaven I swear, I tender dearly,
> Him will I tear out of that cruel eye,
> Where he sits crowned in his master's spite.
> Come boy, with me, my thoughts are ripe in mischief.
> I'll sacrifice the lamb that I do love,
> To spite a raven's heart within a dove.   (v. i. 125–31)

It is a dangerous moment. It is the moment of incipient disaster, of incipient tragic possibility, for which the remedies in comic plots provide a providential salvation.

The remedy in *Twelfth Night* is, of course, the appearance of Sebastian, which closes the gap opened at the beginning of the play by his loss at sea – so far as Viola knew; and it is at the point in the narrative sequence when the comic device – Viola's disguise as a boy – is pretty well exhausted, unable to be useful any longer, that he reappears. The exhaustion of the device has been hilariously brought out by her *cri de coeur* when she is faced with the now unavoidable duel – 'A little thing would make me tell them how much I lack of a man.' She is saved by Antonio at that point so that Sebastian will be able to make his own appearance at precisely the moment in the sequence when it will be most effective, conclusive and clarifying.

It is an *anagnorisis* in the fullest sense. A recognition scene in which the characters' recognitions and the audiences' larger cognitions fall harmoniously into place. When Sebastian appears in Act V, scene i, he supplies at once the brother Viola believes lost, the husband Olivia believes she has married, and the key to the mystery of the 'dissembling cub' Orsino believes he has cherished to his own disadvantage. But what we have particularly to take in, and what precipitates our understanding of the play is more than this neat solution to the errors and mistaken identities caused by Viola's disguise. What I believe we are invited to take in is the unequivocal manliness of the young man Sebastian. He, as it appears from the broken coxcombs, has made his appearance as the 'firago' both the dauntless duelsters believed the other to be. He has laid about him to such good effect that poor Andrew calls him the 'very devil incardinate'. True, Andrew's is perhaps not the last word on martial valour, but his broken pate and Toby's are there in evidence. Barber has noted that 'To see this manly reflex is delightful – almost a relief. The particular implausibility that there should be an identical man to take Viola's place with Olivia is submerged in the general, beneficent realization that there is such a thing as a man.'9 I would like to press the point further. Sebastian is the male figure that the play, one of Shakespeare's subtlest dramatizations of the battle of the sexes, needs: He embodies a proper masculinity and the proper playing of a masculine role.

It will be remembered that when we first see him in the company of Antonio we witness his firm but gentle rejection of Antonio's passionate devotion – yet another mirror image of misdirected love:

> Antonio   If you will not murther me for my love, let me be
> your servant.
> Sebastian   If you will not undo what you have done, that is,
> kill him whom you have recover'd, desire it not. Fare ye well
> at once; my bosom is full of kindness, and I am yet so near the
> manners of my mother, that upon the least occasion more
> mine eyes will tell tales of me.   (II. i. 35–42)

That he possesses sensibility, is no mere macho, the gentleness of these 'manners of my mother' attests. And in this he is the perfect counterpart or double to his sister Viola in whose nature, too, the presence of a blend of feminine and masculine traits is potentially harmonious and benign.

Sexual identity has been in some way disordered, frustrated, displaced, diverted or deficient in every one of the chief *dramatis personae*, and in the chief buffoon-impostor Malvolio. It is this subtle imbalance of the personality as much as outward circumstances which has caused their 'madness'. It is this that the comic device entangles in absurdity, that is self-exposed and mocked in the counterpoint Malvolio plot, and that is caricatured in the sexless ninny Andrew. And it is the remedy to this manifold deficiency that is heralded and embodied by Sebastian. The entry of Sebastian is a living image of the sanguine masculinity that Viola, as cheeky Cesario, put on; that Olivia, a Penelope badgered by suitors, needed; that Andrew Aguecheek aped; that Malvolio pretended to, would have exploited and abused, and grotesquely fails to understand; and that Orsino, out-of-date lover, lacked, until his page brought it out in him.

Alexander Leggatt makes the excellent point that 'in other comedies a single personality is extended by disguise, but the extension is temporary and finally withdrawn; this is the only case in which the new figure created by disguise has also an objective reality, a life of its own'.[10] This is in keeping, he maintains, with the miraculous birth the feast of the Epiphany celebrates, but I cannot agree with him when he says 'the ending takes little account of the reasons for particular attachments; it is a generalised image of love'. Neither this 'generalization' nor Kott's Dionysian saturnalia celebrating 'man's eternal dream of overcoming the boundaries of his own body and of his sex'[11] seems to me to catch the brilliant individuality of *Twelfth Night's* realization of the comic principle.

Feste's ministrations to Malvolio in prison travesty cure, though they have their own rough curative effect just as had Dr Pinch's in *The Comedy of Errors*. But the cure of souls that is conducted homeopathically at the main plot level is the peak achievement in the orchestration of comedy game and human comedy which crowns the early plays. When Orsino says to Viola

Your master quits you; and for your service done him,
So much against the mettle of your sex,
So far beneath your soft and tender breeding,

And since you called me master for so long,
Here is my hand – you shall from this time be
Your master's mistress.   (v. i. 321–6)

the words reverbrate retrospectively through the entire play, setting to rights Shakespeare's most finely conceived comic perversity, and resolving his most brilliant essay in comic remedies. Nor
should the autumnal mood of Feste's final song disturb our pleasure in the play. Feste is the most detached, observant (his livelihood depends upon it) and ironic of Shakespeare's fools, and the
tutelary spirit of a play whose marvellous fooling is as serious as it
is funny. If he knows that no festivity can put a stop to time, this is
not to detract from time's benign moments, but to make them
doubly valuable.

NOTES

1 Barrett Wendall (1894), quoted by Kenneth Muir, *The
Sources of Shakespeare's Plays* (London: Methuen, 1977), p.
132.
2 See T. W. Baldwin, *Shakespeare's Five-Act Structure*
(Urbana: Illinois University Press, 1947), p. 715.
3 Jon S. Lawry, *Shakespeare Studies*, vol. 6 (1970), p. 89.
4 Joseph H. Summers, 'The Masks of *Twelfth Night*', *The
University of Kansas City Review*, vol. XXII (1955).
5 Lawry, p. 89.
6 Jan Kott, *Shakespeare Our Contemporary* (London:
Methuen, 1965), pp. 196, 213.
7 C. L. Barber, *Shakespeare's Festive Comedy* (New Jersey:
Princeton University Press, 1959), pp. 240–57.
8 This excellent point was observed by H. Jenkins, 'Shakespeare's *Twelfth Night*', Rice Institute *Pamphlet* XLV (1959).
9 Barber, *Shakespeare's Festive Comedy*, p. 246.
10 Alexander Leggatt, *Shakespeare's Comedy of Love* (London:
Methuen, 1974), pp. 147–8, 251–2.
11 Kott, *Shakespeare Our Contemporary*, p. 220.

XII

COMIC REMEDIES

Twelfth Night pinpoints with peculiar lucidity the question which haunts contemporary criticism of comedy. How subversive is the comic muse? Is the comedy of *Twelfth Night*, in other words, saturnalia masquerading as epiphany or epiphany masquerading as saturnalia? Which of the Nietzschean contraries does it assert — Dionysian de-structuring or Apollonian form?

'A comedy may end in an aura of benevolence and solidarity and yet be mainly subversive and even demonic', Gurewitch tells us in a recent study.[1] And many have read *Twelfth Night* in a manner which leaves them troubled by some sense of a great flux of anomalous and unordained passions and energies. There is Malvolio's unslaked menace, for instance; and Feste's strangely melancholy song in which the events of a whole life-time seem to melt away and dislimn in the rain that raineth every day. And are we really sure that wayward Eros is safely ensconced and safely controlled? or have we been swept away by Jan Kott's 'universality of desire which cannot be contained in or limited to one sex'.

> Every disguise involves not only an invitation to Cythera, a call to orgy, but is a diabolic invention in a much deeper sense . . . it is a dream of erotic experience in which one is one's own partner, in which one sees and experiences sensual pleasure, as it were, from the other side.[2]

How radical *is* the comic muse? Does comedy divert us, enter-
taining us the while with the absurd follies and errors, the ribald
misdemeanours or riotous exploits of its characters, so that, when
our vicarious participation ends we may return, liberated and
enlightened, to a balanced and rational and orderly existence? Or
does it subvert, rather than divert, undercutting the structure of
norms and *mores*, of the accepted, the comprehensible, turning
upside-down the assumptions and values, the accustomed
responses and distinctions upon which our rational personalities
are constructed, and leaving us with a world as unformed as
Orsino's ocean itself in which nought enters 'of what validity and
pitch soe'er,/But falls into abatement and low price'. And if it is
subversive, is it nevertheless ultimately socially therapeutic?

Bakhtin, most radical of recent theorists, insists upon the latter,
upon the creative decreation of the comic.[3] Orsino's words could
serve as epigraph for his paean to the incomplete.

> True ambivalent and universal laughter does not deny serious-
> ness but purifies and completes it. Laughter purifies from dog-
> matism, from the intolerant and the petrified; it liberates from
> fanaticism and pedantry, from fear and intimidation, from didac-
> ticism, naïveté and illusion, from the single meaning, the single
> level, from sentimentality. Laughter does not permit seriousness
> to atrophy and to be torn away from the one being, forever in-
> complete. It restores this ambivalent wholeness.   (p. 123)

It is a wholeness which combines 'the negative element of
debasement and destruction' with 'the positive element of
renewal and truth' (p. 260). Bakhtin's masterly analysis of the
language and imagery of the comic in its folk-carnival forms, its
celebration of the body as unfinished and unlimited, open at all its
cavities, monstrously protuberant and uncompleted, continuous
with nature in its capacity for material metamorphoses, decom-
position and parturition, copulation and procreation, digestion
and defecation, an ever-living, ever-changing member of the
world's body, fertile, growing and abundant beyond the death or
dismemberment of the individual, throws light upon certain
aspects of the Dromios, of Bottom, of Falstaff and Touchstone.
But Bakhtin regards comedy as monistically antinomian and 'low'

comedy in and of itself as sufficient to regenerate and renew society and culture. For this reason, Bakhtin can tell us nothing about the protagonists of Shakespeare's romantic comedies, nor of the subtle interrelationship and interplay between the protagonists and the fools, nor of the formal coherences and patterns which also release the powers and energies of imaginative recreation. Such comedies must be indeed, in his dialectical materialist ideology, 'idealist' lapses, romantic-bourgeois deviations (from the true and primal, choral unity of 'the laughing people') into subjective and individualistic byways (p. 125).

Bakhtin to be sure, annexes Shakespeare, together with Rabelais and Cervantes, to his radical, saturnalian view of comedy; 'the logic of crownings and uncrownings' he acutely observes, 'organises both the serious and the clownish elements' in Shakespeare's drama, and the 'pathos of radical changes and renewals is the essence of his world consciousness' (p. 275). But this, as I hope I have shown, and shall continue for a few pages more to argue, is a partial view of Shakespearean comedy. The great principle of the uncompleted, the open-ended, the unformed which Bakhtin finds at the root of the comic grotesque, in its images of the body as belly, as disintegrating, procreating grave and seed-bed, is only a contained part of the Shakespearean whole. In Shakespeare's comic art rational and irrational interpenetrate in a dialectic that is not materialist; preposterous unrestraint is both exhibited and contained, outrageous fantasy exorcizes itself through excess, the confusions, transformations and disorientations of the *processus turbarum* lead eventually to self-possession and self re-formation, and clarities of form are educed from the chaos of Orsino's ocean.

The Greeks, who invented it, recognized the therapeutic value of the drama, but the two great Greek voices are at odds on this issue. The arousing of emotion by the artists troubled Plato, as everyone knows. And as everyone knows, *The Poetics* attempts an answer. Aristotle saw that catharsis was an answer to Plato in the matter of raising and casting out the emotions, but he also knew that the end of art is not to trigger a spill-over of emotion, like having a good cry or a good laugh (beneficient as these may be) but to order perception at the highest level of intensity, clarity and coherence. To articulate form in other words. Minds so engaged are safely disengaged from the phenomenal flux, cease to be immersed in the flood of dread and desire in which men live their vulnerable lives. In the compression of his argument the question of catharsis is slurred, and so has remained probably the most debated issue in literary criticism to this day, as any censorship board faced with the problem of violence and pornography in the cinema, for example, knows to its cost. For no such board has yet to my knowledge received definitive, unambiguous empirical data from the social psychologists in answer to the question whether the arousal of emotion by the stimulus of art, or by imaginative participation in represented fictional events, allays or exacerbates the anarchic, irrational witches' cauldron of the passions of which Nietzsche speaks in The Birth of Tragedy.[4] The fatal sentence in The Poetics is ambiguous: 'the imitation of an action that is serious, and also as having magnitude, complete in itself ... with incidents arousing pity and fear wherewith to accomplish its catharsis of such emotions' (Bywater translation, section 6). What is the meaning of the genitive link? Are the emotions purged, or are we purged of the emotions? And what is the meaning of the metaphor? Are the emotions purged, or purified? Do we emerge from the theatre empty vessels, or vessels full of an emotional life sublimated, refined, distilled, contemplated, distanced, ordered, composed and mastered? The truth of the matter is that it is not a problem of translation from the Greek, but of the complexity and mystery of the phenomenon itself. How much more so when comedy, not tragedy, is in question, and not only do we have to make up our basic theory for ourselves, Aristotle's having got lost, but we seem to be faced with a human phenomenon of even denser opacity and ambivalence. Comedy, Kerenyi tells us, 'the Dionysian diastole, or expansion', is older than tragedy, 'the Dionysian systole, or concentration', in its inchoate, unformed, archaic expression, though younger in its forms,[5] and more dependent upon actual physical clowning for its effects. You can tell a tragic tale artlessly and your audience will find it moving to some degree. You cannot tell a joke, or play the fool, without at least a minimum of histrionic or pantomimic verve. And the charisma of the clown is an unreliable quantity, morally speaking. We may find ourselves enjoying the *Schaden-freude* of invective and abuse far more than we remember to disapprove of its objects, or of the uncharitable asperity of the speaker. We may fall in love with the unruly, unregenerate Falstaffian rogue. We may take too unsanctified a glee in the cathartic pleasures of smashing and stripping. Ben Jonson was aware of the danger, as well he might have been, since the exuberance of the wicked in his plays is often infectious. In his prologue to *Every Man in His Humour* he writes of comedy's objectives as being

> persons, such as comedy would choose,
> When she would shew an image of the times,
> And sport with human follies, not with crimes.
> Except we make them such, by loving still
> Our popular errors, when we know they're ill.
>
> (prologue 22–6)

There is no ethic, probably, which has not been exercised by the question whether liberation from the passions or liberation of the passions is the key to the good life. The neo-classical tradition was sturdily moralistic, and solved the problem by means of didacticism and the doctrine of poetic justice. We were to be delighted by the just rewards of virtue and the censure or ridicule of faults and, hopefully, might 'become wise to avoid such vices'; in the sentimental phase of this tradition hearts of gold would be discovered in libertine exteriors, and hypocritical sycophants exposed and expelled. But by that time the comedy of disinhibition was all but extinct in the polite theatre and eking out (from the literary point of view) a semi-underground existence in the puppet shows of the Punch and Judy booths and in vaudeville.

The single Aristotelian or post-Aristotelian fragment we possess, the *Tractatus Coislinianus*,[6] by means of a slight but significant expansion of the Aristotelian formula for tragedy together with an equivalent for comedy, brings out one vital point.

> Tragedy removes the fearful emotions of the soul through compassion and terror . . . It has grief for its mother. Comedy is an imitation of an action that is ludicrous and imperfect . . . directly presented by persons acting, and not given through

narrative; through pleasure and laughter effecting the purgation of the like emotions. It has laughter for its mother.[7]

'Of the like emotions' is puzzling. For while neither laughter nor pleasure is a panacea for human ills – laughter can be cruel, or demonic, or the fierce derision of the psalmist's God – yet surely only an ideal of stoic *Apatheia*, a total anaesthesia of the affective life, would demand the purging, as opposed to the purifying, of pleasure and laughter. 'Of the like emotions' is therefore puzzling unless its anaphoric referent is to be found in the first paragraph. Thus: tragedy removes the fearful emotions through compassion and terror. Comedy removes *these same* fearful emotions through pleasure and laughter. And in that way is cathartic, and medicinal, and therapeutic to the human condition.

That drama was therapeutic rather than didactic, though obscured in late neo-classical criticism, had been consistently recognized in the earlier phases of the classical tradition. The medical analogy between the progress of a comedy and the progress of a disease towards amelioration is persistent. The influential Landino five-act formula of 1482 ascribes to the fourth act 'the bringing of a remedy for the obstructing ills'.[8] Willichius, in his commentary on Terence's *Andria* in the edition of 1550, the text which, we are told, was very probably used in the grammar school at Stratford, explains the five-act Terentian scheme and says:

The third has the sequence of turbations with the complication of the argument, and the stirring of all the difficulties. The fourth exhibits the desperate state of the matter . . . The fifth brings a remedy for the great ills, gives all persons what they desire, and fills them with great joy. (p. 233)

The last two formulations are slightly differently phrased in his commentary on Horace's doctrine of the five acts: 'The third has the increment of turbations and contentions . . . The fourth seeks a medicine for the turmoils and is, as it were, preparatory to the catastrophe, which the fifth demands by right for itself'. In 1565 Christopher Johnson of Winchester compared the three parts of comedies with the three parts of life and the three stages of disease: augmentation, state, decline. This was a medical commonplace of the time and is to be found in Minturnus (1564) and Blundeville (1574) who both describe comedies as proceeding from beginning, through increase, state and decline to end. Scaliger, who was well known among the Elizabethan scholars and a physician himself, like Johnson, uses the medical analogy in his definition of catastasis (the fourth act): 'the full vigor or state' of the disease, or play. Ben Jonson, whose metaphors tend to stress (except in *Bartholomew Fair*) the malady rather than the remedy, has 'a source of ridiculous matter may break forth anon, that shall sleep their temples, and bathe their brains in laughter, to the fomenting of stupidity itself, and the awaking any velvet lethargy in the house (*The Magnetic Lady*, Act 1, scene i), and the 'bleeding' of all the vices at the end of *Volpone*. Dryden is entirely didactic, but Milton's preface to *Samson Agonistes* has an interesting account of tragedy as homeopathic:

> Tragedy is said by Aristotle to be of power by raising pity and fear, or terror, to purge the mind of those and such like passions, that is, to temper and reduce them . . . by seeing those passions well imitated. Nor is nature wanting in her own effects to make good his assertion; for so, in physic, things of melancholic hue and quality are used against melancholy, sour against sour, salt to remove salt humours.

Shakespeare has Hamlet echo the Ciceronian commonplace for comedy: an imitation of life, a mirror of custom, and an image of truth, as well as the Sidneyean moral note, when he says that the end of playing is 'to hold as 'twere the mirror up to nature: to show virtue her feature, scorn her own image, and the very age and body of the time his form and pressure' (III. ii. 21–4). But the effect of the player's speech upon him, (his own choice, one remembers) together with his impatient request 'Say on, come to Hecuba', and his decision to 'tent the King to the quick' with a play, could serve as a key text for the theory of catharsis developed by our own present-day master of those who know. 'O what a rogue and peasant slave am I' is Hamlet's self-punishing repetition, his working through of his own compulsions and obsessions. The transference has been triggered by the experience of the player's recital, deliberately sought and doubly vicarious

(Priam is double to both King Hamlet as victim of Claudius, and Claudius as projected victim of Hamlet) and it issues, at least temporarily, in a state of exultant release and anticipated mastery.[9] The foreshadowing of a Freudian view of the drama of psychic life is extraordinarily impressive. I do not refer to the specific Freudian diagnoses, like Ernest Jones's, which are over specific and reductive, but to the symbolic structures of displacement, of self-dramatizing re-experience, 'remembering, repeating and working through' to which Freud's analyses pointed,[10] and of which he himself spoke. It is after all well known that Freud was a devoted Shakespearean, and that he toyed at one point with the idea of naming his psychoanalysis by the ancient, honourable and ambiguous Aristotelian term, catharsis.[11]

I am persuaded by study of the early plays that Shakespeare conceived of the spectacle of these follies as cathartic in a uniquely interesting way.[12] In them we perceive the emergence of a mimesis which embraces both character and audience in its double interaction. As in all forms of dramatic irony, the informed audience witnesses what befalls unwitting characters. But here the process of looking before and after is so finely articulated that the audience, too, undergoes a restructuring of experience analogous to that of the characters, though from a higher and more comprehensive vantage-point. His comic device is itself thematically remedial. Even in early Ephesus the resolution of the enigmas follows Dr Pinch's attempted exorcism of Antipholus' 'madness'. And consider, in each of the plays, who plots what and for what purpose. There is the taming of the Shrew, and of Titania, and of the lovers' frenzies; there is the bringing to their senses of the young Lords of Navarre, one of whom is to be homeopathically cured of joking by joking in hospital; and the bringing to their senses of the headstrong 'sworn bachelors' of Messina; there is the 'curing' of the love-sick Orlando, and of the love-sick Malvolio. The notorious prevalence of disease in 2 *Henry IV* presages the replacing of a comic remedy by a deathbed scene. Then there is the remedying of Vienna's ills, though that is outside the scope of this book, as are the problematic medicinal skills of Helena, the French physician's daughter. The whole construction is like nothing so much as the house that Jack built. The remedial devices produce errors, that trigger complications, that bring out or induce quiescent follies, instabilities, compulsions, humours, that extruded − expressed − reach a maximum point of exhaustion that generates remedies. We have a multitude of metaphors for a process of excitation, discomposure and recomposition that we do not understand. We speak variously of exorcism, of sublimation, of homeopathy; of safety valves, of syphoning off, or rechannelling; of release.

Shakespeare's early comedies provide us with a variety of dramatic models for this medicinal, benign and restorative process which, embodied in the stories themselves, provide homologies for the spectators' re-constructing experience.[13]

Thus Shakespeare saves us from the trap of bi-polarity, of mutually exclusive alternatives: *either* the antinomian, de-structuring, disinhibitory and subversive pleasures of catharsis *or* the authoritarian, moralistic and repressive catharsis of pleasure, Shakespeare devises a form which liberates from the passions through the passions; at once inflaming and energizing our deepest interests and impulses and reducing the inflammation, to use yet another medical metaphor, with the cool compress of the ludicrous. The more farcical the *processus turbarum*, the more it reveals itself as a working out of the psychic material: the obsessions, anxieties, fantasies which inhibit the achievement of desirable solutions; and the more absurd these antics patently become. The higher intelligence which comes upon the characters in the process of exhausting and eliminating their follies is the audience's, too, but to a lesser degree. For the audience has not only had superior knowledge all along, but has also been invited, by the mocking *raisonneur* fools, to conceptualize and to distance the events as they unfold. Hence Shakespeare's comedies, for all their sentiment, are ironic rather than sentimental, hard not soft. They do not deny the dark side of saturnalia or disinhibition, the ruthless, violent, destructive other face of nature's energies; they occupy always a danger zone of potential radical harm to the individual. Yet they take a tolerant and genial view of the vital spontaneities, the imperious instincts, the recalcitrant emotions and the chaotic appetites and desires. Respecting these, they set out to remedy disorder, tension and deficiency by individual hazard, individual inventiveness and creativity. And so if they are 'romantic' it is not only because they deal with lovers, but because they represent a dazzling, if brief, adventure in the discovery and exploration of what is humanly possible.

NOTES

1 Gurewitch, *The Irrational Vision* (Ithaca: Cornell University Press, 1975), p. 15. See also an interesting recent comedy which treats the problem, Trevor Griffiths, *The Comedians* (London: Faber, 1976).
2 Jan Kott, *Shakespeare Our Contemporary* (London: Methuen, 1965), pp. 196, 220.
3 Mikhail Bakhtin, *Rabelais and His World*, trans. H. Iswolsky (Cambridge, Massachusetts: M.I.T. Press, 1968).
4 *The Birth of Tragedy*, trans. Francis Golffing (New York: Doubleday, 1956), pp. 25–6.
5 C. Kerenyi, *Dionysos: Archetypal Image of Indestructible Life*, trans. Ralph Manheim (New Jersey: Princeton University Press, 1976), pp. 333–4.
6 Translated and discussed by Lane Cooper in his attempt to reconstruct the missing Aristotelian treatise on comedy. *An Aristotelean Theory of Comedy* (New York: Harcourt Brace, 1922). Cooper finds that it is 'the sense of disproportion' from which men suffer in daily life that is 'relieved or purged away by the laughter of comedy ... By contemplating the disproportions of comedy, we are freed from the sense of disproportion in life, and regain our perspective ... To Aristotle, this process of settling into our true selves is pleasure' (p. 181).
7 As Marvin Herrick shows, *Comic Theory in the Sixteenth Century* (Urbana: University of Illinois Press, 1964), this Aristotelian tradition survived through the Middle Ages and into the sixteenth century, when Paccius printed a dual-language Greek–Latin version of *The Poetics* in 1536. Riccobonus, in a Latin version of *The Poetics* (1587), with an

attempted reconstruction of the absent section on comedy, writes that '[tragedy] by means of pity and fear; [comedy] by means of delight from the laughable, incites a purgation of the spirits' (p. 52).

8 T. W. Baldwin, *Shakespeare's Five-Act Structure* (Urbana: University of Illinois Press, 1947), p. 232 and see pp. 312–46 passim.

9 I have discussed Hamlet and the players from a rather different angle in *Tragic Form in Shakespeare* (New Jersey: Princeton University Press, 1972), pp. 143–50.

10 Among recent neo-Freudian approaches to this interpretation of Shakespeare I find Murray M. Schwartz, 'Shakespeare through Contemporary Psychoanalysis' particularly relevant in its emphasis upon the interplay of contraries in life as in play: self and other, masculine and feminine, freedom and dependency, reality and fantasy. Murray Schwartz' paper was read at the International Shakespeare Association Congress held in Washington, 1976, and later published in *HSL* (*Hebrew University Studies in Literature*), vol. 5, no. 2 (Autumn, 1977).

11 In 1895, subsequent to his work with Breuer on hypnosis and the re-enactment of traumatic experiences in the treatment of hysterias. See *The Origin and Development of Psychoanalysis* (1919; reprinted Chicago: Regnery, 1960) and *The Standard Edition* (London: Hogarth Press, 1955), vol. 11.

12 Sherman Hawkins, 'The Two Worlds of Shakespearean Comedy', *Shakespeare Studies*, vol. 111 (1967), whose argument differs from mine in its typological bias and in many details, interestingly anticipates and confirms this central conclusion.

13 Cf. C. L. Barber, *Shakespeare's Festive Comedy* (New Jersey: Princeton University Press, 1959) who has argued persuasively for the theory that Shakespeare's early comedies not only deal with, or centre on or refer to seasonal festivities, but are structured to conduct both characters and audience 'through release to clarification'. See also Michael Long, *The Unnatural Scene* (London: Methuen, 1976) where Barber's

idea is developed to accommodate the tragedies as the contrary 'traumatic perspective' of minds for which the volatilities of unstructured experience hold terror not release'
(pp. 9–11).

APPENDIX:
SCANNING
A SHAKESPEARE
PLAY

Act V of *Love's Labour's Lost* is extraordinarily long. It contains the planning of 'The Nine Worthies', the Muscovite masquerade, the return of the lords in their own habit to be discomfited yet again, this time by the ladies now unmasked, the pageant of 'The Nine Worthies' itself, and the entrance of Mercade, not to speak of the Princess's edict to the lovers and the final songs. And it runs to 1086 lines in the Riverside edition. It is no wonder that there has been a certain amount of uncertainty in the criticism as to what such a plenitude of unravelling actually unravels.

The play's construction appears altogether very odd. For if Act V is a smorgasbord, Act III is a shotten herring. It consists of one scene alone, of 205 lines, which presents the advancement of the incarcerated Costard to the rank of double messenger, first by Armado and then by Berowne. In terms of received Terentian doctrine this must surely strike one as a strange central Act. Where are the impediments and turmoils and knots of error? The 'growing on and continuance of all the hot sturre and trouble . . .'? 'The increase and progression of perturbations'? (*Andria*, ed. Kyffin, 1558; see Baldwin, *Five-Act Structure*, 1947, p. 318). None are to be perceived except, at a pinch, Berowne's rueful confession, 'And I, forsooth, in love . . .'. And even this, though it is certainly an ironic reversal is no more than the necessary initial complicating response to the appearance of the ladies, and therefore theoretically the main business of a *second* Act. The marked success with which Costard carries out his mission we discover in Act IV, when both letters are delivered to the wrong addressees, and the grand ironic exposures of the eavesdropping scene, in which each of the lords in turn is caught by his self-confessed perjury, are climaxed by Berowne's own incriminating epistle. This surely constitutes the main reversal, or set of reversals, the chief of which is brought about by the comic device of crossed letters. But it comes at the very end of Act IV.

Something is surely wrong. *Love's Labour's Lost* is excessively top-heavy. The Riverside line count shows up its queer shape at a glance: I. i and ii: 490; II. i: 258; III. i: 205; IV. i, ii, and iii: 698; V. i and ii: 1086. Can we suppose even early Shakespeare – particularly early Shakespeare, steeped in Renaissance precept and the discipline of Terentian analysis – to have constructed so ungainly and monstrous a shape? The classical tradition laid down no fixed number of scenes per Act, but five to eight was regarded as optimal (Baldwin, p. 238). A glance through the comedies shows that Shakespeare has many short fourth Acts and some very long second ones, but in no other comedy does he devote the whole of Acts II and III to one short scene each, and in no other play has he contrived so huge a disproportion in the size of one Act, nor such a hodge-podge in its content.

It is the first Folio which introduces Act divisions into the 'Newly corrected and augmented' Q text of 1598. But that famous volume proves to be an unreliable guide. It mistakenly heads the fifth Act (as well as the fourth) 'Actus Quartus', and makes no mention of an Actus Quintus at all.

I submit that the solution to this knot of errors is simpler than it seems. It lies in the supposition that Shakespeare did not, in fact, devise the unwieldy and formally senseless order which is accepted in all modern editions, and that generations of editors have inherited a mistaken analysis of Heminge and Condell's (or Jaggard's) mistake.

Suppose the Folio's error lay not in calling the fifth Act Actus Quartus, but in calling the *third* Act Actus Quartus and forgetting to mark Act V? In other words, suppose what the Folio calls Actus Quartus the second time really was Act IV, thus marked in one or another of the sets of original papers, or prompt books, or actor's copies available in the Globe library and used, as Dover Wilson, supposes (*The First Folio*, Oxford, 1955, p. 66) together with the Q text for copy?

This hypothesis gives us two errors for one, since we must now find a true Act V and a true Act III. But the gains, in terms of a greater formal likelihood and the interpretation of the inner dynamic of the play, are considerable. And we have not far to seek. An Act V is very easily identified despite the absence of a change of scene. Immediately after the Muscovite masquerade, and before the men return in their own attire, there is a nearly empty stage. The ladies exchange mockeries at the mens' expense and decide to torment them still further on their return. In the midst of this they are warned by Boyet: 'Ladies, withdraw; the gallants are at hand' – which they do, to the Princess's rhyming command: 'Whip to our tents, as roes (run) o'er land' (v. ii. 308–9). With Boyet alone remaining on stage the men then return, to the Folio stage direction: 'Enter the King and the rest'. As a marker for Act V (with Boyet providing a certain continuity across the shift in mood and tone) this is more than merely feasible. It would seem to be flying in the face of all probability not to see here a clear Act division. Why then has it never been taken into editorial account?

The answer is first of all that it has been so taken, at least once. Theobald divided his 1773 edition in just this way, thus splitting the enormous Act V into two acts of 464 and 622 lines respectively. He saw furthermore that Act III must be no other than the first of the two acts called 'Actus Quartus' in the Folio, and that no more is needed than this change of nomenclature, and the absorption of the Folio's Act III with its single scene, into Act II, also containing one single scene, for a perfectly coherent, symetrically balanced and rhythmically sensible structure to emerge: 490; 463; 698; 464; 622; and one moreover that would have obtained the blessing of the Renaissance scholiasts themselves.

In Theobald's division Act I 'unfolds the argument' by setting up the little academe; Act II 'shows the beginning of the play' with the arrival of the ladies, the succumbing of the gentlemen and (I would add), the initiating of the comic device in the shape of the sending of the letters. Act III, with its crossed letters, its deceptions and counter-deceptions and its hierarchy of eavesdroppings, gives us the canonical 'sequence of turbations' or 'increment of turbations and contentions', the 'complication of the argument' and the 'stirring of all the difficulties' (*Andria*, ed. Willichius, 1550; Baldwin, pp. 232ff.). In Act IV the discomfiture of the men in the Muscovite masque seems remarkably apt for the 'desperate state of the matter' (ibid.), while the staging of 'The Nine Worthies', which is planned in Act IV 'as a medicine for the turmoils' (or at least as a palliative for the ladies' displeasure) will provide occasion for a double 'catastrophe': the announcement of Jaquenetta's pregnancy, and the announcement of the death of the Princess's father. With the former the pageant crumbles into the (unresolved) deadlock of impending fisticuffs between Jaquenetta's two cavaliers; the latter apparently breaks the deadlock between the wooing lords and the sceptical ladies, but only at the expense, as I have argued in Chapter V above, of a properly *comic* resolution, giving us homiletics rather than celebrations, morals rather than marriages, and a disgruntled protagonist.

Remarkably enough (is it the baleful influence of the Queen of Dunces?) Theobald's Act division has been ignored from that day to this. It is a fact which throws an interesting light upon the relation between the perception of dynamic dramatic form and the written text. It has become traditional to regard Act division as mere literary convention, action being continuous on the stage, and 'intervals' in the modern theatre a mere matter of convenience having little or no relation to the original conception. But when a play is conceived as simply a succession of scenes into which pauses can be arbitrarily inserted, it is clear that a text is being read, but that no dramatic rhythm is being imagined. It is rather as if a line of traditional verse were to be scanned without any attention being paid to positions, that is to say, without taking into account the occurrence of strong syntactical-intonational stresses in metrical weak positions, or vice versa. Such mechanical scansion obliterates the tension between regularity and randomness in any complexly modulated line of metrical verse, abrogates rhythm and makes it impossible to perceive that elusive interplay of absence in presence which, in the creations of art or of nature, constitutes form. To press the analogy: Act division is to classical dramaturgy as prosody is to traditional verse or grammar to articulate speech – the hidden structure never itself available for observation (except as an abstracted scheme) but ever controlling the variant transformations, the significant modulations, the expressive recurrences of its embodied paradigms. The case of *Love's Labour's Lost*, I suggest, brings out with particular clarity the virtues of appropriate 'scansion' for the reading of a Shakespeare play.

SELECTIVE
BIBLIOGRAPHICAL NOTE

T. W. Baldwin, *Shakespeare's Five-Act Structure* (Urbana, Ill., University of Illinois Press, 1947), and Marvin Herrick, *Comic Theory in the Sixteenth Century* (Urbana, Ill., University of Illinois Press, 1964), are invaluable sources for information concerning the Donatan tradition and its ramifications during the Renaissance. Lane Cooper, *An Aristotelean Theory of Comedy* (1924), translates and discusses the *Tractatus Coislinianus* during his attempt to reconstruct an Aristotelean treatise of comedy. Leo Salingar, *Shakespeare and the Traditions of Comedy* (Cambridge: Cambridge University Press, 1976), and Giacomo Oreglia, *The Commedia dell' Arte* (tr. Edwards; New York: Hill & Wang, 1968), give most thorough, detailed, and perceptive accounts of comic tradition in England and Italy respectively. C. Kerenyi's *Dionysus* (tr. Manheim; Princeton, N.J.: Princeton University Press, 1976) is a brilliant reconstruction and analysis of the Dionysian cult festivals of antiquity, and the work of C. L. Barber, *Shakespeare's Festive Comedy* (Princeton, N. J.: Princeton University Press, 1972), and Mikhail Bakhtin, *Rabelais and his World* (tr. Iswolsky; Cambridge, Mass.: M.I.T. Press, 1971), fill out our understanding of the nature of long-continuing folk traditions of the comic upon which Elizabethan drama drew. Ian Donaldson, *The World Upside Down* (second edition; Oxford: Oxford University Press, 1974), pursues a particularly central theme in this tradition; and Michael Long, *The Unnatural Scene* (London: Methuen, 1976), develops Barber's idea to accommodate the tragedies as the contrary 'traumatic perspective' of minds for which 'the volatilities of unstructured experience hold terror not release'. The view of comedy as essentially irrational is well presented by Morton Gurewitch, *The Irrational Vision* (Ithaca, N.Y., Cornell University Press, 1975), and its counterpart, comedy as the supreme embodiment and enactment of rationality, by James Feibleman, *In Praise of Comedy* (New York: Horizon, 1970). Erasmus, *The Praise of Folly* (tr. Radice; Harmondsworth: Penguin, 1971), and W. J. Kaiser, *Praisers of Folly* (Cambridge, Mass.: Harvard University Press, 1963), throw important light on the dialectic of folly and wisdom. Standard works in the fields are Enid Welsford, *The Fool* (London: Faber, 1968), Robert H. Goldsmith, *Wise Fools in Shakespeare* (East Lansing, Mich.: Michigan State University Press, 1968), H. B. Charlton, *Shakespearean Comedy* (London: Methuen, 1966), and Muriel Bradbrook, *The Growth and Structure of Elizabethan Comedy* (London: Chatto & Windus, 1955). Bertrand Evans, *Shakespeare's Comedies* (Oxford: Oxford University Press, 1960), gives a definitive account of Shakespeare's manipulation of audience knowledge in a study that deserves to figure prominently in any newer 'affective' approach to the poetics of theatre, while Richard Levin, *The Multiple Plot in English Renaissance Drama* (Chicago, Ill.: University of Chicago Press, 1971), following W. Empson, *Some Versions of Pastoral* (London: Chatto & Windus, 1968), provides a valuable analysis of the relationship between plot levels which makes parody possible.Sister Miriam Joseph's two books, *Shakespeare's use of the Arts of Language* and *Rhetoric in Shakespeare's Time* (New York: Harcourt Brace Jovanovich, 1965), give a comprehensive and lucid account of the figures of speech familiar in Shakespeare's day. Arthur Koestler, *The Act of Creation* (London: Hutchinson, 1969), skillfully adapts Freudian views of the genesis of the comic in a comprehensive account of creativity, which includes jester, poet, and man of science. Freud himself, of course, is everywhere a mine of insight into the therapies of comedy, as is R. D. Laing, *The Divided Self* (London: Tavistock, 1960), into the psychic ailments which require therapy. René Girard, *Deceit, Desire and the Novel: Self and Other in Literary Structure* (Baltimore, Md: John Hopkins University Press, 1976) applies analogous theory to the related genre of the novel in a way which proves fruitful for the criticism of the drama as well. Northrop Frye's taxonomies and analyses of generic symbolism (*Anatomy of Criticism*, Princeton, N.J.: Princeton University Press, 1957) are indispensable to any study of a genre and generate insight even when most productive of disagreement. Stimulating individual studies of the plays are to be found in Ralph Berry, *Shakespeare's Comedies* (Princeton, N.J.: Princeton University Press), J. Russell Brown, *Shakespeare and his Comedies* (London: Methuen, 1957), Larry Champion, *The Evolution of Shakespeare's Comedy* (second edition; Cambridge, Mass.: Harvard University Press, 1973), Jan Kott, *Shakespeare Our Contemporary* (London: Methuen, 1967), Alexander Leggatt, *Shakespeare's Comedy of Love* (London: Methuen, 1974), Thomas McFarland, *Shakespeare's Pastoral Comedy* (Chapel Hill, N.C.: University of North Carolina Press, 1972), and in the abundant periodical literature to which every critic of Shakespeare is constantly indebted.

INDEX